The Babylonian Planet

Also Available from Bloomsbury

Édouard Glissant: A Poetics of Resistance, Sam Coombes
Transcultural Ecocriticism: Global, Romantic and Decolonial Perspectives, ed.
Stuart Cooke and Peter Denney
Radical Animism: Reading for the End of the World, Jemma Deer
Playful Intelligence: Digitizing Tradition, Henry Sussman

The Babylonian Planet

Culture and Encounter Under Globalization

Sonja A. J. Neef

Edited by Martin Neef

Translated by Jason Groves

BLOOMSBURY ACADEMIC

LONDON • NEW YORK • OXFORD • NEW DELHI • SYDNEY

BLOOMSBURY ACADEMIC
Bloomsbury Publishing Plc
50 Bedford Square, London, WC1B 3DP, UK
1385 Broadway, New York, NY 10018, USA
29 Earlsfort Terrace, Dublin 2, Ireland

BLOOMSBURY, BLOOMSBURY ACADEMIC and the Diana logo are trademarks of
Bloomsbury Publishing Plc

First published in Great Britain 2022
This paperback edition published 2023

Library of Congress Cataloging-in-Publication Data

Names: Neef, Sonja, author. | Neef, Martin, editor. | Groves, Jason, translator.
Title: The Babylonian planet : culture and encounter under globalization /
Sonja Neef ; edited by Martin Neef ; translated by Jason Groves.
Other titles: Babylonische Planet. English
Description: London ; New York : Bloomsbury Academic, 2022. | "Translation of Der
babylonische Planet (1st edition) is published by Bloomsbury
Publishing Plc by arrangement with UNIVERSITÄTSVERLAG WINTER." |
Includes bibliographical references and index.
Identifiers: LCCN 2021025489 (print) | LCCN 2021025490 (ebook) |
ISBN 9781350173231 (hb) | ISBN 9781350173248 (paperback) |
ISBN 9781350173255 (epdf) | ISBN 9781350173262 (ebook)
Subjects: LCSH: Globalization–Social aspects. | Culture and globalization. |
Intercultural communication. | Political science–Philosophy. | Language and languages. |
Planetary theory–Social aspects.
Classification: LCC JZ1318 .N432 2022 (print) | LCC JZ1318 (ebook) | DDC 303.48/2—dc23
LC record available at https://lccn.loc.gov/2021025489
LC ebook record available at https://lccn.loc.gov/2021025490

ISBN: HB: 978-1-3501-7323-1
       PB: 978-1-3502-1488-0
       ePDF: 978-1-3501-7325-5
       eBook: 978-1-3501-7326-2

Typeset by RefineCatch Limited, Bungay, Suffolk

To find out more about our authors and books visit www.bloomsbury.com
and sign up for our newsletters.

Contents

Illustrations

Acknowledgments

The editor and publisher gratefully acknowledge the permission granted to reproduce the copyright material in this book. Every effort has been made to trace copyright holders and to obtain their permission for the use of copyright material. The publisher apologizes for any errors or omissions in the above list and would be grateful if notified of any corrections that should be incorporated in future reprints or editions of this book. The third-party copyrighted material displayed in the pages of this book are done so on the basis of 'fair use for the purposes of teaching, criticism, scholarship or research' only in accordance with international copyright laws, and is not intended to infringe upon the ownership rights of the original owners.

The Babylonian Planet

We have come to a moment in history where we see that human imagination needs all the world's languages [. . .] multilingualism does not presuppose the coexistence of languages, nor the knowledge of several languages, but the presence of the world's languages in the practice of one's own; that is what I call multilingualism.[1]

Babel reloaded

Today, as in biblical times, Babel remains a bewildering word with many divergent meanings. The ancient myth, which ushered chaos into the book of Genesis, has begun to run amok once again. Its countless adaptations and interpretations across a broad spectrum of media have sparked an abundance of critical discussions among academics. The wikis and search engines of the World Wide Web give an impression of the interminability of Babel-inspired creations. According to them, we find that Babel comprises the name of an international chatroom, an Iraqi newspaper, a series of books by Jorge Luis Borges, a mountain in Quebec, and a Dutch soccer player's name, to name but a few examples. And each time we refresh the search engine, new hits pop up.

With its spiral-shaped staircase surrounded by arched windows, the tower has survived as the most iconic symbol of Babel in the West. Pieter Bruegel The Elder monumentalized this structure in *Tower of Babel*, a painting that continues to define the contemporary cultural imaginary: in television, it can be glimpsed in images of the space station in the science fiction series *Babylon 5*; in film, it appears in the city Minas Tirith in Peter Jackson's *Lord of the Rings: The Return of the King*; and even architecture draws on this image in the European Parliament in Strasbourg.[2] It is no coincidence, then, that the oldest large-scale film studio in the world, *Babelsberg*, exists under the sign of the tower. Fritz Lang's legendary film *Metropolis*, which was produced there, focuses less on the figure of the tower than on the city itself, staging it, in Dietmar Steiner's fitting words, "as a symbol of *Moloch*, the unplanned, all devouring, ungovernable, misanthropic Megalopolis."[3] By contrast, Alejandro González Iñárritu's film *Babel*, one of the medium's most recent appropriations of the myth, brings city and tower into close proximity within a global context. The film's multi-narrative montage transforms the globe into an intercontinental "mosaic,"[4] a complex construction of individual sets of situations and characters that, no matter how far removed from one another, still brush up extraordinarily close to one another.

The Babel myth has also been staged as a world project by the Belgian choreographer Sidi Larbi Cherkaoui. In his 2010 stage-piece *Babel (words)*, the myth comes to life in the form of residential "living-containers" raised on stage at the Cirque Royal in Brussels. Bringing together sculpture, theater, live concert, and dance, Babel becomes a *Gesamtkunstwerk* in which the large-scale project of building is closely entwined with the project of language, in particular with a living language comprising speech, breath, and body, and more precisely with singing in all of its contrapuntal, polyphonic, and cacophonous possibilities. Analogous to the biblical narration, Cherkaoui's opera never only deals with the founding and legitimation of a heralded abode, but also with the motifs of expulsion and exodus, including migrant and refugee movements in modern-day transitory living spaces. Akin to the biblical myth, *Babel (words)* takes up the fundamental question of the origin of language, balancing the utopia of a perfect language against an apocalyptic identity crisis engendered by a confusion of tongues. Today, under conditions of accelerated globalization and the consolidation of planetary interrelations, such themes continue to occupy our interest with undiminished force.

It is no mere coincidence that critical theories of encounter and of difference converge in linguistic concepts undisturbed by the end of the so-called linguistic turn: the central concepts of cultural studies include "polyphony" (Michael Bakhtin), "creolization" (Édouard Glissant), "translation" (Walter Benjamin, Gayatri Chakravorty Spivak), "monolingualism" (Jacques Derrida), and "accent" (accented cinema studies). Even our current media culture is fascinated with the age-old notion of a Babylonian language. This idea has inspired various art installations, as in Danica Dakić's *Zid/ wall* and Stephan von Huene's *Lexichaos*.[5] Another case in point is *Babelfish*, an online translation user-interface that automatically—but inadequately and sometimes also confusingly—translates texts and websites word for word. The program is inspired by the eponymous fictional artifact in Douglas Adams' *The Hitchhiker's Guide to the Galaxy*; in the novel, as in its adaptations into television series, movies, and computer games, a glibbery cyborganic interface slips into and hatches in Arthur Dent's ear, making the languages of the galaxy instantly universal, directly accessible, and without any loss in meaning for the famed protagonist. Unlike the more or less imperfect translation programs on the World Wide Web, the fictitious Babelfish succeeds in a miracle of translation that is in no way inferior to the Pentecost miracle of the fiery tongues.

Global flows

This book looks back yet again at the ancient myth of the tower of Babel in order to look forward to emerging forms of cultural encounter. Again and again, diverse disciplines with their different approaches and considerations have made evident the highly-charged nature of Babel. Well aware that the age-old question surrounding this myth remains unanswered—for it is, indeed, unanswerable—it must nevertheless be set forth anew. It remains the initial question. For that which the question of the origin, unity, and diversity of languages and cultures is aimed at not only directs the questioner's gaze into a long and dynamic occidental cultural history, but also requires them to think Babel further and to reformulate the associated question ever further and with undiminished emphasis, but also with different nuances. Further, that is: one more time, another time, anew.

The task of defining Babel today can be seen as a mode of *reloading* an object from biblical times and thus giving this ancient myth a twenty-first-century update. The present moment is commonly referred to as the era of globalization, insofar as a new spatial logic of the globe—in which every point on the earth's surface in principle maintains a relation to every other point—has emerged out of worldwide transportation systems, media, and trade. These relations are manifold. They pertain to encounters between languages and cultures, markets and social systems, as well as the complex relationships between ecosystems and a global climate. They encompass the cultural artifacts and customs that now stream around the globe in so-called "flows." With this world-picture in mind, Manuel Castells conceptualizes globalization in terms of "spaces of flow," by which he means process-networks of capital, communication, transport, and information flows.[6] Arjun Appadurai employs similar concepts to think of globalization in terms of "global cultural flows" and "scapes" (so-called ethnoscapes, financescapes, mediascapes, ideoscapes, and technoscapes) in which tourists and immigrants are mobilized by the very economies, information, data, images, and ideologies—and the corresponding technological innovations—

that they themselves help to mobilize. The suffix "–scapes," as Appadurai emphasizes, refers to the fluid and free-flowing forms of the disjunctive worlds in which moving images momentarily register in increasingly mobile audiences.[7]

Building Babel

If one thing is clear, it is that Babel can no longer be thought of outside these worldwide flows. Babel signifies less an act of founding and identity formation and much more a mission *to build* in the sense of a project of being articulated by Heidegger in his famous essay *Building Dwelling Thinking*. It is no mere coincidence that language leads Heidegger to understand how building yields a mode of thought that touches on the essential properties of being:

> The Old English and High German word for building, *buan*, means to dwell, [...] to remain, to stay in a place. [...] Where the word *bauen* still speaks in its original sense it also says *how far* the nature of dwelling reaches. That is, *bauen, buan, bhu, beo* are our word *bin* in the versions: *ich bin*, I am, *du bist*, you are, the imperative form *bis*, be. [...], [I]*ch bin* [...] mean[s]: I dwell.[8]

This "I am, ergo I dwell" becomes much more nuanced once Heidegger explains that "dwelling is not experienced as man's being; dwelling is never thought of as the basic character of human being."[9] Heidegger thinks of the human as essentially homeless: underway to a dwelling and an abode, underway to a relentlessly denied home. Karsten Harries' brilliant reading of Heidegger adds even greater nuance to this concept of dwelling, when he writes:

> Heidegger here understands man as ever again having to seek the nature of dwelling, having to learn how to dwell. This plight of dwelling is more worthy of thought than the all too apparent housing shortage. But can it be the task of architecture to eliminate this plight, which, Heidegger here suggests, is bound up with the very essence of human being? Is the task not rather to understand this plight in its ineliminable necessity? And might such understanding not lead to the only kind of homecoming that does not do violence to our being? Part of such a homecoming would be the renunciation of anything resembling a secure possession of home. To find the home which alone would allow for an authentic dwelling, must we not first learn that the home of which we sometimes dream and whose here and there encountered traces seem to promise some deeply longed-for happiness must always elude us?[10]

The paragon of a "homecoming" humanity is the container-resident of Cherkaoui's Babel opera, who renounces the primal comfort of a "house to call home" and for whom the abode is an aporia and the act of building an eternal mission. In *The Babylonian Planet*, Babel is thought of as such a construction site, one that does not proceed in a strategic and targeted manner but rather through a series of ongoing projects. In this way, it recognizes and performs the long and often misleading course—one that is spiral-shaped and thus modeled on the tower—that being-in-search-of-home must take.

The basic program of this Babylonian construction project consists of the process of entering into relationships. In Iñárritu, Cherkaoui, and others known for their contemporary inter-medial stagings of Babel, echoes of the myth reverberate in the equation of "one tower" with "one world" and in the equation of tower construction workers with a world community. The Babylonian world is a planetary space of relation: relentlessly it seeks to encounter, to translate, to fuse, to confuse, to accentuate, to creolize, to *babylonize*.

The concept of the Babylonian planet thus extends beyond an unsophisticated patchwork culture theory. Neither then or now do the building materials of this grand tower simply emerge from a cultural melting pot that would provide a mold for the eradication of difference and the final amalgamation of all humanity. Babel is to be understood rather as a process of encounter among different linguistic and cultural systems, a process that is never placating, but is always complex, full of misunderstanding and (productive) dissent. More than this one city in antiquity, the tension-ridden dimension of the myth of Babel has for some time now concerned all of urban space and civilization, taken as a fundamental attribute of the human, the one who dwells.

The tower casts an overarching shadow. Insofar as we see the blueprint for Babylon today as being shot through with portents of destruction of the global city and the confusion of a global tongue, this blueprint also forecasts the ecological threats that an industrialized and nuclearized civilization poses to the planet, its climate, and its singular habitability. Seen in this way, Babel can also signify an "ecosophical praxis" that structures human–planet relations in view of what Félix Guattari describes as "the perspective of an ethical-political possibility for one to choose diversity, creative dissidence, and responsibility in regards to difference and alterity."[11] The site of this "Ecosophy" is literally the "house" (*oikos*) in its capacity as a habitat and a habitation for wisdom (*sophia*) and responsibility. Insofar as this takes the form of a "house" of a "society," it will continue to serve as the building block of that Babylonian city, tower, and world.

What Babel means

Let us return to this first question, the one that has incessantly arisen from Babel: What does Babel mean? Does it mean anything at all, and if so, in what language does it mean something? How can one translate it? To be sure, Babel is a name, first and foremost, and it is a name that discloses, as mentioned earlier, a number of contradictory cultural codes:

1. In the Judeo-Christian tradition, the word, as it appears in Scripture, refers to a biblical "city and a tower whose apex reaches the heavens" (Gen. 11.9, 4),[12] built by Noah's descendants on a plain in Sinai. Here, rumors surrounding the confusion of languages, the palace where Nebuchadnezzar II became insane, and of Jewish exile all ran amok throughout the city. In the West, it quickly garnered ill-repute, becoming a kind of sin city, an anti-Jerusalem.

2. In other cultures, by contrast, Babel was held in high esteem as a founding city of high culture and holiness. Dedicated to the god Marduk, it became a cosmopolitan and polyglot metropolis whose tower Etemenanki was praised in the creation epic *Enûma eliš*. Ancient authors raved about the Hanging Gardens of Babylon, regarding it as an architectural apotheosis of the ancient world; the Ancient Greeks even included the gardens in their list of the Seven Wonders of the World.

3. Modern archeology further discloses a *secular*, non-mythical meaning of Babel we have yet to consider, namely the name of an ancient city-state in Mesopotamia that ran highly sophisticated state, legal, trade, and finance systems. A veritably cosmopolitan and polyglot metropolis, its architects built impressive structures and its scribes composed an elaborate constitution, multilingual dictionaries, catalogs of stars, even calendars.[13] Ever since the excavation and decipherment of cuneiform in the nineteenth century, the contours of this historic world-metropolis have become sharper; digital techniques such as high-resolution satellite imagery and laser holography, used to replicate dug-up artifacts, round out the new image of Babel. This is another sense in which Babel has been reloaded.

4. In these mythical and scientific depictions alike, the question of Babel finds its answer either in the demonization or in the recognition of the formidable legacy that ancient Near Eastern civilization bequeathed to the West, shaping artifacts and ideas to this day; its presence continues to

resonate in mythology, iconography, architecture, and—at least in the case of the calendar as well as the names of celestial bodies and their constellations—the history of knowledge. Last but not least, Babel has definitively inspired cultural and linguistic critique in the humanities and social sciences.

Even with this laudable diversity of answers, our question remains fundamentally unaltered. Or more precisely, this central question drives us relentlessly further, expanding the horizons of an originally linguistic question into dimensions of culture and history that traverse academic disciplines and practices. Our new question thus diverges from, but remains homonymic with, our original one: What does Babel mean?

BBL

In his famous essay on the theory of translation, *Des Tours de Babel*, Jacques Derrida situates the question of Babel within a structural-systemic context prior to any discussion of its cultural-historical significance. According to Derrida, one must first decide whether Babel is to be understood as a "proper" or a "common" name. In the first case, the question of meaning is obsolete insofar as the proper name is "the reference of a pure signifier to a single being."[14] In other words, as a proper name, Babel is untranslatable, just as "Peter Miller" cannot be addressed as "Pierre Meunier" without running the risk of causing confusion. The functioning of a proper name is, therefore, essentially based in precluding the possibility of its translation. In this respect, Derrida distinguishes proper names from common names, which are easily translatable ("Müller," "meunier," "miller," "aceñero," etc.).

However, it is plainly evident that the city's name in the book of Genesis had been translated. In ancient Near Eastern languages, "Babel" is a word that contains multiple meanings, which vary considerably and sometimes even completely oppose each other. Ancient Near Eastern Studies have called into question whether the word "confusion" in Gen. 11.9 is at all an adequate translation of the word "Babel." Philologists, on the other hand, simply attribute this translation to an error on the part of the author of Genesis. Vowel-sounds remain largely unrecorded in Old Babylonian cuneiform, and since only its consonants ("BBL") were ever recorded—leaving its vowels to be guessed by means of interpretation—the ultimately proper spelling of the word "Babel" remains undetermined.[15] When the Jewish author of Genesis translated "Babel" as the word "confusion," it is likely that he took a Sumerian root as its basis because the name of the city may have sounded to the author's ear as akin to the Hebrew word *Babal*, meaning "mess." But if one were to trace the root of "BBL" from the Babylonian-Akkadian language, this would give *bâb ili*, meaning "gate of God," "house of God," "gate of the gods" (*bâb*: gate).[16]

In his monumental work *The Tower of Babel*, Arno Borst approaches this error of translation from its historical context, seizing the opportunity to offer a sophisticated cultural critique. The saga of the confusion of languages, according to Borst,

> [...] could only emerge where the difference between languages and cultures had become a problem, and this was not the case in Ancient Babylon, where a natural and historical diversity prevailed. The Babylonian-Akkadian language was until Egyptian the international lingua franca of the second millennium [...]. The world [of the world dominators] established itself as a well-ordered cosmic state whose regime remained unaffected by the multiplicity of languages and origins; people and language are in no way bound-up together and have little to no significance in a kingdom whose rulers refer to themselves as the "king of the universe".[17]

Evidently, the author of Genesis conjured the word "confusion" with the impression in mind of this ancient city as a hub of languages and cultures, frequented by travelers, merchants, even prisoners from all over the world. In addition to the business and literary language of Akkadian, one could hear languages from many different linguistic communities being spoken, including the languages of Aramaeans, Assyrians, Mitanni, Medes, Hittites, Edomites, Moabites, and Jews.[18] It may be pure coincidence that the Sumerian literature has an epic of Enmerkar containing a myth of linguistic misunderstanding between the gods Enki and Enlil. The inspiration for the author's translation might have been drawn from such circumstantial evidence, but Borst decisively argues that the translation of "Babel" as "confusion" was actually a consequence of the author's lack of understanding of the multicultural openness that defined this cosmopolitan state.

The author of Genesis apparently had but one language in mind, ignoring the many "urban" languages and dialects spoken at the time, in particular the business and literary language of Akkadian, as well as Sumerian, Aramaic, Assyrian, and many others. The only language that this author ever considered to be true and holy was the language of "Canaan," or, as it was known since the age of Hellenism, "Hebrew."[19]

The question of Babel, our initial question that we have pursued unabated thus far, reappears here once more and *in nuce*: What is to be regarded as more "real, true or sacred": the idea that "the whole earth was of one language, and of one speech," or the colorful diversity of languages?[20]

Tower and ruin

Upon closer observation, Derrida also takes his point of departure from this philological debate by posing the question of what language we are dealing with when we speak of Babel. His answer, at least at first glance, comes across as redundant: "In what tongue was the tower of Babel first constructed and deconstructed? In a tongue within which the proper name of Babel could also, by confusion, be translated by 'confusion.'"[21] With this formulation, Derrida precisely discerns the Babylonian predicament. When the author of Genesis translates the word "Babel" as "confusion," he does not conceive "Babel" as a proper name, that is, as a word that acts as a "pure signifier," referring to a specific "city," "people," or "language" (Gen. 11) as a unique "being."[22] Rather, Babel was treated as though a translatable common noun.

For Derrida, the egregious violation of a norm does not solely consist in the slip-up, which can be accounted for by a translator confusing two languages. This actual scandal bears on something much more fundamental, namely, that the proper name was translated in the first place. This violation of a norm touches on the fundamental structure of translation. For the process of translation assumes an intact semiosis; it must insist on maintaining a strict separation between proper name and common noun. Derrida's reasoning comes by way of his reading of Voltaire's article on Babel in the *Dictonnaire philosophique*. Voltaire addresses the meanders of this case of translation as follows:

> I do not know why it is said, in Genesis, that Babel signifies confusion, for, as I have already observed, *ba* answers to father in the eastern languages, and *bel* signifies God. Babel means the city of God, the holy city. But it is incontestable that Babel means confusion, possibly because the architects were confounded after having raised their work to eighty-one thousand feet, perhaps because languages were then confounded.[23]

Derrida sets out to trace in detail Voltaire's treatment of the translation error. Voltaire does not only describe this error "with calm irony," as Derrida stresses; moreover, he perpetuates the Babylonian confusion by suggesting yet another translation. When Voltaire, following up the findings of Near Eastern Studies, translates Babel as "the city of God," he does not simply undertake a philological correction, but rather uncovers yet another abyss of translation. He not only translated the untranslatable name of the city, but also, according to Derrida, brushed up against the name of the Father, the untranslatable divine patronym:

> In giving his name, a name of his choice, in giving all names, the father would be at the origin of language, and that power would belong by right to God the father. And the name of God the father would be the name of that origin of tongues. But it is also that God who [...] annuls the gift of tongues, or at least embroils it, sows confusion among his sons, and poisons the present (*Gift* – gift).[24]

This is contentious for any concept of translation. Ultimately, this act of divine naming establishes the "God-Father" as a monotheistic singularity, whereby he, by the way, carries out the most radical thinkable break between the Jewish and Babylonian world. This "God-Name" does not manifest itself here simply as a simple singular character or sign as a proper name would allow; instead, it has been contaminated with translatability, moreover a bewildering translatability that takes place in the play *between* languages, in the relationship *between* one language and another. Derrida concludes from this:

> In giving his name, God also appeals to translation, not only between the tongues that had suddenly become multiple and confused, but first *of his name*, of the name he had proclaimed, given, and which should be translated as confusion to be understood, hence, to let it be understood that it is difficult to translate and so to understand it.[25]

This is to say, the name of the one true God establishes the law of translation, and it does so by virtue of his own untranslatability. The law of Babel, according to Derrida, is built on this paradoxical structure. Effectively, the law requires translation and forbids it at the same time; the law provides a name in the act of divesting it, making the translation a kind of irredeemable task. The "true" translation remains—like the Tower—unfinished. In this sense, the Babylonian law is both name-giving and name-expunging; it is always simultaneously under construction and in decay, both tower and ruin, eternally unfinished, a non-finalizable provision.

This provision demanded by Babel consists neither of the simple correction of an obvious error in translation nor of the uncritical affirmation of melting pots by a single-minded cultural theory, but least of all does it consist in the demonization of multiculturalism, as Borst attributes to the author of Genesis. This provision presents itself far more as a task to translate *between* languages and *between* cultures.

Language and stars

In the case of Babel, the unfinished and unfinishable aspect of translation manifests itself in terms of construction—of "deconstruction," as Derrida proposes in his own account—and thus of building and architecture.[26] Indeed, Babylonian building projects have been interrupted and reconstructed on many an occasion, from Nebuchadnezzar II to Robert Koldewey, who relocated the Ishtar Gate along with the Processional Way to Berlin's Museum Island, and ironically to Saddam Hussein, who replicated the Ishtar Gate and the dilapidated excavation site in their original location near Hillah in modern Iraq, adorning it with a cheap and "sun-faded copy" of a shabby "Disneyland-palace," apparently signaling the absence of any achievements of advanced culture with this undignified memorial.[27]

Voltaire speaks to the bewildering and megalomaniac aspect of building when he inquires about the builders themselves, who were perhaps "confounded or confused" after having built a tower 81,000 feet tall (according to biblical measurements). This delusion of grandeur primarily—and literally—refers to the incomprehensible complexity of chaotic numbers. In this way, the confusion of languages finds a correspondence in architecture, which in turn has a numeric value: 81,000.

In Mesopotamian writings, Babylonian architecture is repeatedly described as a numerical system. This mathematical dimension becomes all the more peculiar when we inquire into the function of the towers in their respective historical context, considering that, as Borst points out, they were "not a document of human hubris, but rather of pure piety."[28] Archaeologists now agree that the zikkurats in Babylon were dedicated to the astral gods of the universe and foremost the city-god Marduk. Knowledgeable of astronomy, mathematics, omens, rituals, and mythology, the priests who were officers of the temple attempted to communicate with the gods through signs, whereby the temple became a kind of tracking station for data-transmission. The round towers were likewise astronomical observatories as well as sacred sites of the law.

With the same authority that the astronomers, through their practice of observation, sought to make celestial phenomena accessible to divination, they invented mathematical techniques to forecast the calculation of lunar and solar eclipses, as well as units of time and distance. The cuneiform tablets of *Enuma Anu Enlil* (second millennium BCE) project the gods Anu and Enlil as figures in an astronomical text applying sexagesimal systems to 360-degree circles, as well as dividing the year into twelve months and the hour into 60 minutes.[29] In this way, the towers "made connections between heaven and earth, serving like ladders to heaven."[30]

In their search for cosmic laws, the Babylonians frequently made use of the symbolic number 72, as Arno Borst has noted, in such instances as the astronomical pentacle of the goddess Ishtar (Venus), where each page is cut at 72 degrees, or in the *Gilgamesh Epic* (7, I, 43), where Enkidu attempts to summon the order of the Stars and Heavens by "angrily crying at the wooden entry door of the forest of *Humbaba*: 'Your height amounts to six times twelve cubits, your width amounts to two times twelve cubits.'"[31] As Borst explains, "according to the Sumerian sexagesimal system previously invented by the Sumerians, 72, or half of 12 times 12, kept reemerging, appearing next to the numbers 6, 12, 24, and 36, numbers that rendered honor to the Stars as the secret language of the Heavens."[32] The number 72 indeed embodies the Babylonian order of the cosmos, 12 times 12/2 or $12^2/2$ as the formula of stars *and* languages. According to Borst, the belief that 72 languages and 72 nations emerged through God's miraculous intervention persisted well into the Middle Ages.[33]

It is remarkable that the author of Genesis did not resort to bewildering numbers to convey the Babylonian enigma, engaging neither Borst's 72 nor Voltaire's 81. Instead, he repeatedly mentions another integer: the discussion concerns *one* language and *one* form of speech, *one* city and *one* tower, "whose apex reached up to the Heavens," and *one* name that brings together the sons of Shem to prevent them from "scattering over the whole earth" (Gen. 11.1–9). Rather than any great number, the author of Genesis numerically quantified the tower of Babel with the number one. In effect, the gesture brings to light a chiasmus: he translated the Babylonian "Babel" (God's gate) with the Hebrew word for "confusion," whereas he translated the Babylonian number 72 (or 81) with "one." In this distortion, the translator glimpses the iniquity of the tower-builders: in the misuse of "one" as the one paradisiacal primordial number.

"The whole earth was of one language," according to the book of Genesis (11.1). The phrase "of *one* language"—inclusive of *one* world—could just as well describe the utopia of a distant past as the present vision of our future. It persists in the most varied of cultural paradigms from past empires into the present with its worldwide flows on an anglicizing planet. It refers back to that primal scene of the creation story in Genesis when God created heaven, earth, and man, to whom he gave language. In Eden, God always spoke to Adam in a single sacred language, albeit one relative to the cultural reception of the Scripture: first Hebrew, later Greek for the Eastern Church, Latin for the Western Church, and finally Arabic for Muhammad.

If the Babylonian *nomos* assumes the value of one, then this number is also valid for the single, singular, and untranslatable name. At the same time, and with the same legitimacy, the name Babel tallies with its translation as "confusion." The Babylonian order ("BBL") egregiously equates the number one with confusion, such that the paradisiacal unity of one becomes discernible in the large number that Voltaire marks in biblical feet with respect to the height of the tower (81) and that Borst discovers in the ubiquitous mystical number that corresponds to the Babylonian sexagesimal system, that is, the 72 languages into which God's word is divided in the miracle of Pentecost and the 72 languages in which the name of the Father remains ineffable, or the one single holy language.[34]

The whole earth

In the dense texture of his essay on Babel, Derrida weaves yet a further thread, an earthly one. His considerations of language take particular note of the mechanisms and rhetoric of belonging employed by language users: origin, ancestry, gender, generation, nation, genealogy. It is in this regard that Derrida points out how Chapter 11 of the Book of Genesis narrates a family history in which the sons of Shem, one of the families of the children of Noah, seek "to *make a name for themselves* in a universal tongue that would also be an idiom" and thus "to assure themselves, by themselves, a unique and universal genealogy."[35] This is foretold in Chapter 10 in a detailed genealogical account. There we encounter the story of "the descendants of the sons of Noah, both kin and a people," who are spread out "on earth after the flood" in a "plain in the land Sinaer" (Gen. 10.32; 11.2). In this instance, the foundation of the language goes hand in hand with the foundation of a family tree.

While Derrida first takes up this thread in Genesis, he further traces it in Walter Benjamin's essay on translation. In it, Derrida re-encounters the motifs of "family" and "life" in connection with the work of translation. When Benjamin speaks of "kinship among languages," from the "life" and "survival" of the original text, from "holy growth" and "germs of language," and when he writes that the task of translation consists in "bringing the seed of pure language to maturity," these motifs serve him to want to see the work of translation as an assignment, or, as Derrida specifies, as a duty or a debt, a "to translate."

The task of translation, according to Benjamin, "seems to be insoluble, determinable in no solution."[36] If languages aim towards a "pure language" through translation, Benjamin holds translation to be an infinite, non-satisfiable task, a non-redeemable debt, an essential incompleteness of a "totality," of "one whole." It is precisely this whole wherein Derrida recognizes "language itself as the Babylonian event," namely as a unity erupting into a multiplicity: "the being-language of the language, tongue or language *as such*" means a "unity without any self-identity, which makes for the fact that there are languages and that they are languages."[37]

The idea of a "Babylonian planet," as it is developed in this book, proceeds from Benjamin's figure of the genealogical imperative "to-be-translated," yet traces the motifs of "growth" and "descent" in another direction. Seen from a planetary perspective, the relationship between the scattering of languages and the scattering of humans across the face of the earth comes into focus. In this way, the concept of native language or mother tongue also finds itself entwined with the fatherland, another term understood genealogically. In the final analysis, Babel also tells a story about a country in which the descendants of Noah have scattered but now seek to gather back together, to settle on the plain, to inhabit it, to build a city and a tower in order to help their family lineage become a proper name, and thereby to establish, literally, a nation, a *natio*, a "genesis."

Derrida sees the language of Genesis not as a straightforward idiom, but rather as Babylonian, a multilingual language in which the name Babylon is both possible and impossible to translate. Like the Babylonian language, the nation of Genesis is not simply a delimited or detachable territory. The mythical country from which the new—though yet to be founded—nation emerged and across which it spread is not the typical fatherland to which homecoming sons return, but rather a *planetary landscape*: homeland and habitat to-be. From a historical perspective, the repeatedly emphasized phrase "the whole earth" includes not only the entire Mediterranean but moreover all *terra incognita*. Thus, it is written that the nations were "divided in the earth after the flood" (Gen. 10.32); the "whole earth was of one language" (Gen. 11.1); people did not want to be "scattered abroad upon the face of the whole earth" (Gen. 11.4); Yahweh, as he gazed at their tower and their language, "confound[ed] the language of all the earth" and "scatter[ed] them abroad upon the face of the earth" (Gen. 11.9).

The story of Exodus takes place across this "whole earth." It is about flight and expulsion as much as the longing to settle down, the desire to build, to live, and to provide an abode for being. In the process, the story imagines a fatherland only from within a movement of diaspora and nomadism, and it imagines a mother tongue as an idiom *to-be-translated*. This dispersion and dissemination that inhabit translation turn out to be an event related to migration and exile, to being-underway, as well as to the "task" of building. In connection with these crisis-ridden experiences—the loss of a homeland, a sense of belonging, an identity, and a proper name and the demand for their return—translation also calls for an ethics of the Other.

The planet of the Other

Derrida dedicates much of his efforts to engage the ethics of translation as they pertain to notions of "obligation" or "debt." In his Babel essay, he speaks of the task of translation as a "requirement for the other as translator," who takes upon himself the obligation to respond as an invitation to survive.[38] The Other is devised as an endless task, a non-redeemable debt with respect to Benjamin's "pure" or "true" language.

In his later work, Derrida came to repeatedly emphasize this obligation to the Other in a variety of contexts. At the same time, a concept of the Other that is at the core of the philosophy of language continues to develop, especially with regard to the laws of hospitality and the commitment to cosmopolitanism.[39] For Derrida, the Other is never understood as a mere next, the friend, sister or brother, neighbor or fellow citizen; the Other is also, if not foremost, the distant "alien" Other who speaks a different language, has different customs and habits, who is none other than the subject with whom we must share the earth.

In such a cosmopolitan context, Babylonian thought becomes planetary thought. It consists in imagining the whole of Babylonian society spread across the face of the earth, literally holding the spherical shape of the planet before our imagination. This image calls for a far-reaching revision of the state of humanity: in view of such a spherical shape of the earth, political, economic, cultural, or ecological relations across the globe can no longer to be thought of independently from one another. Historical movements of colonization are no exception, ranging from Europe and over great oceans westwards and eastwards, making the world one whole for the global-reaching neo-colonial flows of technology, capital, images, and ideas in our present time of globalization. It should be emphasized, however, that the notion of a "Babylonian planet" does not simply assume the planet to be an uncomplicated, uniformly round body, but instead along the lines of a unity wondrously divided in 72 ways.

The figure of the Other serves as a link between "Babel" and "planet," and in this capacity it demands a reimagining of the question of the one and one's own as well as the entire spectrum of ideas pertaining to so-called "identity"—mother tongue, fatherland, rhetorics of "belonging" (religion, race, gender, property relations and so on)—as a question of the Other. This world-Other reformulates the question of fellow nations as the question of fellow humans, and in this way accords with Gayatri Chakravorty Spivak's plea for an imperative to continually reimagine the planet. What is at stake in Spivak's plea is the opposition of unifying modes of thinking about the globe with another, a so-called "planetary mode of thinking," whose essence Spivak understands as an "ethics of difference":

> Globalization is achieved by the imposition of the same system of exchange everywhere. It is not too fanciful to say that, in the grid work of electronic capital, we achieve something that resembles that abstract ball covered in latitudes and longitudes, cut by virtual lines—once the equator and the tropics, now drawn increasingly by other requirements [. . .] of Geographical Information Systems. The globe is on our computers. No one lives there; and we think that we can aim to control globality. The planet is in the species of alterity, belonging to another system; and yet we inhabit it, on loan.[40]

The shift in thinking that takes place in the move from "globe" to "planet" demands a whole series of new readings: digital media world-networks become suspected of neo-imperialist universalizing assaults on a planet we inhabit *on loan*, and this notion of a loan is derived from an ecosophical and environmental awareness rather than from the financialization of markets and capital. Spivak is suspicious of the cultural techniques that are conducive to the consolidation of the world into a unity, above all the promulgation of a distinctly Western conception of development and democracy, the rise of English as a world language, the Latin alphabet as a global script, and so on and so forth.

Against various possibilities offered by globalization, Spivak posits the planet as the locus of a persisting demand for the *impossible*. The planet does not offer a basis for rights but rather responsibilities and the ongoing attempts to learn "the Aboriginal way of living as a custodian of the planet."[41] The focus of this responsibility is the earth itself, in the sense of a "human habitation in community."[42] The prototypical world-Other that Spivak has in mind is the migrant. Spivak takes up arms for the refugees and migrants of the world when she pleads for a "re-constellated planetary imperative to responsibility seen as a right pre-comprehending becoming-human."[43] Seen this way, the figure of the world-Other stands in closest connection to the laws of hospitality, the right to residence, to build, to dwell, "to settle down," in the biblical sense, and "to make a name for oneself."

Taken as a whole, the concept of the Babylonian planet articulates many contemporary demands: the task of translating, a commitment to the world-Other, and an imperative to reimagine the planet. It further differentiates these linguistic and cultural-philosophical positions by placing them on a historically broad base of cultural artifacts. In a series of detailed case studies, both the Babylonian concept of the encounter and the planetary concept of the whole-earth serve as guiding figures of analysis. The intertwining of these concepts promises a renewed cultural understanding receptive to—especially in view of the historical surges of globalization—the forms of cultural encounter to come.

2

Europe: Myth and Translation[1]

When a translator translates from a constituted language, whose system of inscription, and permissible narratives are "her own," this secondary act, translation in the narrow sense, as it were, is also a peculiar act of reparation—toward the language of the inside, a language in which we are "responsible," the guilt of seeing it as one language among many.[2]

The Mediterranean Sea

Starting from Babylon, follow the waters of the Euphrates and the Tigris upstream, tracing the advancement of the Assyrian Army through grasslands and shrublands, always moving westward. This route follows the displacement of the center of the world, from Mesopotamia to the Mediterranean, in early antiquity. This route also follows the journeys of Phoenician and Greek seafarers. They landed on distant shores, colonizing coasts and inland areas while cultivating Mediterranean vegetation, in particular the olive tree, in these foreign landscapes. For them the Mediterranean acted as a maritime artery of dissemination and dispersal but also as an artery of information, transportation, and commerce that connected the mother cities with their colonies and foreign trading posts, and in this way, this body of water provided for the centralization, homogenization, and universalization that characterized the world-concept of the *medius terra*.

The process of standardization accompanying the above movements provides an occasion for Édouard Glissant, the visionary of a "Whole-World" (*tout-monde*), to pose the Mediterranean against the Caribbean: "the Caribbean Sea differs from the Mediterranean in so far as it is an open sea, a sea that diffracts, while the Mediterranean is a sea that concentrates."[3] With its openings, thoroughfares, and passages, the landscape of the Caribbean is home to a young, complex, rhizomatic, and creolized culture of the chaos-world, according to

Glissant, one which stands in relation to the world-totality and which embodies an archipelagic thinking. In opposition to this, Glissant posits the established, continental cultural form of a systemic "root thinking," which assumes "that every identity is a root-identity."⁴ This thinking appeals to founding myths and "the idea of a filiation, i.e. a continuous connection from the community's present back to this Genesis."⁵

Indeed, established cultures offer innumerable and fabulous founding myths that fuel phantasms of origin and kinship as well as collective ideologies of divine election, privileged status, and religious vocation. Epic poetry—as Hegel called it—extends in old Europe from the *Old Testament* to the *Iliad* and the *Odyssey* up to *The Song of Roland* and to *The Legend of Arthur* and *The Song of the Nibelungen.*⁶ It encompasses the myth of the tower of Babel as well as the myth of Europe. And although both myths tell the story of a founding history and a naming, they are neither root-like nor gathered into the integer one; instead, they are scattered, if not outright Babylonian, a confusion of tongues. Glissant even emphasizes in the scope of his argument that over time no so-called "identity" can evade the encounter of languages and cultures known as creolization. All cultures, even the established ones with founding myths, are exposed to "the abundant panorama of all the languages of the world today": even "Europe is 'archipelagizing.'"⁷ Like the myth of Babel in Mesopotamia, the myth of Europe is a "root-thinking," a refounding and an act of naming; yet it is equally characterized by the fluid movement of languages and cultures as they encounter one other. The scene of this encounter is the Mediterranean. We will zoom in on it in this chapter.

The myth of Europe

Since early antiquity, people have been telling each other the legend of Europe, the Phoenician king's daughter, who was spotted by Zeus, the father of the gods, one day when she was picking flowers with her friends on the beach of her native land. Enthralled by Europe's grace, Zeus fell in love with her. In order to approach her, he transformed himself into a fine-looking bull to get her attention. She began to stroke and caress this tame animal and decorate his horns with flowers until she trusted him enough to climb on his back. Then the bull leaped up and carried the princess across the sea to Crete, from Asia to Europe. There, he had an affair with her and later married her off to the king of Crete, Asterios. She bore three sons and gave her name to the continent.

In the process of being handed down, the myth of the abduction of Europe has been translated countless times: from oral to written, from one literary version to another, from mythography into historiography, from Ancient Greek to Latin and from there into all modern languages. Scenes from the story have also been visualized in various artistic forms, such as pottery, reliefs, frescoes, paintings, collages, and installations.[8] In this confusion, there is no one true story of Europe, for no story can be elevated above another. There is also no one original that brings with it a series of translations, but always only a tumultuous mess. Put another way, the multiple translations constitute the myth itself; they construe it belatedly, so to speak.

What is ultimately indebted to the concept of translation is not only the textual type of myth, which touches on the principle of translation, but moreover the material of the myth's story, since the bull carries (*translata*) the princess from her homeland into a foreign country. Depending on the myth's narrative version, the foreign land is depicted as either friendly or hostile, and Europe's "migration" is staged accordingly, namely as a form of carrying off women in the sense of abduction, a common practice in the context of the Persian wars (like Io), but occasionally also as seduction and the fulfillment of a deep longing for the Other, the foreign. Significantly, the direction of Europe's journey leads from east to west, as if the historical conflicts between Orient and Occident, between East and West—the Cuban missile crisis, the building of the Berlin Wall, as well as the horrors of 9/11—have been apodictically programmed into this myth.

This chapter will focus on the breaks that emerge with each new enactment of Europe, in particular when the specific translation also involves a rewriting into another medium. The central objective of this chapter is to conceive of the idea of Europe with the framework of its translations in this sense, namely both as a procedure that produces intermedial transcriptions of a deferred original and as a migration between homeland and diaspora, thereby setting two remote places in relation to one another. Specifically, I would like to develop this objective based on four cultural objects that elaborate the concept of Europe in various medial modes: 1) linguistically, Europe as name; 2) mythographically, in the version of the epyllion by Moschos; 3) cartographically, with respect to the Prime Meridian; and 4) graphically, based on the frescoes by Tiepolo in the grand staircase of the Prince-Archbishop's palace in Würzburg, Germany.

A name, a legend, a cartographic element, and an architectonic painting, these media-cultural translations of Europe will be analyzed more closely below.

Europe as name—or the politics of translation

Let us first look at "Europe" as we looked at "Babel" in the previous chapter, posing the decisive question anew: What kind of name is Europe? Does it have a meaning? In which language does it have a meaning? Can "Europe" be translated?

That translation presupposes a distinction between a translatable common noun and an untranslatable proper name has been explored in the previous chapter on the basis of Jacques Derrida's theory of translation. In this connection, it is important to note that mythographers and classicists do not understand "Europe" as a monosemic proper name, which, to take up Derrida's definition once again, would maintain "the reference of a pure signifier to a single being" and thus would be untranslatable.[9] Instead, they understand "Europe" as an eponym: a name that refers to a mythic figure, place, or people. It is indisputable that "Europe," as eponym, is a translatable common noun, but translation becomes a serious matter of discussion the moment that one must decide how to translate "Europe."

In *Paulys Realencyclopädie der Classischen Altertumswissenschaft*, Hugo Berger, author of the article on Europe, states that the name is "composed of ευρύς 'broad' and όπ 'eye'."[10] The English Wikipedia site points in the same direction with the claim that the name *Eurṓpē*, stemming from Ancient Greek, "contains the elements εὐρύς (*eurús*), 'wide, broad,' and ὤψ (*ōps*, gen. ὠπός, *ōpós*) 'eye, face, countenance,' hence their composite *Eurṓpē* would mean 'wide-gazing' or 'broad of aspect'."[11] This conclusion does not conform exactly with Berger's translation, which does not go so far as to attribute a definite subject or object position to Europe.

Other dictionaries offer still another translation, one which Berger regards as "incorrect" and that is also mentioned in the English Wikipedia. It surmises, in the Greek *Eurṓpē*, a derivation of the Semitic word for "evening" and a family relation to the Phoenician word *ereb*, or "dark" and "downfall," as in *ereb shamshi*, "sunset." Accordingly, the meaning of "Europe" would be "evening-land" (as German *Abendland*) or "occident," comparable to *Maghrib*, and its antonym would thus be "morning-land" (as German *Morgenland*), or *Anatolia, Asia, Levant, Orient*, and *Nippon*.[12]

The three translators of "Europe" cited above seem to not entirely agree. They differ from each other not only in that they probe into the history of language at varying depths but also in that they use different sources, which they treat with varying conceptions of what constitutes scholarly standards. But a red thread runs throughout the confusion caused by the translations of Europe. For the three readings of "Europe"—one who sees far; one who is seen from afar; that (sun) which is setting—all define Europe from a distance. No matter how much the proposed translations might diverge, in each case "Europe" is not brought into relation to *here* but rather with a *distance*, with a *distant* land, one seen *from afar*, one who looks toward or even occupies the place where the sun sets.

What unfolds around Europe in all three readings is a complex scenario of vision, a situation of seeing that takes as its premise an external gaze, insofar as the representation of the *Abendland* always proceeds from an exterior vantage point located in the east and directed towards the west. "Europe" does not merely refer to a country, but rather to a *distant* land, a not-here that is always remote and never one with itself, because it is derived from the fixed point of the *Morgenland*. Europe in the sense of the *Abendland* does not merely refer to the occident but rather the occident *in its relation to* the orient, or even: as its *translation*.

The matter does not become any less ambiguous if we cease to inquire into how the common noun "Europe" is correctly translated and instead focus on which mythic or even historic figure the proper name "Europe" stands for. Even Herodotus admitted to not knowing where the name originated:

> As for Europe, no one knows whether or not it is surrounded by the sea, or where it got its name, unless we say that it came from Europa, the Tyrian woman, and before her time was nameless like the others. But it is clear that Europa was an Asiatic and never visited the country that the Greeks now call Europe, only sailing from Phoenicia to Crete and from Crete to Lycia. So much for this subject.[13]

Who Europe was, in which country and in which language she was at home, of which country she was a citizen, and which cultural identity she took with her when the bull carried her off—all these aspects remain quite vague in the myth's polyphony. Some authors name her as the daughter of Telephassa and Agenor, King of Sidon or Tyre. Others record Okeanos and Parthenope as her parents, Thrake as her sister, and Asia and Libya as half-sisters. According to Hesiod, in turn, Okeanos and Tethys are her parents. The later portrayals of a flower-picking Europe often go back to Moschos, who passes her off as the daughter of Phoenix and Telephassa.[14] On the whole, Europe's identity—her proper name as much as her genetic offspring or biometrical fingerprint—remain as polymorphous as the myths involved. She does not sign with an unambiguous identity, a juridically valid signature, and the confusion around her origins parallels the uncertain genealogy of the texts and artifacts that together form her myth.

At stake in the question of the proper name is not only the whole complex of lineage—the affiliation with a family and a people—and its relation to the archaic figures of blood and soil as well as those of nationality. What is also at stake in the proper name is the relation to the father and the fatherland as well as the mother and the mother tongue. From antiquity to modern political systems, the prevailing law states that only one who is in command of a proper name can assert, through a birthright regulated by law, a claim to a standing achieved by ancestors.[15] Seen in this way, the proper name is also a political issue; its politics consist in providing a subject with certain rights and duties while in its territory, and it also regulates the conditions in which a subject may rightfully leave the borders of its territory and, once abroad, which rights it enjoys as a visitor or guest.

Since, in this cascade of textual variants, Europe cannot invoke a patronym with any certainty, misgivings persist not only in regards to the identity of the beautiful princess, her original kingdom or fatherland, and the language in which her name would have meaning, but as a migrant, she arouses considerable suspicion. With nothing more than the clothes on her body, she crossed over the sea; entry and right of residence are admitted to her only because the native who carried her across the border acts as a guarantor for her, and through the status of marriage her stay will become permanently legalized.

In the ear of the Other: the epyllion of Moschos

Out of the endless reverberations of the Europe fragments and adaptations that have coursed through ancient literature ever since the *Illiad*, one poem in particular has achieved distinction—the epyllion of Moschos of Sicily from the second century BCE—because it is known as the "first completely preserved poetic treatment of the myth of Europe."[16] Winfried Bühler has translated it from Ancient Greek to German with great philological care. In doing so, he made a decisive turn from the most prominent translations until then, namely those of the Swabian school, which range from the pedagogically correct "Germanization" of Gustav Schwab to Eduard Mörike's word-for-word translation.[17] As he states in the preface, Bühler's translation does *not* raise "the claim to represent the linguistic effect of the original."[18] The translator thus spares us from what Walter Benjamin calls the "monstrous examples of such literalness" that were produced in abundance during the nineteenth century.[19] He also does not succumb to the mistake—in Benjamin's words—that "fidelity in the translation of individual words can almost never fully reproduce the sense they have in the original."[20]

Instead, Bühler makes an appeal to a different strategy of translation, claiming that his translation would "merely show how the text has been understood."[21] He attempts to evade the "irresolvable conflict" between freedom and fidelity in translation by positing a fictive historical recipient. Bühler then concedes, in all modesty, that he does not wish to reproduce in his readers the linguistic effect that the original text made on this historical recipient in his own day. Instead, Bühler wants to "merely show" how the text has been understood *by an historical* Other, that is, how it sounded "in the ear of the ancient Other," quite evidently out of the firm determination to know what resounded in that person's ears and head.[22]

The gesture of generosity with which Bühler offers his services as a translator involves bringing the Other into the center of this endeavor, yet it has less to do with "lending his ear to the Other" and more with speaking in the name of this Other, *for* the Other; it is a case of "lending a mouth" rather than an ear, and in this way, the Other is belatedly installed as a *Fürsprecher*, an advocate of a historically distant culture. Recent theorists of translation, however, diverge from Bühler with their suggestion that the language of the Other should persist in its very otherness. As Derrida has argued, from the Other comes what Benjamin has called the non-translatable, ungraspable, and non-communicable of language, which is what is at stake in translation.[23] Not only to tolerate this otherness but moreover to invite it into one's own language: this constitutes the task of translation.[24] Seen this way, the politics of translating proves to be an "ethicopolitical practice," as Spivak proposes in her reading of Derrida.[25] Furthermore, the encounter with Moschos' antique text shows how a politics of translation cannot be considered without an ethics of the *historically* Other.

In this sense, and with this task before our eyes, we want to turn to Moschos' epic of Europe, as the text presents itself to us today. Even if it has given rise to a naïve theory of translation, Bühler's German version has also produced an optimal text for an in-depth consideration of this chapter's opening question of who Europe was, in which country she was a citizen, and in which language she was at home.

Phoenician–Greek: between the languages, between the letters

In Moschos' epyllion, we meet Europe on the morning of her abduction, when picking flowers with her companion from a meadow by the beach. Before reaching the passage where Zeus transforms himself into a beautiful bull and

approaches her, an authorial narrator with an Olympian omniscience provides a
sketch of Europe, the other figures, their actions, their intentions, as well as
information about the family ties of the gods and the royal family. At this point,
the narrative switches into direct speech, and for several lines we hear Europe
speak in her own voice and her own language, when she directs her speech to her
companion:

> Come away, dear my fellows and my feres: let's ride for a merry sport upon this
> bull. For sure he will take us all upon his bowed back, so meek he looks and mild,
> so kind and so gentle, nothing resembling other bulls; moreover an understanding
> moveth over him meet as a man's, and all he lacks is speech.[26]

No indication is given as to which language Europe speaks. On the left side of
the page is Moschos' Ancient Greek text, while Bühler's text on the opposing
page is printed in German. Ostensibly, Europe is speaking in her mother tongue,
the language of her parents and of the royal house. What is also remarkable
about this "direct speech" is that Europe does not *directly* speak to the bull,
although he appears friendly and sensible, almost a human being. Well
considered, she directs her words to her female companion rather than to him;
since he lacks speech, the bull himself remains for the moment the dumb object
of her speech act.

Only later, during the crossing of the sea, does the king's daughter address the
bull directly: "Whither away with me, thou god-like bull? And who art thou [. . .]
'tis plain thou art a god" (vv. 135, 140). Probably, Europe again speaks in her
mother tongue, which ought to have been altogether foreign to the uncommon
stranger, the animal or God, but which he still appears to understand, for this
beautifully horned bull promptly answers her: "Be consoled, virgin, and fear not"
(v. 155). The beautiful princess and the divine bull each speak in their own
language, she in a royal human language, he in a divine animal language.
Miraculously, the one understands the other without requiring any translation
or without the one needing to awkwardly enter into the language of the other.
And yet they understand each other.

As to the question of precisely which languages were spoken, the epyllion
gives at best circumstantial evidence. From a cultural-historical perspective, the
very different languages of Phoenician and Greek suggest themselves, the one
Canaanite (northwest Semitic), the other belonging to the Indo-European family.
Moreover, each has formed differing writing systems: Phoenician is a dextral or
leftward-moving consonantal script, while Greek is initially a boustrophedonic
and later a sinistrograde or rightward-moving *scriptio plena* of a full alphabet.

Yet, the languages in the myth of Europe are, in a fantastic way, not entirely foreign to one other; what connects them is not a family relation in a linguistic sense but rather what Walter Benjamin describes as a "suprahistorical kinship between languages," according to which "in every one of them as a whole, one and the same thing is meant. Yet this one thing is achievable not by any single language but only by the totality of their intentions supplementing one another: pure language."[27]

Benjamin unfolds the idea of a kind of universal language that does not follow from the sum total of idiomatic vocabularies and grammars but rather from an urge or "intention" of individual languages to want to speak. A "pure" or "universal" language does not require another language in order to express a meaning. As far as the pragmatics of speaking goes, only one thing is missing: insofar as this language is an unredeemable guilt or unfinishable task, it is denied to mortals.

In the conversation between Europe and the father of the gods, this translation miracle may have been successful. But in the diaspora in Crete, when the Phoenician princess becomes the wife of the Cretan king, she will have been exposed to the troubles of earthly communication. Away from her fatherland, her mother tongue will have been transformed into a foreign language, the language of the Other, of the immigrant, the guest, or the one living in exile, until it becomes foreign to herself.

Similarly, the script that she will have used to sign her name at her marriage when legitimating her move and giving her name to the continent was both foreign and novel to the Cretans. Herodotus characterizes it as "Phoenician letters" (Φοινίκηια γράμματα) and even as the "letters of Kadmos" (Κάδμηια γράμματα), in the supposition that the Phoenicians who immigrated with Kadmos, in search of his missing sister, also brought their sciences, arts, and writing to the Greeks.[28] In this instance, mythography and historiography reveal themselves, as they do all too often, as joined discourses, because from the perspective of language history, the Phoenician alphabet numbers among the first non-pictorial, stabile, and abstract alphabetic scripts. It is indeed assumed that the principle of phonetic letter script—likewise Europe herself—has traveled from Phoenicia to Greece and that precisely this translation can be seen as the birth of modern Western alphabetic scripts.

Harald Haarmann provides a pertinent example when he points out that "the ancient Cretan expression for 'writing' [is] *phoinikázein* (literally, 'writing in the style of the Phoenicians')." Furthermore, Haarmann refers to an archeological find, according to which in Crete at the end of the sixth century BCE "the title for a person subject to the chancellery is given the expression 'Φοινίκηια γράμματα,' which refers to one who writes with Phoenician letters."[29] Europe may have written precisely in this way: in the style that the Phoenician immigrants wrote in Greece.

The handing down of the script across the Mediterranean and along the trading routes of the Phoenician seafarers is usually presented by historians of writing as a history of innovation and a transfer of technology, whereby the innovative moment of this new way of writing consists of a remarkable *encounter* of very different languages *in an alphabet*. The Phoenician script, though, had one deficiency: as a pure consonantal script, it completely lacked vowel letters. Only in the course of the relocation and the accompanying cultural encounter would this deficiency be ameliorated, namely through an event that could be characterized as an adaptation or assimilation: in a regraphetization process, a writing system that was developed for a Semitic language was adapted to the needs of an Indo-European language. Two striking examples are provided by the letters *Aleph* and *He*: *Aleph* no longer stands for the glottal stop and *He* no longer for the aspirate in Semitic; instead, they designate the vowels Alpha and (H)eta.[30]

It is thus conceivable that Europe, while riding astride the bull's back, took the letters across from Phoenicia to Greece in her belt bag. Writing her signature, and thereby giving her name to the continent, Europe may have first used those Phoenician letters for which she found an approximate phonetic correspondence in Greek: . . . *Resh* . . . *Peh* . . . It is not inconceivable that those empty spaces were filled by the Phoenician letters that first seemed useless in Greek: *Heh Vav* . . . *Ayin* . . . *Het*.[31]

This transcription, which is not a simple transfer but rather a misappropriation of the Phoenician or a confusion of the existing relation between letter and sound, constitutes Europe's real achievement, insofar as it gave rise to something completely unanticipated. With this new and henceforth Greek signature, the inventive immigrant gives the continent not only a name but also the initial spark for a first complete alphabet and thereby for a new mode of thinking, one which renegotiates the entire relationship between logos and voice. It is no mere coincidence that Eric Havelock characterizes the invention of the Greek alphabet a "cultural revolution."[32]

It should be noted that this new script is not only due to the *encounter* and mixing of two writing systems, two languages, and two cultures; it is also based on a deficiency, namely the absence of vowel signs, that is, the absence of a foreign element in the indigenous.

The prime meridian

Hesiod (*Histories* 4: 147) tells us how Europe's father sent his sons to look for his abducted daughter. Their travels took them to Thera, Kadmos, and Delphi, where, having failed to find their sister, they became colonists and founded new settlements. The exploration and conquest of the continent by these and other seafarers at that time found its spatial equivalent in a series of ancient worldviews. If in Homer (2: 251–91) the name Europe still applied restrictively to the Greek mainland, quite soon it was broadened to include other parts of the Mediterranean. Herodotus (*Histories* 4: 42) divided the then-known ecumenical world into three continents: Europe, Asia, and Libya. Europe's horizon was further extended to the coasts of Iceland and Norway by Pytheas of Massalia's legendary journey into the northern lands, together with a number of other major discoveries, which were mapped by Eratosthenes of Cyrene, a Greek cartographer, polymath, and director of the Library of Alexandria, resulting in a new worldview (see Figure 2.1). In his cartographic works, Eratosthenes shows himself as possibly the first planetarian, insofar as he plotted the spherical form of the earth in a coordinate system, indicated the distribution of water and land on the surface of

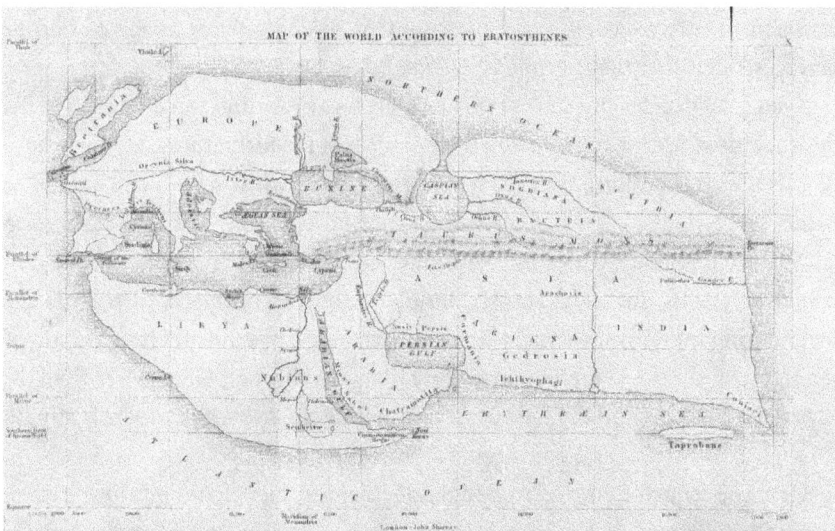

Figure 2.1 Nineteenth-century reconstruction of Eratosthenes' map of the known world, c. 194 BCE, Edward Herbert Bunbury, *A History of Ancient Geography among the Greeks and Romans from the Earliest Ages till the Fall of the Roman Empire* (London: John Murray, 1883), 667, https://commons.wikimedia.org/wiki/File:Mappa_di_Eratostene.jpg (public domain).

the globe, and furthermore calculated the circumference of the earth with spectacular accuracy.[33]

As a result of the campaigns of the Romans, Europe finally acquired political contours as reflected in Ptolemy's major worldview (completed around 180 CE), in which the borders of Europe coincide with those of the *Imperium Romanum*.[34] Instead of being written in Greek letters, the name *Εὐρώπη* began to be written mostly in Roman letters; instead of representing a mythological figure, "Europe" began to refer to a continent. Europe had become Europe.

The tripartition of the known world, as in Herodotus, sometimes changed. For example, Poseidonius translated the worldview of Eratosthenes into a cartographic map in which the inhabited world took on the form of a rhombus "by connecting the longest longitudes and latitudes," with "Europe as the northwestern triangle." Europe also formed "the northwestern quadrant" in the subsequent "round map again undertaken by the Romans."[35] This ancient theory of zones resulted from the need for a measuring unit, not just for mapping the known world, but also for grasping the *terra incognita* and for positioning it in relation to a homeland. Here, a further signature of Europe becomes apparent. It is executed by drawing a graphic line, which forms neither Phoenician letters nor Greek or Roman letters, but which is still something like a signature. For in the style of the writing or drawing hand that draws the coastline and divides ecumenism into zones, it is not the case that a geographical image of Europe emerges, but rather that Europe is invented.

Even today, such a line cuts across Europe. As a brass line, it is engraved in the floorboards of Meridian House on the premises of the former Royal Observatory in Greenwich (London): the prime meridian of the world, on which Greenwich Mean Time (GMT) is based. Tourists from all over the world flock here to admire the line that divides the world into east and west. In a glass case and lit from below, this line runs across Meridian House's courtyard, disregards the neighboring buildings, and continues on, first as a brass line, then as a chain of red lights, and next as an imaginary line that cuts through Greenwich, the UK, across the Channel and the European continent, across seas and oceans, running through all of Africa, and converging at the center of the poles.

Like the equator, the zero longitude divides the globe into two equal hemispheres. However, the equator of the earth is also a celestial equator, insofar as it traces from the earth the zenith of the solar orbit within a year, just as the tropic of Cancer and the tropic of Capricorn represent the northern and southern limits of the ecliptic, respectively (the highest summer and winter sun positions on the northern and southern hemispheres, respectively). Thus, while the latitude lines are derived from the relationship between the sun and the earth, the longitude lines do not owe themselves to such "cosmic" authority, but are purely earthly results of cultural and ideological codes.

Among these lines of latitude and longitude, the zero degree of longitude in particular is a political issue. After all, as a measure for determining global space and global time, it literally delineates the seam of the world. Hence, it has been subject to renegotiation throughout the course of history. For example, for Ptolemy, who designed the first comprehensive world atlas in about 150 CE, the prime meridian coincided with the western edge of the then-known world, near the current Canary Islands, close to Africa's northwest coast.[36] Over the years, therefore, all great centers—Rome, Copenhagen, Jerusalem, St. Petersburg, Pisa, Paris, and Philadelphia—claimed it for themselves, until 1884 when Greenwich was officially declared by the International Meridian-Conference to be the reference point for the global coordinate system.[37] In the end, this line was drawn by the hand of a sea power, which positioned its ships by relating the chronometric time of day (*Uhr-Zeit*) on board in combination with the sun's position to the "arche-time" (*Ur-Zeit*) of this universally valid zero-line. In this way, that faraway foreign land that was to be discovered and conquered was measured, framed, and mapped from the point of view of nowhere else than the observatory of a European royal house. Reason enough for Joseph Conrad—in his literary fantasy in *The Secret Agent* (1894)—to blow up the Greenwich Observatory in an effort to hit the imperial metropolitan center at its heart.

Tiepolo's *Treppenhaus*

Just as the practice of cartography today is predominantly a digital art of simulation, from the very start it was in liaison with painting, a liaison that has lasted over many centuries. Thus, zero longitude, with its logic of spatial organization along a zero point, finds a media-cultural equivalent, or translation, in figurative painting. If cartography, with its "panoramic point of view of the map," had already established a tradition in painting, the imagery of the Renaissance era pursues—according to Christine Buci-Glucksmann—a further, "perspectivist point of view."[38] The concept of a zero point in painting was first introduced by the Italian architect Brunelleschi in the fifteenth century. It refers to that specific point in perspectivist drawings, also called the vanishing point, from which represented objects seem to vanish into the distance. The trick of this zero point lies in giving viewers the illusion of a three-dimensional reality mediated on a two-dimensional plane in that they find themselves in the same position vis-à-vis the represented world as the painter.

The idea of the Renaissance zero point is exemplary, particularly with respect to a conceptualization of Europe, in Tiepolo's famous representation of the continents in the Baroque grand staircase (or *Treppenhaus*) of the Würzburg palace (1752). The vaulting of the *Treppenhaus* brings together the four continents in one painting: the center frieze represents heaven including the sun god Apollo, with Africa on the east frieze, Asia on the west frieze, America on the north frieze, and Europe on the south frieze. The inspection of the staircase frescoes is subject to difficult optical conditions, which are related to the curvature of the vault as in the geographical survey of the spherical shape of the earth. What is important when visiting the staircase is the perspective zero point from which the continents of the world are seen. In *Tiepolo and the Pictorial Intelligence* (1994), Svetlana Alpers and Michael Baxandall have analyzed this in detail.[39]

Viewed from the angle of visitors who have walked up the lower stairs and now find themselves on the staircase's halfway landing, their gaze falls directly onto the vault's south side and meets the front-frieze: Europe (see Figure 2.2). The European attributes are all represented: the bull and the horse; temple, cross, and crozier standing for religion; and moreover the tools of war and those of art, including painting on the left in front of the bull, the musicians further back on the right, and the sculptor even further to the right.[40] Alpers and Baxandall argue that the composition of the frescos, as well as the lighting effects and the architectonic structure of the staircase, put Europe into a privileged position in relation to the other continents.[41] Upon entering the *Treppenhaus*, Europe is

> [...] the first of the four parts of the world to be seen as a whole from an unstrained angle of view, from the landing at the turn of the stairs [...]. Its design is specific to this point of view. It is from here that its perspective [...] works. And being viewpoint-specific to this extent [the continent of Europe] is different from the other three friezes, which are calculated to work for a beholder on the move. In fact, perhaps one has no business looking at Europe from the same upper gallery from which one looks at Asia, Africa and America. If anything, one should look from Europe.
>
> Having walked from the half-way landing to the gallery, it is from below Europe that one first fully addresses Asia, Africa and America. The initial character of Europe goes rather beyond this sense. Even when one moves off from the south end of the gallery and wanders about the upper gallery beneath the friezes, it still remains [...] the point of view. Asia, Africa and America are depicted in their relation to Europe. Europe is the rubric, the initial code [...]. The ostensible frame of reference is Europe with the other three parts of the world as tributary.[42]

Figure 2.2 Giovanni Battista Tiepolo, ceiling frieze *Europa* (1752) in the grand staircase of the Würzburg palace. Author: Welleschik, CC BY-SA 3.0, https://commons.wikimedia.org/wiki/File:W%C3%BCrzburg_tiepolo_1.jpg.

A problem confronts the visitor entering the grand staircase of the palace, a problem that once again links up to the opening question(s) of the chapter: what does Europe mean—the one who *gazes broadly*; the one who *is seen* from a distance; or the one who lies where the sun sets (in the *Abendland*)? And is Europe translatable? Tiepolo formulates his answer in a visual mode, insofar as the transfer of Europe across the Mediterranean is laid out precisely according to this logic of a zero point, which is assumed to be the ideal point of view. His answer turns out to be complex, if we follow the analyses of Alpers and Baxandall, according to which the first frieze is the one that is both seen by the visitor "as a whole from an unstrained angle of view" and is set as the ideal perspectival point of view, *from which* one has "the first complete view of Asia, Africa, and America."

Europe thereby occupies the position that is seen without distortion and from which the other continents can be seen in their entirety. The perspective resting points of the grand staircase are organized from Europe, namely the southern pole, which is intended for a resting beholder, and secondly, the opposing, northern pole, which offers the beholder a point of rest, from which he can observe the world without moving. The perspectival disturbances and distortions are minimal at these two poles. To the beholder who moves away from these two poles and, for instance, turns his eyes from Africa to Europe, the continents offer a deformed perspective. In the staircase, there is only one "correct" worldview: it is—literally—the Eurocentric one.

Alpers and Baxandall point out that this perspective is a purely artificial one: "in the same way as Mercator's map projection show the globe, [Tiepolo's maps] show a view that no one—not even Tiepolo himself—has seen."[43] This is so because the optical organization of the *Treppenhaus* is illusory: it shows the structure of the world from abstract, quasi-geodetic ideal poles that try to cunningly counteract the restrictions of the field of vision with a natural horizon. The *Treppenhaus* presents an architectonic world-stage that condenses the world into a single hemisphere. Significantly, the perspective is not that of the planetarium, which perceives the world from a position that is beyond the earth or even beyond the solar system; rather, Tiepolo's perspective is that of the *theatrum mundi*, which perceives the world as a whole from a position *within the world*.

Tiepolo's *Treppenhaus* extends beyond any simple or unambiguous treatment of a fixed Eurocentric perspective; rather, with the same means of architectonic painting it formulates a theory of world movement that presupposes a rotation around a middle axis (the stairs), which is needed in order for the entire world and all of the continents to be able to be seen. In this movement, the perspective resting points are destabilized, while images of Europe become visible from the problematic, secondary, and formerly excluded vantage points, namely Africa and Asia.

Evidently, Tiepolo took the assignment of Europe's transfer seriously. For the distortion that arises when the world is translated into signs never ceases; at no point in the gallery or on the steps of the staircase does the entire world become visible to the beholders in an undistorted way. They have to accept a skewed perspective no matter how they position themselves. But the distortions become bearable—at best—when the viewers remain within the orbit of the rotary motion, and from there try to compensate in what amounts to an ongoing cybernetic movement. This is the incomplete and unfinishable task of translation before which Europe places the visitor in the *Treppenhaus*.

M/Other

Like the cartographically and artistically rendered Europe, already the mythical Europe was not completely disinterested in the foreign. At the end of the chapter, we turn back to Moschos' epyllion. This time, we do not look at the famous scenes of the transformation and the transfer across the sea, but rather the little-known beginning of Moschos' poem, which deals with a dream of Europe that she dreamt in the early morning of the night before her abduction:

> [S]he dreamt that two lands near and far strove with one another for the possession of her. Their guise was the guise of women, and the one had the look of an outland wife and the other was like to the dames of her own country. Now this other clave very vehemently to her damsel, saying she was the mother that bare and nursed her, but the outland woman laid violent hands upon her and haled her away; nor went she altogether unwilling, for she that haled her said: "The Aegis-Bearer hath ordained thee to be mine."[44]

Of these two mothers, one resembles a foreigner and the other a native, and Europe appears attached to both. Moschos proceeds to say that Europe, awakening from her dream, was speechless with terror. Still confused about the clarity of the appearance of the two women, she finally spoke timidly in monologue:

> Who was the outland wife I did behold in my sleep? O how did desire possess my heart for her, and how gladly likewise did she take me to her arms and look upon me as I had been her child! I only pray the Blessed may make the dream turn out well.[45]

There are no day-residues in a Freudian sense told in this dream, but according to the "dream theory" of antiquity a statement of fate by the gods to the mortals. This fate may break on Europe by force, but she does not resist it. On the contrary, the prophecy awakens a longing in her heart, not for her biological, native mother, who claims birth and protection for herself, but for the other, the non-native one, and with her for the land that lies opposite the continent of Asia. This auspicious stranger, however, appears to her as a mother.

Like a wedge, Europe's desire, her homesickness for the non-home, drives itself between the traditional connection of blood and native soil, birth and homeland, mother tongue and fatherland. The basic statement of the mother, of which one cannot say anything but "I only have one mother, a single one, a unique one," is complemented here by this other, impossible sentence, "she is not mine." The mother is the origin of my mother tongue, and that language, like the mother, does not belong to me. In this split, a native language is invoked that, in correspondence with the Derridian concept of monolingualism, is never "the one language of self-understanding," but always originally foreign.[46] Europe's longing for the foreign cannot only be understood here as a symptom of something that according to Derrida should be seen as the core work of translation, namely an alienation or separation of that which precisely lays most claim to genealogical identity: the mother herself and with her the mother tongue.

It is not all that surprising that Derrida developed his concept of monolingualism at the very moment that cultural studies—in light of the new intermingling of the world on the occasion of the fall of the Berlin Wall and the rise of the World Wide Web—began to celebrate polyphony and polyglotism as dialogical principles, after Bahktin.[47] Derrida defined monolingualism as a language that one has and which one claims as a "mother tongue," a language that one is bound to speak, whether through birth, heritage, or nationality, and which—like the mother herself—in its very intimacy can never be replaced by another language.

At first glance, Derrida seems to place not only multiculturalism in question, but also formulates a highly contradictory demand: "Consequently, anyone should be able to declare under oath: 'I have only one language and it is not mine.'"[48] With this expression, Derrida's concept of "monolingualism" literally takes up the integer one, the very biblical cipher that takes on highly confusing traits in the myth of Babel, when "one city," "one tower," "one name," and "one language" are mentioned.[49] But upon closer inspection, it turns out that for Derrida these numerals do not cancel one another out: bilingualism does not take the place of monolingualism or multilingualism. Insofar as monolingualism is marked by the Babylonian division into the multiple, it is thus accompanied by a deep longing for the other language, that is, for the language of the Other. For Derrida, language always necessitates a "turn to the other," who gives "its word or rather [...] the possibility of giving its word."[50] Monolingualism is always furnished with this supplement of the Other:

> We only speak one language—and, since it returns to the other, it exists asymmetrically, always for the other, from the other, kept by the other. Coming from the other, remaining with the other, and returning to the other.[51]

Seen this way, Europe's language does not belong to her, and even the sons that she bore in Crete have no claim—whether a birthright or hereditary right, whether of blood or soil—to this language. The mother tongue always comes from the Other, who provides what is proper and peculiar of one's own language. Acknowledging the foreign in the self: this is the basic condition for every concept of cultural identity, in language and beyond.

Europe teaches us that so-called "cultural identity" can never be thought of as singular and root-like, never as completed and pure, but always as hybrid, as a poetics of relation. It is no mere coincidence that the prime meridian serves as an exemplary figure of hybridity in Robert Young's *Postcolonial Desire*. He explains his notion of hybridity through the image of a subject who in Greenwich is standing right on the line, with one foot in the western hemisphere and the other foot in the eastern hemisphere. Following the cartographic logic, a single step to the left is enough to designate this subject as occidental, or, for that matter, as oriental after a single step to the right. Thus, what was initially regarded as homogeneously Western starts mingling with the Other.

It cannot be emphasized enough that hybridity in Young's sense means less a resolution of the former opposites through assimilation than the challenge that Europe, by fixing the prime meridian to Greenwich, also acknowledges that the totality, homogeneity, and uniformity of the West is always also riven by the difference produced in Greenwich, that it thus experiences itself as originary different.

If language and culture are thus conceived as hybrid, the task of translation is not merely that of a tourist's multicultural approach to the Other, as demonstrated by Greenwich as a site for globetrotters and hemisphere hikers. Generally, the hybrid of the Babylonian planet cannot be equated with a polyglot internationalism or with Esperanto, these truly laudable attempts to form a borderless dialogue. Rather, the Babylonian planet is marked by the figure of the Other, who contaminates his own language—precisely in its phantasmatic form of a mother tongue—with otherness. Thus, the work of translation implies working on one's own language, which not only has to "become" foreign, but also, as Michael Wetzel emphasizes, has to be actively "made foreign."[52]

Regardless of whether she is riding astride the bull's back with the Phoenician letters in her belt bag, being transferred from Asia to the west over the Mediterranean, and regardless of whether she measures the world in a coordinate system, or unremittingly reinvents herself in the distortion of Tiepolo's *Treppenhaus*, Europe is never fixed but is instead a space of movement and flows, or, as Glissant writes, a Mediterranean "archipelago." Whether in Moschos, Greenwich, or Tiepolo, Europe is never something that is unproblematically identical with itself. Instead, sometimes as personal name and eponym, sometimes as cartographic line or architectonic drawing, Europe embodies this Babylonian task, in recognition of the globular form of the planet, of making the foreign familiar and the familiar foreign.

3

On the Shores of the *Cité nationale de l'histoire de l'immigration* in Paris[1]

How can one understand the stranger other than in a paradoxical way, in which one appeals to a universal right? This difficulty is highlighted by the interpretations of human rights [. . .] that were raised by the debate about the citizenship rights of blacks, Jews, and Protestants [. . .]. After all, this paradox of strangeness literally characterizes the discourses that aim to announce a declaration of rights as a—universalizable—French program.[2]

The grand capital

Since the dawn of the modern age, the world was discovered and measured in the course of the great sea voyages embarking from Europe on a trajectory that led beyond the Mediterranean Sea to the oceans and the most remote continents until the entire planet had been circumscribed. In an age of advancing scientific, technical, and medial innovation, both old and new Europe bethought themselves of the sustainable principles of global responsibility that would come to be collected under the names of the *Enlightenment, Aufklärung*, and *Lumières*. Just as the Enlightenment and colonialism formed joint discourses, recently post-Enlightenment and neo-colonialism have entered into a highly productive liaison. Our age posits anew the old questions of fellow man, of the distribution and transfer of resources, and of the translatability of cultural and ethical values and norms. But this time, it does so under the conditions of our contemporary phase of globalization. Then as now, these questions are bound to a peculiar rhetoric of place. Even though relevant for the entire planet and the human in and of itself together with his so called "universal" rights, they are based on a highly particular logic of the local.

On the world stage of occidental values and norms, certain places tower with a seemingly eternal permanence. Athens, Rome, and Jerusalem are followed by Byzantium, Paris, London, Brussels, and Berlin. In this chapter, we will pay a visit to one of these places. It is regarded as the capital of the great revolutions for human rights, for equality, freedom, and fraternity. Paul Valéry is only one among many Europeans who sees in it the capital of capitals, not only that of France or Europe but the capital of the world.[3]

Among the many palaces of France, the Élysée Palace is the most powerful. It sees itself, today as well as in the time of its founding, not only as a political, financial, or economic center; rather it claims an ideological, religious, cultural, and even a linguistic role in the world. This is the capital that we will visit, though not to inquire into the grandiose themes of world politics, trade, finance, or rights. Rather, our search is directed at what upon first glance may appear much more secondary but in truth touches upon all of these themes more than superficially. In a word, our inquiry approaches the capital as the epicenter of language, where the French language opens out into a world language. Instead of heading for the heart of the capital, we will seek out a small palace on the periphery of the city, where we can study the contemporary treatment of the fundamental questions of the Enlightenment with a concrete single case that is exhibited there within a few square meters.

In 2008, on the outskirts of Paris, the *Cité nationale de l'histoire de l'immigration* (CNHI) was opened, a French national museum dedicated to the history of immigration. According to its name, the museum does not see itself as a museum but rather as a *Cité*, that is, as a place or neighborhood, whose location is less privileged and in which social encounters take on a mostly unofficial, chaotic, and polyphonic character. Thus, the elevation of the *Cité* to an official, national site of commemoration also raises the expectation that the official, centralized discourses of French and European history will now be observed from a certain position on the margins.

This confrontation between the center and the periphery is announced already in the title of the museum, insofar as a *Cité nationale* indicates the institutional status of a French national museum. Two diametrically-opposed concepts, that of the *Cité* and that of the *nation*, are linked here, and with them two completely distinct ways of speaking. The nation is in equal parts monolithic and monologic. Oblivious to Derrida's concept of monolingualism—an alienation and deconstruction of the mother tongue, the city, and the tower— here *one* people (the French) speak in *one* nation (France) in *one* monologic language (French) and thus in an instance of what Michael Bakhtin calls "official discourse." While the nation stands for a kind of anti-Babel, the *Cité* is characterized by a babbling "intimate familiar" way of speaking.[4] In the formulation of a *Cité nationale*, a rhetorical energy is liberated, one that is nourished on the contradiction of this oxymoron. The effects of this energy damage the plausibility of both the concept of the national—and with it the related concepts of the republic and the state—and that of the *Cité*. The aporia that opens between *Cité* and *nationale* will be examined more closely in the following sections. This task involves tracing this aporia in the discursive order of the museum as well as in the language of which the museum avails itself: French.

A postcard from the edge of language

Before we examine the museum itself, let us look at an artifact that we encounter at the threshold of the museum, namely one of those little souvenirs that one can acquire in the gift shop and with which the museum advertises its visual concept far beyond the city limits (see Figure 3.1). This postcard appears friendly and cheerful: two hearts pierced by arrows smile at the viewer on a pink-pop

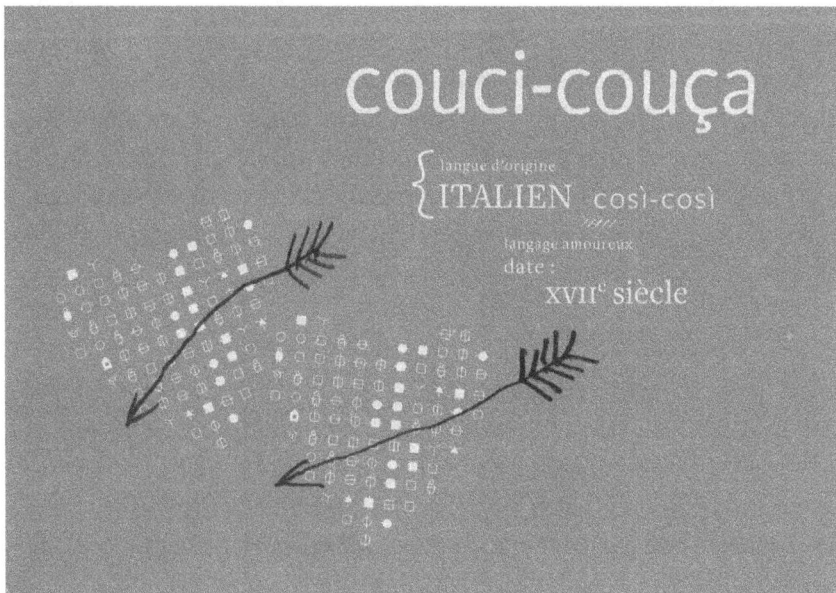

Figure 3.1 Postcard, Cité nationale de l'histoire de l'immigration; graphic conception, Pete Jeffs, *Réunion des musées nationaux*, Paris, 2007.

background. The hearts consist of small symbols that recall pictograms and script in general, yet they do not follow any conventional code. This idiosyncratic writing system was designed by Pete Jeffs especially for the CHNI.[5] The hearts affectionately lie next to one another, in harmony yet without actually touching. Only the two arrows, directed to a single but invisible target, promise to intersect, yet this point lies outside of the frame and waits there like the promise of a caress that is only suggested but is all the more tenderly signaled.

Couci-couça reads the legible inscription on this postcard. Like the pictured hearts, this phrase stems from a *langage amoureux*. In everyday speech, *couci-couça* answers the compassionate question, *comment vas-tu?* with a non-answer along the lines of *ni bien ni mal*, neither good nor bad.

- – How are you doing?
- – *Couci-couça.*
- – Are you content?
- – *Couci-couça.*

However, this answer is far more indifferent than *comme-ci comme-ça* (like this, like that). As a response, *couci-couça* contains the suggestion of a token of love for the caring attention of the questioner, since the phrase *faire cosi cosi* indicates an erotic sphere. The tenderness of this idiom does not lie solely in its erotic connotations; what we have here is an act of caressing that language itself provides.

Couci-couça is one of those *mots voyageurs*, a traveling word that at first glance appears to be truly French, or even, if you will, monolingual French. At the same time, the expression with its amorous meaning appears to be both estranging and stimulating. Marie Treps traces *couci-couça* etymologically back to an Italian origin: in the seventeenth century, *cos* meant *ainsi-ainsi*, literally "so-so."[6]

- – How are you doing?
- – Things are going so-so.

This *ainsi-ainsi* is pure (undecidable) rhetoric. It communicates nothing and translates nothing; it stands for nothing extralinguistic, and it is missing a grammatical object in which a comparison—X is like Y—can begin to make sense. It is the basic figure of metaphor *ab absurdum*: instead of establishing a meaningful relation of similarity to an other—a third in the sense of *a tertium comparationis*—the expression refers back to the object itself. With *couci-couça*, however, we have a different state of affairs. Although a self-referential metaphor in contemporary French, through the lens of linguistic history the expression is revealed as the encounter of *two languages*. When the French *comme-ci comme-ça* came into contact—through the familiar and intimate language of recent immigrants—with the Italian *cosi cosi*, what emerged was the mixed word *couci-couça*. In this neologism, the metaphorical structure remains enigmatically hermetic and without reference to an outside: whoever says *couci-couça* compares his state of mind to itself and thus implicitly claims to be fully at one with himself in a kind of monadic, tautological ipseity, uncontaminated by any outside, in this way affirming the condition of a self-contained "identity."

But the sheer self-referentiality of this expression also brings to light the innermost poetic capability of language: in this case, a single word—drawn from a native and a foreign language, French and Italian—intimately fuses two languages together and thereby reveals the sensibility of language for physical affection. Language, in the sense of *langue*, first of all means the individual language, the national language, the language of culture and literature, or, in the case of France, the language of the republic, of the *Lumières* and the *sens commun*.[7] The claim of a linguistic identity always appeals to at least one of these two myths of origin: a genealogical bond to the blood of the "mother tongue" or a territorial bond to the soil of the "fatherland." In response to such dogmatically based claims of mono- and multiculturalism, or of mono-, bi-, or multilingualism, Derrida counters with the concept of the "monolingualism of the Other," as discussed in the previous chapter, particularly with reference to the structural unpossessability and unmasterability of a national language like French. The conceptual coupling of language as abode and homeland in the sense of being-underway (Heidegger) or of an unfinishable "task" (Benjamin) takes on a particular accent in view of Francophonie. For when Derrida situates "his" Francophonie "on the shores of the French language, uniquely, neither inside it nor outside it" but rather "on the unplaceable line of its coast,"[8] he is referring to a geopolitically defined shore of Europe and in particular France that occasionally extends into the most distant overseas regions. In Derrida's personal experience of so-called "language acquisition" in a French school in colonial Algeria, Francophonie was split, from the very beginning, by the hyphen *between* the adjectives "Franco-Maghrebian." Inherent in the desire of language, however, is the traumatic experience of the terror inside languages, one which is related to French colonial policy.[9]

In this sense, *couci-couça* emerges as a textbook case of an expression that offers a healing reconciliation *in* language that became necessary by dint of an injury *through* language. This expression demonstrates not only the fusion of two idioms in two individual languages in an etymologically documented case, but also intimates the myriad possibilities for the encounters of languages. Creolization emerges in this startling neologism as the basic structure of every *langue*, in the sense of a monolingualism that—even when it concerns a native language, a *Muttersprache* that thereby summons genealogy, origin, background, and blood and soil as authorities—always stems from the Other.

Michael Bakhtin has spoken in a related context of a "double-voicing," a "dialogue of languages" that entails the "possibility of never having to define oneself in language [. . .] of saying 'I am me' in someone else's language, and in my own language, 'I am other.'"[10] According to Bakhtin, the dialogical principle brings forth a "double-voiced and internally dialogized" discourse in which "a potential dialogue is embedded, one as yet unfolded, a concentrated dialogue of two voices, two world-views, two languages" and that is possible, "of course, in a language system that is hermetic, pure and unitary."[11] Two idioms echo polyphonically in a single word. Just as two lips form speech, these two idioms form a single organ, one that touches itself, one that folds in on itself, one—recalling Luce Irigaray's formulation—that is split in its unity.[12] *Ainsi-ainsi*, says language, *so so*: just as the lips touch each other in speaking, so too does language affect itself and render itself as always already rent in two. Two languages, two historical idioms, two spheres, and two cultures meet each other, and in their confrontation emerges a *novum*, a third, which jubilantly calls to us and invites us into the pink multicultural world of the *Cité*. In eager anticipation, we make our way to visit the museum on the edge of Paris.

On the edge of the capital

Ever since the world's fair of 1931, the *Cité* has been a favored excursion for both Parisians and Paris tourists. It recalls trips to the beach: you pack a bag for the day, meet up with friends or family, and head out of the city. If you were to start from the historical heart of Paris, with its grand museums and the "official discourse" of their text panels, you would take Line 8 on the metro eastward past the Bastille until just before the Boulevard Périphérique, where the city ends and the *banlieue* begins. Just before the final station lies the Porte Dorée in the 12th arrondissement, today a middle-class district within the city limits, but once a notorious area on the edge of time that was known as "the zone" up to the 1920s.[13]

Around 1900, all of Paris beyond the city wall was encompassed by a 250-meter-wide military zone. This was a *non-aedificandi* zone, an empty area where all construction was prohibited, in order to guard against potential invasions and to maintain an open field of fire. Provisional wooden structures, however, were tolerated. Even after the fortifications were demolished, this zone remained a no man's land outside of the city, serving as an area of settlement for the rootless, recent immigrants, and the disenfranchised.[14] Both the Parisian proletariat and the waves of foreign workers fled to this zone in an attempt to escape the horrendous prices of housing. In search of a promised land, they formed a special population, the so-called *zoniers*, that the photographer Eugène Atget has seared onto the retina of our cultural memory. The ragpickers or *chiffoniers* had found accommodation outside the city fortifications not in real estate but rather in wheel estate, settling behind the Porte Dorée in a shantytown of caravans and shacks.[15] Etymologically, the Porte Dorée draws its name from this peripheral setting. The construction that served as the gateway to the city literally lies *à l'orée du bois*: on the verge of the forest of Vincennes, which borders the 12th arrondissement.[16] Over time, *de orée* fused into *Dorée*, and just as this elision dissolved both the boundaries of the words and their original meaning, so too did the *zone* disappear from the city.

Starting in the 1920s, the ragpickers were driven out, the city walls leveled, and the barracks demolished. A new space emerged in the east of Paris, an open space of 110 hectares, on which, in 1931, a new city was supposed to be built, a new promised land: the world metropolis of the *exposition coloniale*. For the occasion, a new metro station was constructed, one that would carry eight million visitors to the exposition space, in order to experience "le tour du monde en un jour" (a tour around the world in a day).[17] Endemic arts and crafts were exhibited, and on this occasion, the French government brought people from the colonies to present them in reproductions of their native architectural styles, such as wood huts and temples. As the centerpiece of the exhibit, an entire Senegalese fishing village was featured in the manner of a European ethnographical exposition.[18]

One single building would be granted architectural permanence: the main building of the *Empire Français*, designed by the hand of Albert Laprade. Then, as now, its ground floor housed the salon of the then-Colonial Secretary Paul Reynaud, as well as the salon of the Field Marshal Lyautey, Governor of Morocco. The grand ballroom extends above the second floor, where the exhibits were located.

Long after the provisional pavilions disappeared from the Bois de Vincennes, the *Musée national des arts d'Afrique et d'Océanie* (National Museum of the Arts of Africa and Oceana) was installed inside this Palace of the Colonies as a permanent colonial museum. Placed under monumental protection, the building remains nearly unchanged except for a new name: "Palais de la Porte Dorée." The name clearly indicates the architectural paradox, given that a *non-aedificandi* law provided the basis for having a historic city gate on the edge (*a l'orée*) of the Vincennes forest. Seen this way, the Palace of the Colonies, with its monumental imperial architecture, defies its own foundational law, namely the construction ban that was supposed to secure the capital by making its beltway into a fortification to guard against foreign invaders. The historical way of writing *Porte de Orée* itself had indicated this construction ban, by mirroring the border between city and forest with the border between the words *de* and *orée*. In this demarcation, writing designated a special kind of emptiness, a literal blank space between letters that mirrored a white space on the map, recalling the law of a taboo territory that can neither be written nor built upon. The Palace of the Porte Dorée was built on this very space that, by virtue of its name and the land use law it invokes, prohibits any building. It is this uncanny house that now shelters the *Cité nationale de l'histoire de l'immigration*.

Shorelines (I)

We arrive at the metro station Port Dorée on the eastern extension of Paris. Instead of an endemic forest, we suddenly find ourselves under palm trees. We listen to the murmur of the water that flows towards us in the *Square des anciens combattants d'Indochine* (Square of the veterans of the Indochina wars) like a wild stream from the fountains of the statue of "France Colonial." During the colonial exposition, this statue stood on a landing in front of the palace; today, it is exhibited just a stone's throw away. Modeled after Athena, the statue is outfitted with the trademarks of the empire: in her right hand she holds a spear, in her left, like a figurehead, she holds an angel. Her headgear, however, recalls a Gallic helmet.[19]

To reach the museum, we only have to cross the boulevard. The building powerfully towers above in a classical style replete with cornices and colonnades. Through cast-iron gates, watched over by two lions, we enter an enclosed courtyard whose surface is strewn with white gravel. A Senegalese fishing boat, moored under palm trees, invites us to marvel at the ingenuity of the boat builder that constructed this sloop out of a single piece of timber. For a moment, we can imagine that we are on the museum's own pebble beach, where the shade cast by palm trees invites us to unpack our beach bag and spread out our towel. On the horizon, ships of the major sea powers, sculpted by Alfred Janniot into the facade of the palace, have set full sail. They bring the riches from the colonies to the mother country: coffee from Senegal, pepper and rubber from Cambodia, rice and corn from Indochina. Between the oceans, life on the mainland of overseas territories is depicted in primal scenes of harvesting and hunting: a flurry of bodies, mouths wide open, spears and tusks thrust out of jungle canopies, primeval animals as proud and wild as the naturally vigorous men that hunt them, bare-breasted women gathering water.

Palm-lined stairs lead to the main entrance. The first thing one encounters in the large entrance hall are the standard museum fixtures: ticket office, information stand, museum shop, and coatroom. From here, stairs lead up to the exhibits of the *Cité*, another stair leads down to the basement where a tropical aquarium that was built during the colonial exposition remains a popular tourist attraction in its own right. The basement, with its natural spectacle of an exotic water world, is linked thematically with the aboveground cultural attractions via a small photographic exhibit, which shows people at the coast, in particular Senegalese villagers catching fish. In the topographic organization of the museum, this ethnographic mini-exhibition is situated in an intermediate zone, namely in the landing between basement and first floor, as though the primitive technology of fishing formed a thematic link or transition space, through which the visitor ascends from a state of nature to the light of civilization.

On the first floor, the large ballroom borders on the entrance hall. Frescoes in the colorful style of posters, stemming from the colonial period, have been reconstructed. The front wall displays Pierre-Henri Ducos de la Haille's vivid *La France et les cinq continents* with the eternal values of occidental civilization in allegorical procession—justice, peace, liberty—magnificently framed by exotic landscapes and sailing ships on the French oceans.[20] On the expansive floor, colorful beach umbrellas invite visitors to loiter. A breeze from abroad wafts through. But neither the breeze nor the aquarium will tempt us; we leave the beach and make our way to the exhibit.

The politics of showing

The *Cité nationale de l'histoire de l'immigration* was a long time in coming. Already in 1990, a group of historians had founded the *Association pour un musée de l'immigration* (Association for a Museum of Immigration), demanding a memorial site dedicated to the history of immigration in France, similar to the one on Ellis Island. It took a number of attempts. The Mitterand government hesitated, while the Chirac government resisted it outright. Only in 2002 did Jacques Chirac, following his re-election, take the project on, entrusting it to his cultural minister, Jacques Toubon. The latter emphasized the necessity for such a museum in his opening address on October 10, 2007:

> The history of France, the construction of its identity and its culture, is largely that of the millions of men and women that have left their homelands in order to settle in France and to become French. Yet this history is as good as unknown and unrecognized [...]. The *Cité* takes on the goal of becoming the place in which the legacy of immigration is not only preserved but moreover given its proper value.[21]

In this speech, Toubon takes on the function of an advocate. He speaks as a representative of the initiators of the museum. By the power of his office as President of the Orientation Committee of the museum, he speaks "for" the *Cité*, "for" the advisory board and the council of historians. Grammatically, Toubon speaks in the name of a third person, "the *Cité*," whose advocate he is. In the discursive order of the museum, however, he fills the role of the first person of that authoritative speech act which lies at the base of every national museum.

In her theory of the museum, Mieke Bal underlines the discursive character of showing and compares the museum discourse to a speech act: "In expositions a 'first person', the exposer, tells a 'second person', the visitor, about a 'third person', the object on display, who does not participate in the conversation."[22] The speech act of the museum is held in the first person and it is a constative one: it observes and affirmatively determines the history of France, and it will enlighten the French people regarding an—until now—unknown aspect of its history, a history that is "as good as unknown and unrecognized." The addressee, the authority identified by Bal as the "second person," to which the speech act directs itself is the French people, whose current view of immigration must be changed. The object of the speech act is the history of immigration and the stake of this third person in the development of the French people.

In sum, the *Cité* (first person) speaks to the French people (second person) about the immigrants (third person) with the goal of changing the observer's gaze vis-à-vis the history of immigration. Later, I will examine the peculiar rhetoric of Toubon's editorial note; at this point, though, we will turn our eyes to the exhibition itself. Let's follow Toubon's invitation vis-à-vis the exhibition objects, to not only observe the history of France in view of the problem of immigration, as the dominant tenor in discourses of migration runs, but more to perceive and recognize the achievements of the migrants. With our attention thus sharpened, our interest guides us to the second floor, where the permanent exhibition is located.

Benchmarks of migration

The permanent exhibition is dedicated to the history of immigration in France in the last two centuries. It bears the title *Repères*: benchmarks, points of orientation, from *se repérer*: to get one's bearings. Through nine thematic sequences, the so-called *Repères*, the visitor is routed along a path that leads chronologically from the first wave of migration to France's multicultural present.

1. *Emigrer* (Emigrate)
2. *Face à l'etat* (Facing the state)
3. *Terre d'accueil, France hostile* (Host country, hostile France)
4. *Ici et là-bas* (Here and there)
5. *Lieux de vie* (Living environment)
6. *Au travail* (At work)
7. *Enracinements* (Roots)
8. *Sportifs* (Athletes)
9. *Diversité* (Diversity)

Each of these themes is considered from three aspects: first, the official historical discourse is presented on interactive light tables by means of text, visual, and audio material. Photographs, facsimiles of archive documents, law decrees, and newspaper clippings report on celebrated and dismal passages in France's history of immigration. Secondly, this macro-historical discourse is complemented by those micro-historical, personal, and authentic objects that immigrants were able to save in their hand luggage either on ship crossings to Marseilles or train journeys across the border. These indispensable and portable means of survival in foreign lands include such items as a rice cooker, a violin, a transistor radio, a puppet, tailor's scissors to practice the vocation, as well as the documents of the crossing: letters, permits, and photographs, and eventually the luggage itself.[23] So numerous are the memory objects donated to the museum by the immigrants that a special *Galerie des Dons* was established just for them. Moreover, the exhibit displays individual remembrances in the form of letters and video recordings with contemporary witnesses. Finally, artifacts and art objects add to the mix as commentaries on the authentic historical material: paintings, caricatures, photo series, sculptures, video installations, and interactive play stations.

By its very nature, immigration withdraws from any central point of observation, for its events and objects come from an outside that, from the perspective of a national cultural canon, remains invisible or, to speak with Mieke Bal, silent. The permanent exhibition seeks to cope with this expositional recalcitrance by means of this special exhibition practice whereby the history of immigration is continually narrated in a combination and confrontation of multiple perspectives. For example, the benchmark "Facing the state" exhibits historical visual and audio documents of the policy of the minister André Postel-Vinay, who in 1974 attempted to limit the immigration of foreign workers through stricter laws. The minister's voice is complemented on the same panel by a counter-voice, namely a report by Michel Yapi, one of the *clandestins Africains* (so-called "clandestine" African immigrants) who in a short film with the title *Père clandestin légal* (A legal clandestine father) offers testimony about his status as a French non-citizen.[24] In this museum speech-act, the law splits into two voices that speak simultaneously and contrapuntally: the unofficial speech of the "clandestine" person enters into the arena of the official speech of the lawmaker. In the resulting polyphony of both voices, the status of the so-called *clandestine* proves to be a paradoxical construction, one produced in equal measure by the sheer existence of a human and by the legislation that prohibits such an existence. The *Cité* speaks in the name of the government *and* in the name of the immigrants and bases its historiographic authority on this creolized way of speaking.

In general, the individual exhibits indicate the peripheral position of the history of migration, its legal gray areas as well as the migrants' economic marginalization. With a meta-museal gesture, the museum points at itself and at its interactive techniques of exposition that are laid out in dialogue form, thereby avoiding a misappropriation of the building's history and that of the 12th arrondissement. A small photo series by Eugène Atget from the years 1912 to 1913 refers to the historical setting of the *Cité* as a former "zone." The xenophobia of French politicians and media is put on display. A gallery of photos by Florence Delahaye is dedicated to the graffiti of anonymous sprayers in the explosive Parisian suburbs, another to the immigrants that succeeded in making a name for themselves: Picasso, Goya, Kusturica.

The soccer legend Zinédine Zidane is honored in the "Benchmark athletes," and the celebrated victories of the French national team are presented as impossible without the goals of immigrants. The "Benchmark of living environments" contains a locked compartment whose windows offer various vantage points for visitors to peer in through. The sculpture *Climbing down* by Barthélémy Toguo, which alludes to the accommodation of a newcomer in a dormitory, particularly stands out (see Figure 3.2). The tower of bunk beds reaches up six levels, and each is outfitted with one of the large, sturdy woven plastic bags iconically known as *Türkentasche* (Turkish tote) in German, *sac polonaise* (Polish tote) in French, and *Chinese laundry bag* in the United States. This bag reappears throughout the exhibition, serving as a multicolored pop-icon of a multicultural culture.[25] In a way, they approximate the beach bags that we started out with. In the end, we were looking for such a pleasurable excursion, and we were not disappointed, for the beach appears ubiquitously in the museum as a symbolic place of arrival. As we will see, Toguo's bunk bed tower is in some respects such a beach.

Figure 3.2 Barthélémy Toguo, *Climbing down* (2004). © VG Bild-Kunst, Bonn, 2020.

Shorelines (II)

People on a beach can be seen on an image from Olivier Jobard's photography series *Entrien avec Kingsley* (Conversation with Kingsley). The image is somewhat blurred and underexposed. At first glance, it looks like a badly-staged snapshot at some beach. White foaming surf spills onto a shallow golden shore, as it does on the *terre promise* of a promising holiday resort. In the distance, human figures emerge from the water. At the bottom left, somewhat out of focus, several people are seated and facing the sea; one holds his head in his hands, looking exhausted. Between them and the water, two figures are standing above a body that is stretched out on the sand. There are no beach bags to be seen. At this point, we can recognize this beach as a difference kind of *terre promise*. The absence of a boat or any watercraft begs the question: where did these people come from? The photograph's caption, written by hand, situates the image in a kind of journal

"J'ai coulé puis j'ai nagé aussi vite que possible pour sortir de l'eau glacée. Les autres criaient. Ils se noyaient. Je suis retourné deux fois à l'eau pour les aider à regagner le bord. Puis je me suis écroulé. Il manquait deux personnes à l'appel."

I went under, then I swam as fast as possible to get out of the icy water.
The others shouted. They drowned. I returned twice to the water to help
them stay afloat. Then I collapsed. Two people were missing at roll call.

Figure 3.3 Olivier Jobard, *Entretien avec Kingsley* (2003). © VG Bild-Kunst, Bonn, 2020.

recording the long journey of "Kingsley," which Jobard documented in 2004 with a Leica camera. This journey took half a year and crossed many borders and coasts on its path from Cameroon, across the Niger to Nigeria, through the Sahara, Algeria, Morocco, the Canary Islands, and finally to the European continent.[26]

Again and again, the exhibits in the museum (re)turn to the beach. In countless variations, they gather the beaches of our planet into a collection, and in this way, the exhibits come to accumulate meanings of the promised land—those spaces of transit where the new arrivals reach a shore and set out to make a new life—until, in a meta-museal reflection, the *Cité* comes to resemble a beach.

The language of the republic

France is, without a doubt, proud of its beach stories. With the same political engagement with which he pushed the founding of the CNHI, Jacques Chirac campaigned for wide-ranging changes in the way French history is written. In his address of January 30, 2006 in the Élysée Palace, he ceremoniously announced:

> The greatness of a country is to accept its entire history, both its glorious chapters and its shadows. Our history is that of a great nation. We can look upon it with pride. We look upon it as it is. In this way, a people grows together, unites, and becomes stronger. That is what is at stake with the questions of memory: national unity and cohesion, love for one's own country, and confidence in who one is.[27]

In his public speech, Chirac demands that the history of slavery be recognized as a chapter in the history of France, and he articulates his wish for a national day of remembrance for slavery.[28] Moreover, the topic of slavery should be incorporated into the curriculum of elementary and secondary school. Finally, Chirac appoints "one of the greatest contemporary writers, Edouard Glissant" to plan a national center for the remembrance of slavery, the slave trade, and its abolition. Thus, he turns to the archipelagic thinker of the "whole world" and of creolization, who was once banished from France by Charles de Gaulle and thus from his homeland on the island of Martinique, France's westernmost extension. With this mandate, Chirac once again positioned himself against the formation of a Ministry for immigration and national identity and against the policies of his successor, Nicolas Sarkozy, policies that were already being advertised and which are not at all that unusual in terms of common European immigration policies.

It was no coincidence that Sarkozy was not present at the festive opening of the *Cité* when it should have been honoured and welcomed itself in the role of the newcomer. This attitude toward foreigners is not an isolated one in Europe. The concern to protect the territory from intruders in a unified Europe has produced a highly developed, EU-financed machinery. The name of this agency, The European Agency for the Management of Operational Cooperation at the External Borders, is derived from the French *Frontières extérieures* (External borders), or *Frontex* for short. Its operations are named after its areas of operations, and so it is no coincidence that coastal areas and in particular the Mediterranean are central: *Poseidon* (Eastern Mediterranean), *Hera* (Canary Islands and the coast of western Africa), *Nautilus* (between northern Africa and Malta/southern Italy), as well as *Amazon* (eight European airports; an operation tackling illegal migration from South America) and *Hermes 2011* (solely for the boat migrants on Lampedusa).[29]

The protective measures take the most diverse forms. What is decisive is the proper name, whose acknowledgment, from the perspective of hospitality, is far more significant than the mainstream media's sole focus on visible features of the refugees, namely: skin color (black), gender (male), age (young adult). Only the proper name confers the status of a legal subject to the refugees, a status which, by the power of the law of nations, both obliges Europe to apply, and releases it from, its duty of hospitality. It is a peculiar release. It *produces* deportees in the same way that Europe does, and both deny them asylum.

A strange and anachronistic twist in the development of scholarship consists in the linking of contemporary forms of hospitality with the archaic logic of blood: current proposals regarding the procedures for the intake of refugees call for DNA tests, which would establish identity and family in the sense of blood relations. Sarkozy is not alone in his idea of a "selective immigration," in which asylum seekers' French language proficiency and knowledge of republican values would be documented prior to their entry to Europe.[30] Paradoxically, such knowledge can often be gained only in capital cities. It is written in the large capital of capitals—to use Derrida's formulation from his essay on Europe, *The Other Cape*, which makes use of the polysemy of "cape"—that remains inaccessible to those migrants that reside in more remote areas. The visa that allows entrance into the capital can only be obtained in the capital. And the right to hospitality is reserved solely for those who can be shown to be non-foreign, who—either through ancestry and blood, or through language, education, and culture—already belong to something, even before their entrance is permitted.

With respect to the revolving door, which in one and the same movement both allows and disallows entrance, the dream of a creolized French of the whole world, the dream of Glissant and the *Cité*, faces a large obstacle. Even prior to the opening of the new museum, on May 18, 2007, eight academics resigned from the advisory board of the *Cité* in order to protest against the Sarkozy-promoted *Ministère de l'immigration, de l'intégration, de l'identité nationale et du codéveloppement*. To this day, the resigned university representatives remain in constant dialogue with the *Cité*.

Accent-free Creole

Let us glance once more at Jacques Chirac's public speech, given at the reception in honor of the slavery remembrance committee. At the point where the president entrusts Édouard Glissant with the planning of a research center for the history of slavery, he proceeds in the following words with a plea against forced labor:

> Finally, the fight against slavery is a fight of today. It is a struggle of France and the French-speaking world. Forced labor continues to exist in one form or another on almost every continent today: according to the United Nations, over 20 million people are victims of it. How can we allow the fact that, at the beginning of the 21st century, there are families in the world who, generation after generation, are "chained" in debt bondage?[31]

Chirac's question ("How can we allow . . .?") is admittedly not a serious one. It does not allow for a possible affirmation and does inquire even less into the basis for this state of affairs; instead, assuming a rhetorical attitude, the question articulates a complaint about the injustice of this world. This complaint in turn conceals a command, a command to a current fight, namely a "fight waged by France and Francophonie." Against the slavery of debt, Chirac poses the values of the republic, those of the great country that takes on this responsibility, because it is allegedly the land of human rights. Human rights, however, require a medial form, a book of laws, and its language is in this case Francophonie. In the *Cité*, which is of course a *Cité nationale*, it is precisely this Francophonie that is omnipresent.

C'est ici la douce France? "Is this sweet France?" asks a man wearing a Keffiyeh in a caricature by Georges Wolinski, trailing a line of people wading to shore from a steamship anchored just offshore, while a man with a dog observes their approach (see Figure 3.4). As in Wolinski's caricature, the new arrivals in the *Cité*,

Figure 3.4 Georges Wolinski, *Douce France* (n.d.), *Musée national de l'histoire et des cultures de l'immigration*, https://www.histoire-immigration.fr/collections/wolinski-douce-france.

from all regions of the world, all speak French, even as they are swimming toward the shore from an undetermined horizon. Strangely accent-free, immigrants report in video exhibitions of their deracinations, of their foreignness, of their French as well as non-French identity. Their creole is a peculiar one.

We are approaching the end of the tour. The last milestone bears the title "Diversity" and is dedicated to the encounter of languages. Here, the interpretative panels elucidate the historical relationships between languages: we read that French received Romanesque, Celtic, and Germanic influences, and later Arabian, Persian, Asian, and American ones. We read that of the 60,000 words in the *Dictionnaire Française*, 8,600 have a foreign origin. Then we are confronted with a panel with the inscription "Encounter":

Over the centuries, France has been permeated by the multiplicity of exchanges and of cultural contributions from abroad. The adaptations, borrowings, and mixtures shape the everyday, and over the course of time they contribute to the development of the national heritage, a heritage that is left to us by history.

Once again, it is the first person that speaks from the museum walls. It determines and explains Francophonie on the strength of its expertise. It speaks of diversity, exchange, and mixture and acknowledges a debt, a credit that the foreigner has bestowed upon us. This loan is assessed in connection with a "national heritage" to which homage should be rendered. This "national heritage" is, in the language of the museum, *le patrimoine national,* and the CNHI is dedicated to precisely this concept. Jacques Toubon has unambiguously expressed this in his opening address: "The *Cité* has the aim of becoming the place in which the heritage [*le patrimoine*] of immigration is not only preserved but also appreciated."[32] Jacques Chirac uses the same terminology when he speaks of his plans to refresh the memory of the forgetful French, of the duty toward a "national cultural heritage" that "will have to be preserved, utilized, and exhibited to the public in our museums."

Cultural heritage and inheritance—as with heritage and inheritance in general—deal with the transmission and translation of tradition. This expresses an obligation between generations, one which reaches beyond the individual life and toward the future of the lineage. By law, inheritance is regulated by a contract that pertains to family and that binds the contracting parties on the basis of family relations. In this way, the right of inheritance pertains to a line of descent, a family, or a household and presupposes the familial status of a contracting party. As Jacques Derrida emphasizes in his essay about hospitality, it

> [...] is possible for them to be called by their names, to have names, to be subjects in law, to be questioned and liable, to have crimes imputed to them, to be held responsible, to be equipped with nameable identities, and proper names.[33]

This identity requires notarization; it avails itself of a family name that can be verified with the aid of a signature or, if necessary, a DNA test. Moreover, the French word *patrimoine* signifies that it is the father's name, the *patron,* the *pater familias,* that lawfully grants an inheritance, and that the fatherland in the sense of *la patrie* thereby plays a decisive role.

But what if an immigrant, like Michel Yapi, is *clandestine,* or, following the Saint-Bernard affair, *sans papiers,* undocumented.[34] Which inheritance, which *patrimoine* should he declare in the *Cité*? Or when he arrives with nothing on a beach—as Édouard Glissant writes—not as "the domestic migrant, who comes with his tin trunk, his oven, his saucepans and his family photos"—and it must be added—with his identification papers, but rather as the "naked migrant"?[35] If he arrives illegal and in a certain sense nameless, like Kingsley in Olivier Jobard's photo documentation, not even possessing a beach bag, what donation shall he offer to the *Galerie des Dons*? And how should he reclaim his loan to the French nation—supposing that he has one—and how should he, as creditor, redress the balance if his very identity is prohibited through the immigration laws? If he still possesses the power of memory, but not Francophonie—with particular reference to Kingsley, who has found a translator in Olivier Jobard—how should he ever get a chance to speak in the CNHI, in order to tell his story for the history of immigration? As Derrida describes the law of absolute hospitality, "the first act of violence" toward the stranger is that he "has to ask for hospitality in a language which by definition is not his own, the one imposed on him by the master of the house, the host, the king, the lord, the authorities, the nation, the State, the father, etc."[36] This seems to be the fundamental problem of the CNHI, namely that the historiography of immigration plays out on the edge of sayability. For a foreigner to give an account of foreignness requires a language other than his own.

Couci couça

Let us conclude the tour. As the *Cité* sets out to explain and enlighten, in order to change perspectives on immigration, the exhibit ends with a didactic language game for the visitor—the second person—to the museum. The task consists in mobilizing discrete words to form sentences on a touch screen. On offer are words in a white font on a black screen as well as in a black font on a white screen. Visitors generally comply with the installation's instructions, while children in particular take up the invitation to learn through play. With the index finger, words are pushed around the screen. Instead of making sentences, which would be assembled from white and black words across the board, they sort the words according to another order, one whose color coding could not be more apparent: the black, foreign words to the left, and the familiar, white ones to the right. *Pyma*, they find out, is originally a foreign word, just like *zéro*, *hasard*, *tabou*, and *couci couça*.

In this installation, which is conceived of by the first-person of museum discourse as an exercise in mixture, the creative process of creolization produces entropic effects. French does not turn out to be *one* language, nor *the only* language; rather it conveys about sixty other languages within it. One should bear in mind that Francophonie exposes these foreign elements as foreign and uncanny—in a word, as *clandestines*: as covert and illegal. In the national museum, the second person is shown up by the expertise of the authoritative first person, who befits Francophonie and who will not hesitate, in accordance with his tolerant attitude, to admit the foreigner, who in the process is marked with a certain otherness. This strange marking of the foreigner is an ironic repetition of the earliest scenes of the republic. In 1793, Garnier de Saintes proposed a decree in which the foreigner "who will receive a certificate of hospitality, should wear on the right arm a band with the tricolor on which would be printed the word 'hospitality'."[37] The hospitality of the *Cité* is an unreconstructed monolingual francophone one: it places an armband, with the stigma of the guest, on the foreign words, even long after their assimilation.

Se repérer means "to get one's bearings." Along the *repères* of the museum, the coordinates of *couci couça* shift, and it is exposed as foreign and not indigenous to French. In this way, it supports *ex negativo* the idea of an original and pure Francophonie. In truth, Francophonie is never monolingual; rather, it plays out "on the shores of the French language," as Derrida writes, "on the unplaceable line of its coast."[38] Glissant calls this shore "archipelagic," whereby he alludes to the geographic shore of Francophonie in the Caribbean, which forms the outermost cape of the capital, where the creolophone language has given up a root-identity and instead embarks on a poetics of relation from which the Caribbean sea opens out into "'planetary' influxes."[39] Language arrives on this beach like a new arrival without an origin, turning toward itself in the intimate embrace that *couci couça* holds open for us, namely by speaking unfamiliarly *in one's own language*. The project of the *Cité*, to raise a monument to the cultural heritage of the immigrant in a national museum, remains enigmatic in the sense of an absolute hospitality. Moreover, with regard to the utopia and phantasm of a universal language—taken as the language of a universal republic and a global, even planetary whole-world—it remains an infinite task.

4

Outre Mèr(e): Jacques Derrida and the Mediterranean[1]

The sea in between

Before departing from the European continent, we will linger for a moment in this capital, Paris. What drives us is the question of how languages and cultures encounter one another under the conditions of globalization. Put differently, it is a question of how the concepts of "mother tongue" and "fatherland" change, specifically as they pertain to figures of heritage and community belonging, if existing borders are renegotiated, and if concepts of exile, asylum, and diaspora challenge the idea of homeland. These words—exile, asylum, and diaspora—are very old, and the phenomena that they describe are as old as all of humanity. Although it seems that we are dealing with apparently universal concepts—having a mother and a father is as inalienable a human quality as having the capacity for speech—these concepts must necessarily be studied in single cases. The "case" that this chapter is concerned with bears a name, an untranslatable proper name: Jacques Derrida. Our inquiries into this case take us not only to the Parisian capital and the hallowed halls of its universities, where Derrida's work took hold; rather, we begin our trip in the Parisian suburb of Ris-Orangis, where his house and gravesite are located. More or less in diametrical opposition to the course of Derrida's life, we move from the simple grey granite stone, across all of France, and then, embarking from Marseilles, set sail on the open sea. In the course of this journey, Derrida appears no longer simply as a Frenchman but rather as one who was predominantly a transient.

What is involved in the attempt to illuminate the relationship between Derrida and the Mediterranean? What is involved in the attempt to consider this Mediterranean Derrida on the stage of European thought, with its history, its ideas, its culture and languages? In order to speak of Europe, one must concern oneself with France and its capital Paris with its diverse functions, ideological, political, hegemonic, colonial, juristic, and economical. If Derrida is to be considered as a European and Western thinker, one will have to approach the capital in a twofold movement: first removing oneself from Paris and Europe to head for opposite coasts, then looking back across the distance to the realm left behind. For after all, there is a sea in the middle of the biographical narration centered on the name of Jacques Derrida, dividing it onto two shores and anchoring it at two coasts:[2] *la France metropolitaine*—the "motherland," the "main country," the "France of the capital" Paris—and *la France d'outre mer*, the "oversea" departments and territories of France. Situating these areas *outre mer*, "on the other side" of the sea, the name literally suggests an additional France, because *en outre* means "also, besides, furthermore." In legal and administrative terms, *la France d'outre mer* refers to all French departments outside the European continent; it encompasses the Caribbean as much as Polynesia, Antarctica, and New Caledonia, all areas belonging—mostly as former colonies—to the territory of the French state. Algeria, to be sure, where Derrida was born, is not considered an overseas department any more. Still, Derrida's work reflects the bisection into a main and a marginal aspect in the constant examination and critique of hegemonic structures. And it is no accident that the Mediterranean Sea features prominently in his writings as a structure that constitutes relations between distant places in both separating and connecting them.

The metropolis

The concept of the metropolis contains a bundle of meanings, a tangled mass of ideas that stand to be unraveled and ordered into three aspects. First, the word "metropolis" refers to the capital in the sense of a geopolitical center. In his essay *The other heading* (*L'autre cap*), Derrida observes with Paul Valéry that "the large capital" (*la capitale*), Paris, the capital of capitals, differentiates itself from all other capitals.

> *On the one hand*, it is the capital of the country in every domain, and not only, as in other countries, the political *or* economic *or* cultural capital. "To be in itself the political, literary, scientific, financial, commercial, voluptuary, and sumptuary capital of a great country; to embody its whole history; to absorb and concentrate its whole thinking substance as well as all its credit and nearly all its monetary resources and assets, all this being both *good and bad* for the nation that this city crowns—it is in this that Paris *distinguishes itself* from all other giant cities."[3]

Accordingly, the first meaning of "metropolis" is that of the capital that centrally organizes the diverse actions and events of the nation-state.

The concept of metropolis can also be placed in a larger geopolitical frame. In this second aspect, "metropolis" stands for a supranational area. For societies at the end of the twentieth century and in particular for our changing present, the metropolis stands for a global city that marks a node in a global network—like New York, Berlin, Cairo, Tokyo—and is allocated the political, scientific, artistic, financial, and economic functions of a world center. And moreover, it is recognized as representing the "whole history" not only of a country, a nation, or a cultural, linguistic, or religious community, but rather of global memory itself, for which one nowadays would have to add 9/11, the fall of the Berlin Wall, the Jasmine Revolution, Fukushima, the global financial crisis, and so on.

If the first meaning of "metropolis" defines Paris as a capital of France including its mainland and overseas territories, the second increases the vantage of Paris to encompass its function as a global city. Derrida also recognizes this second view of Paris in the thought of Valéry.

> *On the other hand*, by being distinguished in this way, the *exemplary* capital, our capital, is no longer simply the capital of a country, but the "head of Europe", and thus of the world, the capital of human society in general, or even better of "human sociability".[4]

After he has divided Paris into "on the one hand" the capital of France and "on the other hand" the capital of Europe, and "thus" of the world, Paris can raise the claim to being a global capital of human society and indeed of human sociability itself. On this, the Enlightenment grounded its idea of a universal republic as the idea of a site of absolute and irrevocable values. Derrida chose this citation with care, for it shows with exemplarity the hidden Eurocentric and Francocentric logic of the so-called "metropolis" as a normative center of the world. The idea of a "center" of "human society" and even of "human sociability" conceals a conflict between particular and universal values, which, according to the critics of universalistic thought,[5] presents the essential catalyst of globalization with all of its other forms, such as colonization, Christianization, or even control of the planet through "global" actors such as global capital, trade, media, time.

In view of a global thought inclusive of critics of globalization, this second interpretation of "metropolis" involves a third meaning, which likewise concentrates on the metropolis as a global city, while setting the accent differently. It accounts for the factor that the metropolis, in the complexity of its functions, not only exceeds the national scale, acting internationally or supranationally, but also that the influx of worldwide activities within a single place produces a decentralizing or "chaotic" moment. The very capital that centrally organizes the nation or the confederation is at the same time a metropolis in the sense of a cosmopolitan city with a multicultural and polyglot population, each of whose communities have their own memories, pose their own questions, suggest different answers, cultivate other wishes, and in general feel responsibility in their own ways for the whole planet. In this connection, the metropolis stands not only for a heading (a cape, a chapter, capital) but rather, according to Derrida, always also for an "*other* heading." Derrida emphasizes the polysemy of this concept:

> The expression "The Other Heading" can suggest that another direction is in the offing, or that it is necessary to change destinations [. . .], that there is another heading, the heading being not only ours but the other, not only that which we identify, calculate, and decide upon, but the *heading of the other*, before which we must respond, and [. . .] *of which* we must *remind ourselves*, the heading of the other being perhaps the first condition of an identity or identification that is not an egocentrism destructive of oneself and the other.[6]

The metropolis is also such a heading. Its three functions come together in this concept, insofar as the metropolis, as a capital, has at its command the power to steer the fortunes of 1) a country, 2) a continent, or 3) the whole world. Under "our heading," Derrida understands the capital per se in these aspects as 1) a regional capital, 2) a global capital, and 3) a cosmopolitan city of diversity and of Babylonian mixture. Seen as a heading, the metropolis offers itself as a diverse and also contradictory place, both absorbing and scattering, both central and peripheral, both monolingual and multilingual. From this contradiction, Derrida obtains the analytical potential of his concept of heading when he speaks of Europe as a heading, when he speaks of the complex role of the capital that is oriented, in the totality of these three characteristics, not only toward a nation or a continent but rather the whole planet. The whole planet finds itself envisioned in the capital as an "other heading."

"Mèr(e)"

The concept of the metropolis becomes even more complex when considering the etymology of the word. "Metropolis" is composed of two elements, each of which requires further analysis. The second element, "–polis," calls up theories of the state and thereby related political and jurisprudential theories, which cannot be considered in detail here. At the moment, it must suffice to recall that the *polis* in antiquity was a city-state that consisted of the city and surrounding *chora*. In the case of the city-state, the countryside was not completely subordinated.[7] It was rather a construction that linked up ideas of stateliness with ideas of the city, thereby avoiding a power-political distinction between a country and its capital.

In the age of the large Hellenic colonization, the Greek territory expanded from the mainland and the islands between the Mediterranean and the Aegean to regions on the coasts of the Mediterranean and the Black Sea. The "polis" became a "metro-polis," literally a "mother-city." In the course of time, the Mediterranean world was overspread by such network-like colonial foundations. Later Rome took over the polis-network, as it proved to be useful for the administration of distant regions. While Arabs from the opposite shores referred to the Mediterranean as "the white sea," the Latin name for the sea in the middle of their world empire was *mare nostrum*, "our sea," whereby the possessive pronoun "our" indicates a claim to tie the figure of possession and predominance to an idea of community and belonging. "We" goes back to an idea of a common primordial ground, a fatherland, a people of a nation (*natio*: birth) and thus to a certain birthright. This coupling of political and genealogical claims is expressed literally in "metropolis." The first element of the compound metro-polis, *meter*, denotes the colonist's country of origin as meter, that is "origin," "source," "producer," or "mother." Since antiquity, the relationship between the land of the colonizer and the colonies has been understood as the relationship between a mother and her daughters.

Therefore, it is noteworthy that as a concept linking origin, language, and cultural identity, the figure of the mother is associated with another one that has to be assigned to a completely different paradigm: the sea. Yet it might in fact be by chance that in French the two terms converge in a homonym: *la mère*, the mother, is phonologically indistinguishable from *la mer*, the sea. In written language, they stand for wholly different concepts, while in spoken language, one cannot register a difference. The above excursus on the metropolis underscores this accidental coincidence in the French language, whereby *la mèr(e)* refers on the one hand to the large quantities of salt water that is connected to the large oceans of the planet via straits and headlands and that relates distant shores to each other. The same sound form, but with a different spelling, on the other hand, denotes the woman who gives birth, "her own flesh and blood," as it is said, and who endows origin and identity, the personal one as well as the cultural one with a significance that far exceeds the question of genealogical descent, as it is the mother who is said to be the source of the "mother tongue," the so-called native language.

The above techniques of etymological analysis and word play count among the basic skills of deconstruction and follow a long philosophical tradition. Like Martin Heidegger, Derrida also works with the "accidental resemblance" between words and emphasizes that such resemblances might be accidental but in no way arbitrary; rather, it avails itself of an economic power to place two wholly distinct concepts in a relation to one another. According to this analytic procedure, it becomes inevitable that the concepts of territory and fatherland—which form the basic constituents of the metropolis as a geopolitical institution—become coupled to the concept of genealogical identity and of origin, that is to interlace the ideas of father and ground with the ones of mother and blood.

What, however, are we talking about if we want to speak of this "other," or "further"—*outre*—Derrida, the one of the "other heading," the planetarian? In order to approach him by means of the double figure of *la mèr(e)*, he shall be called by a different name for the time being, a provisional but promising name that separates Jacques Derrida from his proper name, which is first and foremost a patronym, and that also separates him from his own language, which in his essay *Monolingualism of the Other* he repeatedly presents as his mother tongue. This other name of Derrida is not able to deviate ultimately from the original from which it derives; it emanates from it like a distorted *alter ego*, for it is written with the same letters that it merely rearranges anagrammatically to form another name that becomes meaningful in another language. This anagram translates the proper name into another language in which the untranslatable proper name becomes a translatable generic name. In this so-called foreign language, German—for Derrida the language of Husserl, Heidegger, Arendt—"Derrida" becomes foreign to the subject it uniquely designates. Eventually, he will be foreign to himself, henceforth to bear the game name "Jacques Dreirad." But what does "Dreirad" mean as an untranslatable proper name?

Jacques Dreirad

The pen portrait *Jacques Derrida*, written by Geoffrey Bennington (main text) and Derrida himself (footnotes), contains several family photographs, some taken in France, others in Algeria. One image, entitled *Photograph with automobile (I)*, shows Derrida at the age of four, sitting in a toy car in the rue Saint Augustin in El Biar, a suburb of Algiers, where he lived with his parents in the 1930s until he was five years old (see Figure 4.1).[8] The grown-up Derrida, the philosopher whose work keeps coming back to the structures of the proper name and of the autobiography, takes the picture as an opportunity for some reflections on his mother Georgette Derrida. In the passage in question at the beginning of the book, Derrida outlines his memories of the pictured scene and of his mother, even though she is not shown in the image. A linguistic coincidence provides him with the explosive material for his reflections, because the name of rue Saint Augustin reminds him of the original text of the confession: the confessions of Saint Augustine of Thagaste, dedicated to the death of his mother Monica. By the way, Thagaste is the ancient name of a Roman polis in Africa; today, the city, located in the northeast of Algeria, is called Souk Ahras.

Derrida similarly sets out to write a kind of confessions, too (*Circumfessions*). Following the example of Augustin, who regrets the loss of his mother Monica in his confessions, Derrida now reflects the future death of his mother Georgette.

Figure 4.1 Jacques Derrida in a toy car in the rue Saint Augustin in Algiers, in Geoffrey Bennington and Jacques Derrida, *Jacques Derrida*, trans. Geoffrey Bennington (Chicago and London: University of Chicago Press, 1993), 12. Reprinted with kind permission of Pierre Alferi and Jean Derrida.

He hastens to point out that he does not intend to compare his mother Georgette with Saint Monica:

> [M]y mother was not a saint [...], but what these two women had in common is the fact that Santa Monica [...] also ended her days, as my mother will too, on the other side of the Mediterranean, far from her land, in her case in the cemetery in Nice which was profaned in 1984.[9]

Derrida's "unholy" mother resembles the holy Monica in a biographical split, in being divided into two parts, located at two coasts. The holy mother Monica was born on the south coast of the Mediterranean, in Thagaste in Algeria, as was her son Augustine. Yet unlike him, she died on the other side of the Mediterranean, in Ostia, and was buried in the church of Sant' Agostino in the metropolis of her time: in Rome. Derrida claims the same overseas transportation for his mother, at a time when Georgette Derrida is still alive, when her death and burial are yet to come. Thus, being far away from home becomes something that Derrida's mother already experiences during her lifetime. The mother's funeral (at a cemetery in Nice) has not yet taken place. It is her son's text that fixates the mother's split biography, situated both overseas (*outre mer*) and in France. Derrida thus suggests that the mother, every mother—not solely Georgette Derrida—is always affected by a division. In Derrida, the mother—commonly considered the embodiment of origin, home, and security—implies dislocation and dismemberment. The coupling of the mothers in Derrida's autobiography is split into opposites: one dead and one living, each in part on the side of the colonizer and in part on the side of the colonized, as if a mother was always not quite her self, as if the mother was always an irredeemable promise of home.

This deficient quality of the mother, who at the same time gives herself and withdraws, is characteristically already clear at the moment when the childhood photograph of Jacques Derrida was taken in his toy car. For the mother was already absent from the photo in advance, as if her absence, that empty presence, was one of her basic characteristics. The reflection on the places of birth and death of the mothers of these two great Western thinkers—Derrida and Augustin—repeats the double structure of the homonym *mèr(e)*: on the other side of the Mediterranean, the mothers are buried in foreign soil, one in Rome, the other in Nice, and just as the future death of the mother was a threat to her presence already in her living present, so too the land of birth has always been permeated by this other place, that "capital" on the other shore.

Although at the time of writing, her death still lies in the future, Derrida already sees his mother in the cemetery in Nice. Her significance as a mother seems to rest in this consideration, which she repeatedly induced in her son already in her lifetime and on which he grounds his philosophy of difference as deferral. In various contexts, and with a macabre interest in death, Derrida discusses the thought-figure of the mother as the embodiment of an absent presence. Fate seems ineluctable for the mother; an inescapable death is certain already at the moment in which a childhood photograph of Jacques Derrida is taken, a photo in which the mother is significantly absent, as though the absence of the mother, typically figured as an abundance of presence, counts among her most basic characteristics. The thought of a future death of the mother leads Derrida to the cemetery in Nice, which becomes the state for two temporal reflections: it is a place in the future at which the mother will be buried after her death, and *at the same time* it is a place in the past, a place with a history, connected to an anti-Semitic desecration committed in 1984 that has since then become an irreversible and persistent memory. The thought of this will still have a place even in the future, and it will continue to have an effect at the time of the mother's burial.[10]

Called by name and in light of their respective places of birth and death, the mothers of these grand occidental thinkers, Georgette and Monica, testify to one further aspect of the double structure of the homonym *mèr(e)*. These mothers were buried in foreign ground, on the other side of the Mediterranean, and just as the future death of the mother already poses a threat to her presence in the living present, so too is the land of birth also pervaded by the other place, this other heading, the metropolis on the other shore.

The other wheel

Another look at the portrait of the child Derrida in a toy car elucidates what the anagrammatical pseudonym—Jacques Dreirad—helps to clarify. What does this other name mean to us, and how does it place the Derrida of Paris in relation to the Derrida of El Biar? It is, for a start, assumed that the word *Dreirad*— "tricycle"—refers to childhood, to the native land, moreover to the mother, the brothers, and the whole Derrida family that lived in the rue Saint Augustin in Algiers for nine years. Derrida makes his "autobiography" the point of departure for a reflection on "automobility" and on the temporal paradox that expresses itself in the death of the mother and that takes the form of a photograph. In this connection Derrida writes about the

[...] compulsion to overtake each second, like one car overtaking another, doubling it rather, overprinting it with the negative of a photograph already taken with a "delay" mechanism, the memory of what survived me to be present at my disappearance.[11]

In connection with Jacques Dreirad, the photograph becomes a medium that binds autobiography to automobility. In photography, the photographed transforms into a revenant. Similar to how a temporal-spatial order inheres in the death of the mother, in the case of this photograph the paradoxical structure of time opens an ambivalent spatial dimension, whose ambiguity emerges in the word *Dreirad* in a nearly ideal way. The Japanese-German novelist Yoko Tawada narrates in *Überseezungen*[12] that one day she typed the name "Derrida" into her computer's word processer and that it autocorrected the unknown word "Derrida" into the pre-programmed "Dreirad." Tawada comes to the conclusion that "two things that appeared very similar, [could] be *very differently intended.*"[13]

There is of course a long tradition of wordplay and misunderstanding in literary criticism. Out of this tradition, Harold Bloom (in)famously developed a method of "misreading," whereby readers valorize the connotations or secondary meanings and become interested in the coincidences and accidents of the signification process and their resulting possibilities. In looking at the childhood photographs with an analogical process of "mislooking," we might think we perceive a normal vehicle with four wheels, but in examining the photograph carefully, it has to be conceded that only three wheels can be seen: both the left front wheel and back wheel as well as part of the right front wheel, standing out behind the bumper. Experience with vehicles and with the deceptive nature of central perspective permits the assumption that there is a fourth wheel, but the laws of optics prohibit regarding it as visible presence. Voila, Jacques Dreirad. It is the epithet of the philosopher whose work is in large part devoted to the insistent critique of the concept of presence and immediacy. The photo once again recalls the technical conditions of the medium, the two-dimensional flatness, the illusion of the senses, and the phantasmagoria. The same game that confuses the letters in the language confuses the view of the picture, this time with the means of the central perspective.

On closer inspection, however, the viewer of the photograph will discover a fourth wheel on the automobile that is not obviously connected with the other wheels, insofar as it has a different mechanical function, namely the steering wheel, that cybernetic instrument that allows us to choose a direction, head for a destination, change direction, and choose a different course. For the actual fourth wheel of the automobile, however, the steering wheel provides a peculiar substitute that interferes with the visual reading and adds to it a prompt, unpredictable change of direction, namely a reflection on the relationship between the visible and the invisible as well as curiosity about the new goals that can be achieved with the change of course.

This other—*punctum*-esque—fourth wheel of the automobile provides, in connection with Derrida's autobiography, also a reference to the automobility of the philosopher. Jacques Derrida was repeatedly affected by such changes of course throughout his life. In the portrayed Jacques Derrida, he relates a situation in which he found that the southern and the northern coast of the Mediterranean, Algiers and Paris, mirror each other: "I was driving in Paris near the Opera and I discovered that other rue Saint-Augustin, homonym of the one in Algiers where my parents lived for 9 years after their marriage."[14] A further, other, *outre* rue Saint-Augustin on the other cape. Derrida discovered it during a car trip, this time in a real car, with four wheels.

Ever since his childhood in Algiers, Derrida was well prepared for the drive in Paris. He knew not only how to drive, but also how to read the street name signs in Paris written in Latin letters, a script that has a long history. The Latin alphabet was not only useful for the Roman colonists who brought it to northern Africa, but some centuries later after the Islamization of the Maghreb in the course of the seventh century also for the Spaniards and finally, after 1830, for the French. The Latin alphabet served various conquerors, colonists, and settlers in the area now called Algeria as an instrument to implement their goals, be they religious, military, administrative, cultural, scientific, economic, or of a different kind. Alphabetic script was used since the Punic Wars, and every new phase came along with a specific direction of writing: from left to right for Latin, Spanish, and French, from right to left for Arab and Hebrew. The Berber language remained undecided in between for a long time.[15] Even today, the conflict between the Christianized and the Islamized world (as if the planet housed two worlds) is expressed in the form of a different alphabet, literally in the alphabet of the Other, the one who writes in the wrong direction, in an absurd way, and who heads for another cap in scripture.

Arabic

There is no doubt about the direction of Derrida's writing before and after he crossed the Mediterranean. Heading for France, he left Algeria in 1949 at the age of nineteen. He commemorates the passage on the ship named *Ville d'Alger* (City of Algiers) in *Monolingualism of the Other*: "First journey, first crossing of my life, twenty four hours of sea-sickness and vomiting."[16] He took up residence in Paris, studied, did research, and taught. Paris was his dwelling place. Derrida always used the Latin alphabet, always wrote from the left to the right, always oriented towards the occident, and mostly in French, his mother tongue, about which he says that he "had none, precisely, none other than French."[17] Even in writing about belonging to the Maghrebian Jews and about the repressions they were subject to, Derrida does not cease to emphasize that French is the only one language for him, the language that cannot be substituted by any other one: "I am monolingual. My monolingualism dwells, and I call it my dwelling; it feels like one to me, and I remain in it and inhabit it. It inhabits me."[18] The French language is his abode and home, even when, at some point in time, the proper name "Alger" no longer stands only for his hometown, but also for a ship and thus for a journey, a return to his home, also and especially on the open sea in the moments of translation.

The language Derrida speaks of in *Monolingualism of the Other*, however, is not just French, that is to say not the French without any accent spoken in the metropolis. He speaks of the so-called Franco-Maghrebian, a kind of a Babylonian special form of language neither defined by the birth of the speaker nor by nationality or French citizenship but to be grasped in no other way than by describing a particular relationship to the metropolis Paris. For the metropolis is the dwelling place of this language even from the point of view of Algeria. In unmistakable reference to figures of birth and descent, Derrida calls the metropolis the "Capital-City-Mother-Fatherland, the city of the mother tongue," and this country is "near but far away," a "being-elsewhere," an "over there," and, especially in view of the question of language, a "place of fantasy":

> As a model of good speech and good writing, it represented the language of the master. "What's more, I do not think I have ever recognized any other sovereign in my life." The master took the form, primarily and particularly, of the schoolteacher. The teacher could thus represent, with dignity, the master in general, under the universal features of the good Republic. [...] The language of the Metropole was the mother tongue; actually, the substitute for a mother tongue (is there ever anything else?) as the language of the other.[19]

One may of course wonder if there have not been any linguistic alternatives to French in Algeria. Derrida reflects on the status of the various languages of the country, first on the "living"—Arab and Berber—then on the so-called "dead"—Latin and Greek—and on the holy language, Hebrew, as it were in between them.

Since the end of the nineteenth century, when inhabitants of Algeria were decreed French citizenship, the Jewish, Berber, and Arab cultures in Algeria had been shaped by processes of cultural concurrence: assimilation, acculturation, Francization. In this context, Derrida remembers first and foremost an interdict:

> A particular interdict against all Arabic or Berber languages was, as I recall, in effect, and let us provisionally retain this word "interdict." For someone from my generation, this took several cultural and social forms. It was first of all something educational, something which happens to you "at school" [. . .].
>
> Given all the colonial censorships—especially in the urban and suburban milieu where I lived—and given all the social barriers there, the racisms [. . .], given the disappearance, then in progress, of Arabic as the social, everyday, administrative language, the one and only option was still the school, and the study of Arabic was restricted to the school, but as a foreign language [. . .].
>
> The *optional* study of Arabic remained, of course. [. . .] The authority of National Education (of "public education") proposed it for the same reason, at the same time, and in the same form as the study of any foreign language in the French lycées of Algeria. Arabic, an optional foreign language in Algeria! As if we were being told [. . .]: "Let's see, Latin is required for everyone in sixth grade, of course, not to speak of French, but do you, in addition, want to learn English, or Arabic, or Spanish, or German?" It seems that Berber was never included.[20]

For Derrida, whose family lived at the edge of an Arab quarter in Algiers, Arab was "the neighbor's language," the language of a neighbor incorporating the closeness and intimacy of a child's spatial experience on the one hand and still remaining inaccessible on the other hand due to his language, culture, customs, and religion.[21] That neighbor's language, Arab, was a native language, too: native of his own country, city, quarter, school, and at the same time a foreign language, a language of the Other, in fact at just these places: a guest in their own house. Derrida approaches this guest in dialectical terms as "the other as the nearest neighbor," "very near and infinitely far away, such was the distance."[22]

Jewish

In opposition to being French, and similar to being Arabic, being Jewish cannot be understood solely through concepts of nationality or citizenship. Nor does the concept of a mother tongue offer a sufficient definition. In the case of Derrida, one sometimes speaks of being Jewish without Judaism.[23] The history of European philosophy is replete with Jews without Judaism. Hannah Arendt explains in her famous conversation with Günter Gaus that she had no idea that she was Jewish until the moment in which she was called a dirty Jew by classmates at her elementary school in Königsberg. Like Arendt and many other Western philosophers, Derrida came from a secular Jewish family. For a French overseas territory like the Maghreb, which was not immediately affected by the Nazi occupation, one would not expect anti-Jewish measures, at least not like those enacted in Königsberg, Berlin, Paris, or other continental cities. Nevertheless, in *Monolingualism of the Other* Derrida speaks of a "disorder of identity," caused by the circumstance that, at some point in history, an incompatibility arose between a certain cultural and religious identity and French citizenship.[24]

In his history lesson on the Algerian Jews, Derrida refers back to the 1870 Cremieux decree by virtue of which they became French citizens. The mentioned "disorder of identity" that Derrida also describes as "degradation" followed decades later. It was nothing other than "the loss of French citizenship [...] for the same Jews of Algeria," "'under the Occupation', as we say."[25] Derrida places "occupation" in quotes in order to emphasize that the history of French Jews in Algeria requires further specification because

> [...] it is actually a legend. Algeria has never been occupied. I mean that if it has ever been occupied, the German occupant was never responsible for it. The withdrawal of French citizenship from the Jews of Algeria, with everything that followed, was the deed of the French alone. They decided that all by themselves, in their heads; they must have been dreaming about it all along; they implemented it all by themselves.[26]

When the French government enacted the Cremieux decree in 1870, it executed a kind of patriotic unification of the national family, annexing the overseas daughters, the children *d'outre mer*, to the metropolis as if reincorporating them into the womb. This event, however, is decidedly not a sign of conception, of nesting and growing in the uterus, of protecting and nurturing, but rather a gesture of the involuntary imposition of citizenship and thus literally an act of "national" violence. Later, it was the same "mother," the French state, who legally repealed the Cremieux decree following a parliamentary act, thus depriving Algerian Jews of French citizenship. This was in October of 1940, before the Vichy regime was established. Derrida recalls the loss:

> Along with others, I lost and then gained back French citizenship. I lost it for years without having another [...]. I hardly knew, at the time, that it had been taken away from me, not, at any rate, in the legal and objective form of knowledge in which I am explaining it here [...]. And then, one day, one "fine day", without,

once again, my asking for anything, and still too young to know it in a properly political way, I found the aforementioned citizenship again. The state, to which I never spoke, had given it back to me. The state, which was no longer Pétain's "French State", was recognizing me anew. That was, I think, in 1943; I had still never gone "to France".[27]

If the French mother country imposes French citizenship as a national identity onto the inhabitants of overseas territories, this naturalization—literally a "correction" of birth—entails numerous legal and administrative changes to different norms and systems: in law, in finance, in health, and in education as much as with regard to language, script, and history. All of that is given by the metropolis and revoked again after three generations. The repeal leaves all Jews in Algeria not only without nationality, but without any law or welfare system. The just established French mother tongue becomes to the third generation, for whom she is no longer a pidgin, a mysteriously foreign, even a monstrous language. As if in a second birth, the French metropolis produces the Maghrebian—now non-French—Jews again, this time as expatriated subjects of uncertain identity. They are excluded from the womb and, paradoxically, left without a "birth" (*natio*), provided with a lack of origin and called by a name that identifies its bearer as an inadmissible subject.

Uncanny mouth of the uterus

Even after identifying himself as a Maghrebian Jew, Derrida does not cease to insist that French is his only language. "I only have one language": this phrase echoes throughout the essay *Monolingualism of the Other*. Yet whenever the phrase is pronounced, it entails what appears to be its contradiction in the same sentence: "it is not mine."[28] Derrida explains: "For never I was able to call French, this language I am speaking to you, 'my mother tongue.'"[29] It seems that this tension within the French language can hardly be understood but in the context of the Mediterranean. Especially in Derrida's highly autobiographical text on monolingualism, this insecurity in terms of language can be read with regard to the French colonization of Algeria: as caused by the expatriation, by a kind of exile at home. And the fissure within the "mother tongue" is true for the personal historical fate of Jacques Derrida, a fate that is as individual and singular as it is typical and universal. For Derrida's argument far exceeds mere personal circumstances; it concerns the very concept of identity as something that is fundamentally at stake, in passages overseas as well as in the search for a dwelling, a home. It is no coincidence that Derrida prefers the word "identification," which presupposes a process with an agent (to identify oneself/an individual as), to the word "identity": "an identity is never given, received, or attained; only the interminable and indefinitely phantasmatic process of identification endures."[30]

This is the paradoxical gesture of *Monolingualism of the Other*. On the one hand, Derrida insists on being monolingual francophone: "Yes, I only have one language," he keeps saying, just to add, on the other hand, "yet it is not mine." And, what is more, "Yet it will never be mine, this language, the only one I am thus destined to speak, [...] never will this language be mine. And, truth to tell, it never was."[31]

This contradictory logic links the notion of "always" to the notion of "never," or an affirmation to a negation, and scandalously designs the connection as a causal structure as if the second was an obvious conclusion following from the first. The rupture formed by this contradictory sentence is not one that only runs between different languages, between one's own language and a foreign language, but already through the monolingualism of the first language itself. The rhetorical force of this rupture is indeed based on a subtle comparison by which the mother tongue, a cultural concept, is tacitly linked to the natural mother. The phantasms of identity are derived from the figure of the "nature-culture-mother": she vouches for descent and the pertaining birthrights as well as for the affiliation with a certain linguistic or cultural community. Her somatic sign is the cervix, the organ also called "mouth of the uterus," which literally administers both life and language. Hans Bellmer has brilliantly visualized this connection in his image *La Bouche*. On a chair, four legs lie crossed at the knees, and there is a conspicuous gap in the place where the upper thighs touch. A looming red opening against a black background recalls the labia but also, momentarily, the lips of a mouth (see Figure 4.2).

Let us assume someone who said of the mother what Derrida says of the "mother tongue," someone who said, "I only have one mother, who is absolutely unique and irreplaceable; I have never had and will never have a different one," just to add, "and this mother is not mine." And let us assume this sentence was not about accidentally losing the so-called biological mother who might by replaced by a so-called social mother, but actually the impossible assertion, "I have one mother, and she is not mine." The figure of the mother in its function as natural guarantor of a certain identity finds itself entangled in a contradiction, a contradiction that is no way tolerable.

Derrida finds the irreducible impossibility marking any birth or origin, the gap that compromises the idea of an identity, within the concept of the "mother

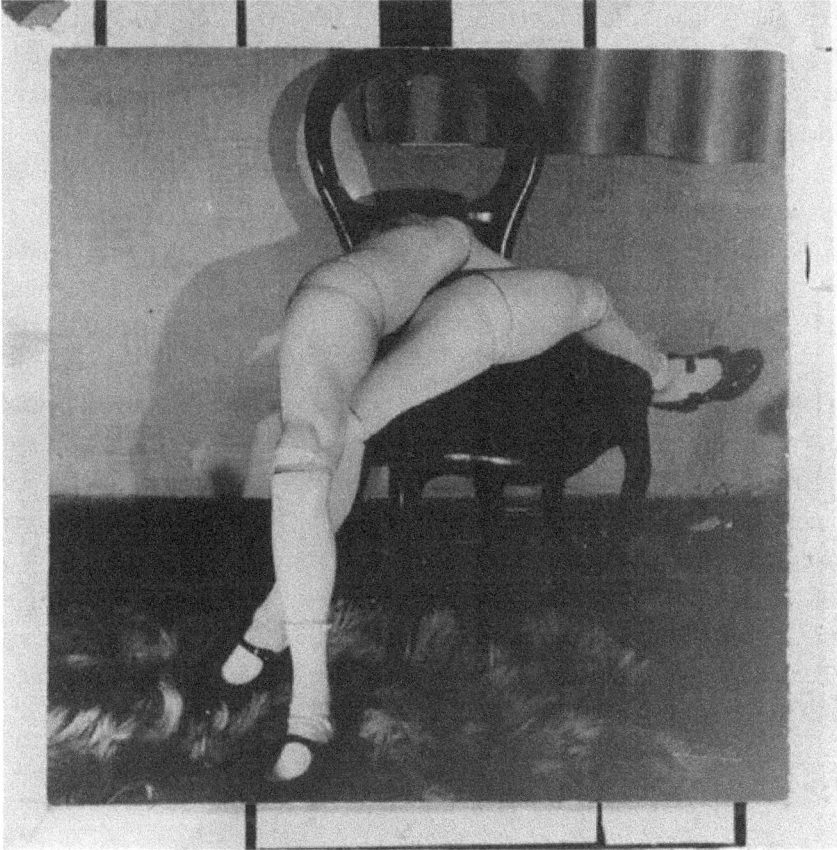

Figure 4.2 Hans Bellmer, *La Bouche* (1935). © VG Bild-Kunst, Bonn 2020.

tongue." The expression "mother tongue" articulates a logic that pertains not solely to this historically particular francophone case but to language as such: every language, even a so-called foreign language, is first and foremost a mother tongue, unique and irreplaceable by virtue of the same law by which everyone has but one biological mother. The natural law of the mother/tongue is based on the strange rhetoric that entangles the known, or native, with the unknown, foreign. It is no coincidence that Derrida calls the encounter with the mother tongue "uncanny": *unheimlich*.[32] The word—occurring in German in the original French version of the text as though a (reverse) translation into a "foreign mother tongue"—evokes the complex semantics Sigmund Freud discusses in a detailed philological analysis. Freud discloses its complex structure by focusing on the basic word *heimlich* that has quite contradictory meanings: it can refer to the confident, the homelike, and the familiar as much as to "what is concealed and kept out of sight," as Freud puts it. *Unheimlich*, however, is not just a negation of *heimlich*. Among "its different shades of meaning the word *heimlich* exhibits one which is identical with its opposite, *unheimlich*."[33] The "uncanny is that class of the frightening which leads back to what is known of old and long familiar."[34] The uncanny intertwines the unknown with the familiar and situates the foreign not in opposition to the own, but in its heart.

For the figure of the *Muttermund*—the "cervix," but literally "the mouth of the mother"—Freud's interpretation of the uncanny produces the disruption that affects the domain of language and genealogy alike. The mother, both as the supposedly closest, most intimately known neighbor and the figure of protection and security, of education, culture, and language, is marked by a strangeness that is not at all exterior. At the same time familiar and strange, she becomes a strange relative, a foreign intimate. The maternal imagery of origin, culminating in the "mouth of the uterus," the organ that opens to both speak and give birth, seems to bind the born child to what is taken to be its first home, vouching for an origin beyond doubt. Yet the maternal imagery reassures only at the price of initiating an incurable homesickness, a debt that cannot be paid off. In *Translation as Culture*, Gayatri Chakravorty Spivak relates the concept of the mother tongue to a debt:

> Translation in the narrow sense is [...] a reparation. I translate from my mother tongue. This originary *Schuldigsein*—being-indebted in the Kleinian sense—the guilt in seeing that one can treat one's mother tongue as one language among many gives rise to a certain obligation for reparation. I'm a slow translator, and for me it is the shuttle between the exquisite guilt of finding the mother tongue or the substitute mother tongue when I translate from French—every "original" is a place-holder for the mother tongue—shuttle between that guilt, a displacement of some primordial *Schuldigsein*, and the reparation of reality-testing, where each of the languages becomes a guarantee of the other.[35]

The *Schuldigsein* in the mother tongue corresponds to the gift of life given in birth. In Spivak's mother tongue, there is a term for this debt:

> [M]*atririn* (mother-debt)—a debt *to* the mother as well as a debt [that] the [place of the] mother *is* [...]. The aphorism: *matririn* is not to be repaid, or cannot be repaid [...]. The mother-debt is the gift of birth, as it is imagined to be, but also the accountable task of childrearing (literally *manush kora* = making human, in my mother tongue). One translates this gift-into-accountability as one attempts to repay what cannot be repaid, and should not be thought of as repayable.[36]

Derrida reflects on the interminable task of translating in terms of debt and the gift (both the English "gift" and the German *Gift*, "poison"). In Spivak, the interminable task turns into an ethical concept and an obligation. The somatic figure of the mouth of the uterus is devoted to carrying out this duty, to keep promising a home and a language beyond all doubt without, of course, ever being able to find and give them.

The ambiguity of the *Muttermund* only exists in German. French must rely on two translations: one for the context of birth (*orifice du col utérin*), another for speaking (*bouche de la mère*). And it is, furthermore, unavoidable that in the process of translation, the other figure of mother and sea—*la mèr(e)*—interferes in the semiosis. The homonym gives expression to the uncanny "m/other tongue" that is (just like the mother) at the same time familiar and from afar, beyond the sea. Not least, it recalls the most distant places of the planet and displays them as continuously being affected by the process of orientation, across straits and headlands. Bound for where? Always home!

5

The Southern Cross: The Planetarism of Alexander von Humboldt and François Arago

I turned me to the right hand, and fixed my mind upon the other pole, and
saw four stars never seen save by the first people.
The heavens appeared to rejoice in their flamelets. O widowed northern
region, since thou art deprived of beholding these![1]

The language of human rights

In the age of the great transoceanic crossings, the Atlantic becomes the Mediterranean of the world. The West expands across it, purports to discover the new continent, and investigates its flora and fauna as well as its foreign cultures, which it harnessed with the use of African manpower. Pioneers cross over it, carrying in their wake waves of emigrants; in the reverse direction, monetary wealth from abroad flows toward Europe. Along these crossings, an idea also sets sail between the continents, one which brings to the colonies independence and to the motherland a law that henceforth declares the rights of man to be a universal law of nature. For the first time in the history of the occident, there arises—after the divine plan of salvation of religions and the scientism of modernity—a law passed by the principles of the modern political system. It declares that all humans are innately, and solely on the ground of their humanity, free and equal in dignity and rights and that these rights are universal, inalienable, and egalitarian.

A law that has as its object the human irrespective of origin, class, religion, language, gender, or race has to deal with the problem that it nevertheless requires a particular language in order to be communicated. Ultimately, its basic condition is that it does not privilege one language over another and that it provides neither God nor king with a proper name, in any language. Since the law knows no other sovereign than that of truth, it cannot be written in a simple, natural language in the sense of a vernacular or national language, for every monolingual composition would inevitably accept the neglect of the other languages. The other language is the language of the Other, who is the very subject of the law. As a point of fact, though, laws require a presence in the media to enable their communication and to obtain legal force in individual cases, even a universal law. Indeed, human rights have received a linguistic form, insofar as the great texts of the Enlightenment were composed in the vernacular or national languages English, French, and German and written in the Latin alphabet. And just as the Enlightenment and human rights have always been written in one language, they are also endowed with one origin, one religion, one sex, one race, and so on. The young French republic of 1789 was no exception. With a grand gesture, it announced the *Déclaration des droits de l'homme*. But at the same time, it held onto the old Code Noir, that decree, developed by Jean Baptiste Colbert while under the rule of the Sun King, which regulated the rights of slaves in the French colonial empire and outlasted the entire French Revolution. While the *Lumières* enlightened the world, their slaves abroad conveniently dropped out of view. "Up there in Paris," as Louis Sala-Molins pithily expresses the hypocrisy, Montesquieu concerned himself with the separation of powers, Rousseau with the social contract, Voltaire and Diderot with art, but none thought of rescinding the Code Noir.[2]

Only in 1848 did a French minister set out to issue a decree that would invalidate the Code Noir. In his brief incumbency as a Secretary of War and Navy in the provisional government of the Second Republic, in April of that year, he abolished slavery in the French colonies. He thereby pledged the Republic to the "universal" validity of human rights, which, as they are unconditional, cannot discriminate based on skin color. It is no coincidence that this Secretary was also an astronomer. The validity of universal values was well known to him from his actual place of employment, the Paris Observatory, and so from then on the light of the *Lumières* was to be trained on him in the parliament hall. His name is among the names of the seventy-two wise men who are eternalized in gold letters on the Paris Eiffel Tower: Dominique François Jean Arago (1786–1853).

Arago's universe

François Arago was just as much a planetarian and an ideologue as he was an astronomer and scientist. The principle of humanity illuminated his universe like the light of stars, and for him both are underlain by absolute, non-negotiable natural laws. But the commitment to the universal can never completely renounce the earthly-profane ideas under which it is formed for the astronomer. As a boarding pupil of the polytechnic school, Arago had two basic requirements to fulfill: first, that he was French by birth, despite his Catalonian ancestry, and second, that he pledged himself to the Emperor of France and thus against the Republic.[3] As so often, politics and astronomy here proceed hand in hand; and with Arago, this two-sidedness is particularly interesting. Still as a student, Arago was summoned by Pierre Simon de Laplace to the Paris Observatory, which at this time was a stronghold of Republican activism.[4] The Observatory was to be his lifelong workplace and his spatial frame of reference, his prime meridian from which he sought to comprehend global systems including celestial phenomena and to which he continually returned. From here, he set out in 1806 with Jean-Baptiste Biot, commissioned by the Bureau des longitudes, to determine the southern course of the Paris meridian arc. Today, the arc, made of brass, is inscribed in the floor of the Cassini-Hall in the Paris Observatory in the 14th arrondissement; at that time, however, the measurement was only carried out up to Barcelona and was supposed to be extended to the Balearic Islands. In a short matter of time, this research trip degenerated into a dangerous odyssey across the Mediterranean, which took a number of dramatic turns due to the extent of Napoleonic interventions. Arago reports on this in his *History of My Youth*, an autobiography that sometimes bears the traces of a classic picaresque novel. The short version is as follows.

At the beginning of 1806, Arago sailed together with Biot under the French flag to the Spanish coast. There, the astronomers wandered with their instruments from station to station, placing their geodetic signal lights on the mountain summits. By determining the latitude of Formentera, they ascertained the southern extremity of the meridian arc. While Arago was undertaking another geodetic measurement on Majorca in early 1808, the French marched into Spain. The Majorcans raised the suspicion that Arago had set up his concave mirrors at his mountain station in order to provide support for the landing of the French troops. Disguised as a Majorcan, Arago fled on June 1, 1808 from an approaching riot to the castle of Bellver near Palma. From there, he escaped on a half decker camouflaged as a fishing boat in which he, a small crew, and his instruments sailed, landing at Algiers on August 3, 1808. Arago procured a false passport for himself and his companion and he abruptly embarked for Marseilles. His fellow travelers—Jews, Arabs, and Europeans—were largely refugees like him; even the Moor captain sailed under a false identity, and the crew consisted for the most part not of mariners; they all sat in the same boat, as foreigners, in the crossing of the Mediterranean.[5]

In the Gulf of Lion, however, the ship fell into the hands of a Spanish privateer who abducted the refugees to the Catalonian city of Rosas and from there, as the city threatened to fall into French hands, further south to Palamos. After three months of imprisonment, the Dey of Algiers finally managed to achieve the release of his ship and so, too, the release of the multicultural crew. Starting from the Costa Brava on November 28, Arago embarked once again for Marseilles. With the French coast in sight and the harbor in front of them, the winds changed and a gust of the mistral sent them back on the open sea toward Africa. They landed in Béjaïa, a port city in eastern Algeria. Since maritime traffic had ceased for the winter, Arago set out overland, accompanied by the Moorish sailors, toward the capital of Algeria some 200 kilometers away, which they reached on Christmas of 1808. Half a year later, on June 21, 1809, he put out to sea one last time in the direction of Marseilles, and this time he reached the French mainland. With changing disguises, sometimes Christian and sometimes Muslim, sometimes French, Spanish, or even Austrian, Arago had made his way to Europe, and, as he had not only mastered many languages but could also imitate multiple accents, he had never been definitively identified as an enemy.

The last stage of his odyssey led him to a lazaretto, a quarantine station for maritime travelers, where he experienced the intake rituals with which the newcomers from Africa were greeted, in Marseilles as well as elsewhere, both then and today. A festive reception occurred only upon his arrival in Paris, which he reached as a national hero, the results of his measurements in his luggage. In the same year, 1809, and only twenty-three years old, he was elected to the Académie des sciences and received the chair of Analysis Applied to Geometry at the polytechnic school in his function as the astronomer of the Paris Observatory, whose director he became in 1830.[6]

While at sea, Arago had determined the longitude of Paris. On land, he then investigated the wavelengths and the deflection angle of starlight, discovered with Fresnel the interference of light waves, demonstrated the constancy of the speed of light, described the connection between electricity and magnetism, and discovered the uses of daguerreotype.[7] In addition, he undertook no less effort to instruct the people in the fundamentals of astronomy, in the conviction that political reason required a broad basis with an enlightened and critical spirit. He dispelled the superstition that meteors are bringers of bad luck, ascertained the harmlessness of moonlight, and taught his people to observe rather than stare, so that during the total eclipse of 1842, an entire army of amateur astronomers stood by his side.[8] From 1813 to 1843, Arago held his famous public lectures on popular astronomy. His audiences were large, up to 900 in number, men and women, and in some cases counted very prominent figures among them, including Victor Hugo,[9] Auguste Comte, and George Sand. The publication of the *Annuaire* of the Observatory was soon read across all of Europe.[10]

In 1845, even the aged Alexander von Humboldt (1769–1859) attended the lectures. Arago maintained a friendly connection to him, which by then had continued for more than thirty years and lasted until Arago's death.[11] The initiative for this friendship proceeded from Humboldt. In his autobiography, Arago recalls the circumstances of their first contact on July 2, 1809, just after returning from Algeria. On the French mainland for the first time after his varying imprisonments and while still in quarantine, Arago received a letter from an admirer, who himself had just recently returned from a long American journey:

> The first letter which I received from Paris was full of sympathy and congratulations on the termination of my laborious and perilous adventures; it was from a man already in possession of a European reputation, but whom I had never seen: M. de Humboldt, after what he had heard of my misfortunes, offered me his friendship. Such was the first Origin of a connection which dates from nearly forty-two years back, without a single cloud ever having troubled it.[12]

The letter was the beginning of a long friendship, which began with the thirst for adventure on a research trip and which then nourished itself on the common passion for astronomy, also and especially in its entanglement with political ideals.

Babylonian friendship

The Parisian letter came of all people from a Prussian natural scientist. It was written—like so many of Alexander von Humboldt's writings—in French. In the nineteenth century, French was not only the language of diplomacy, but also the language of astronomy. Moreover, and this held true not only for the French, it was the language of republican thought. For Humboldt, who nevertheless preferred twenty years of self-imposed exile in Paris to his Prussian homeland, it was the language of science, freedom, and maybe even love. Not much is known about the latter; in the case of Humboldt's relationship with Arago, astronomy was central. As Arago could not speak German, French was the language of friendship between them. The researchers came together in French, and they composed a ponderous correspondence in this language, of which principally

BIBLIOTHÈQUE D'HISTOIRE SCIENTIFIQUE

T. Ier

Bibliothèque
Alfred Giard

CORRESPONDANCE

D'ALEXANDRE DE HUMBOLDT

AVEC

FRANÇOIS ARAGO

(1809 - 1853)

Publiée avec une préface et des notes

PAR

LE Dr E.-T. HAMY

Membre de l'Institut et de l'Académie de Médecine,
Professeur au Muséum

LIBRAIRIE ORIENTALE & AMÉRICAINE

E. GUILMOTO Éditeur

6, rue de Mézières,
PARIS

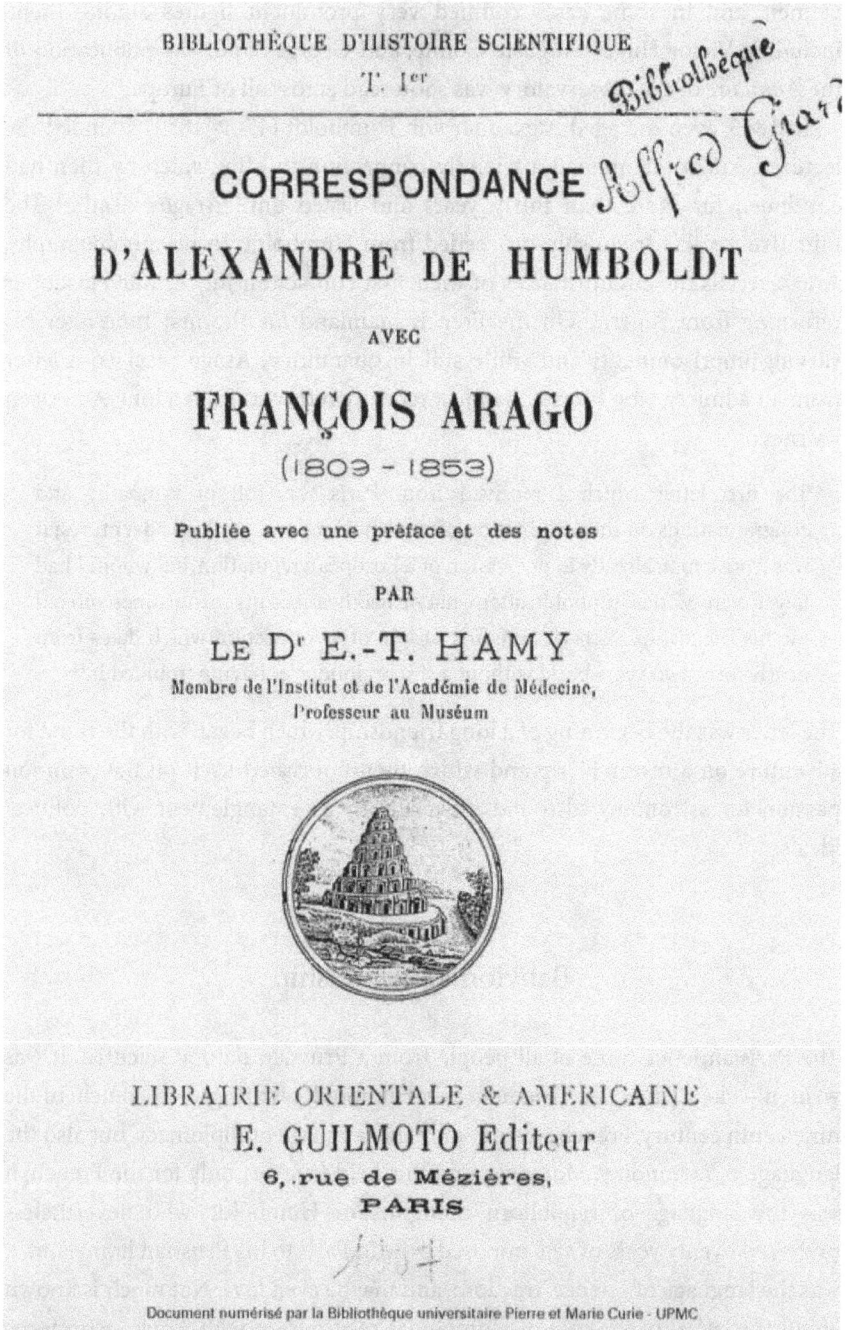

Figure 5.1 Title page of Alexander von Humboldt and François Arago, *Correspondance d'Alexandre de Humboldt avec François Arago (1809–1853)*, ed. Ernest-Théodore Hamy (Paris: Guilmoto, 1907), http://jubilotheque.upmc.fr/img-viewer/fonds-biologie/BG_000015_001/Contenu/JPEG_HD/viewer.html?ns=BG_000015_001_J3_001.jpg.

Humboldt's letters to Arago are preserved since Humboldt did not take care to retain Arago's. Ernest-Théodore Hamy collected the letters, annotated them, and posthumously published them, including an introduction, with Guilmoto in Paris.[13] It is no coincidence that the editor used the emblem of the Tower of Babel as the printer's mark (see Figure 5.1), this symbol of a mythic construction site in ancient Babylon that stands for an interminable task of translating the innumerable languages of the world, through God's heavenly work, into one sanctifying language.

Alexander von Humboldt and François Arago stood bound together for decades. Together, they engaged in science policy in the Bureau of Longitude or in the French Academy of Sciences, and they advocated for research expeditions; as scientists, humanists, and cosmopolitans, they held these to be indispensable for the general comprehension of the world-nexus. They quoted each other's observations and measurements, which they exchanged by post. After Arago's death, Humboldt issued some of his works.[14] Arago's *Œuvres complètes* contain some "introductions" by Humboldt, which for the German edition of the *Gesammelte Werke* first had to be translated into the mother tongue of the author. Humboldt reminisced at the age of eighty-four:

> The thought makes me proud that I, through affectionate devotion and through the persevering wonderment that found expression in all of my writings, belonged to him for a period of forty-four years, and that my name will be mentioned next to his great name every now and then.[15]

Not seldom did the correspondence serve the purpose of Humboldt reassuring himself, via Arago, of findings in his astronomic and meteorological inquiries. Humboldt was dependent on Arago's expertise, especially while writing the third section of *Cosmos* on astronomy and astrognosy.[16] But for the working friendship, astronomy was more than the exchange of information. For both Arago and Humboldt, astronomy was a heavenly language in which the laws of nature are composed, laws which they set out to learn and master. This duty was their obligation and each dedicated himself to it in his own way, the one as an explorer of the universe, the other as a thinker of the cosmos, the one as a Mediterranean and citizen of the *république universelle*, the other as a Transatlantic who had no republic, let alone a nation, and in this regard was thoroughly reliant on a cosmopolitan point of view. The telescope and the sextant—these mobile instruments which traveling research scientists used for location determination, chronometry, and terrestrial cartography—were for them world media. While Arago increasingly resorted to the observatory for his telescopic observations, for Humboldt the journey remained a lifelong basis for research activity. His medium was the ocean, the *mer*, if you will, a fluidly networked space whose orientation markers, the stars, he shared with Arago.

The humanitarian activities of the two researchers are closely interwoven with astronomical research and yet of an entirely different order, for both Arago and Humboldt appeared as impassioned advocates for equality and freedom and as vehement adversaries of slavery. This coupling of astral knowledge and cosmopolitanism is especially pronounced in Humboldt's writings, for Humboldt developed his concept of the cosmos as an ambiguous figure that relentlessly oscillates between astronomy and human rights. The impetus for a theory of the world derives from this vibratory movement.

Humboldt's *Cosmos*

In 1862, the fifth and final volume of Alexander von Humboldt's *opus magnum* appeared. *Cosmos* was the title of the monumental work, which resulted from twenty-five years of work and which, like the Tower of Babel, remained incomplete.[17] It encompassed no less than a synopsis of the scientific exploration of the world, and it advanced within a brief time to become the most prominent science bestseller in the German-speaking world of the nineteenth century. Looking back from the present day, what is worthy of recognition beyond the galactic scope of the work is its methodological achievements, which decisively crossed over the borders of formerly mono-disciplinary research approaches. The vehicle for this crossing was the correspondence with expert scientists of the most varied provenances. It is not for nothing that Ottmar Ette characterizes Humboldt from the standpoint of the contemporary age of global information flows as an intellectual pioneer of "globalized digital networks."[18]

From an epistemological perspective, something anachronistic inheres in the title of this synopsis of world knowledge—*Cosmos*—something significantly more identifiable today than in Humboldt's lifetime. With the great epistemic turns before one's eyes, one recognizes that already in those days the concept of "cosmos," with its totalizing gesture and metaphysical suggestion, hardly fits into the program of a modern description of the world. The title of the book seems to contravene the very principle of the Enlightenment for which it advocated.

Why "Cosmos" as the title for this work?[19] Was not, in view of Humboldt's enthusiasm for Arago's astrophysical research, the term "universe" a more obvious one? Other than "cosmos," "universe" stands for both the demystification of astronomy as well as the disenchantment of every metaphysical foundation, even of a political world order for which both Arago and Humboldt advocated. That this conceptual pair—cosmos/universe—marks the biggest possible caesura in Western thought is, from a history of science perspective, often and explicitly described and furnished with the catchword of the "Copernican turn."[20] The astro-medial innovation of the telescope delivered, together with the new Newtonian physics, the empirical-theoretical evidence for the heliocentric worldview, which, not least with the help of a further media revolution brought about by book printing, set off a revolution in meaning that fundamentally altered the understanding of the "world." In place of the finite, ordered cosmos of the Aristotelian–Ptolemaic nature philosophy—as Alexandre Koyré described this fundamental change—the infinite universe emerged in the seventeenth century, one without hierarchical structures, without a plan of redemption, but full of regularity. The breakout from the medieval cosmos is a process of enlightenment, in which God pulls back from the starry sky and in which the human, with its new experience of time and space, becomes conscious of its place in the world.[21]

In view of this grand revolution of meaning, Humboldt's title *Cosmos* appears, in the year 1862, remarkably backward-looking. Even so, in this period during which nation-states oriented their scientific, economic, and cultural activities preferentially toward the massive projects of colonization and globalization, there prevailed an elevated need for accurate factors in establishing identity. Astronomy seemed decidedly useful for this, as the growing number of national and imperial observatories being founded all over Europe shows.[22] "Openly anachronistic" is how Peter Sloterdijk characterizes the title *Cosmos*. But Sloterdijk assesses the effect of this untimeliness as undeniably productive for a philosophical redefinition of the Western subject:

> It was [...] the historically conditioned chance for this monumentally holistic "physical description of the world" to compensate with the resources of aesthetic education for what modern Europeans had endured through the loss of the firmament and cosmic *clôture* [(en)closure]. Humboldt had wagered that he could present this metaphysical loss as a cultural gain [...]. In panoramic nature paintings, the aesthetic observation of the whole replaced its lost safety in the vaulted universe.[23]

In fact, for Humboldt *Cosmos* was neither about a rebirth of the medieval theory of the spheres nor about the reanimation of a promise of salvation, but rather, as Sloterdijk writes, much more about enlightenment as a "historical chance."

Interestingly, Sloterdijk characterizes the "resources of aesthetic education" as "compensation" and "replacement" for a "loss" that the modern sciences inflicted on the modern worldview. An economic critique looms in this formulation, as though the enlightened concept of the universe was lacking in something that the concept of the cosmos could supplement, and moreover not in the sense of a simple restoration of an old order but rather through another, belated, and "freely anachronistic" concept of the cosmos. In this balance sheet, "cosmos" and "universe" are no longer simple oppositions to one another but rather connected to one another though a complex economy of compensation: they form a system or a partnership, perhaps even a kind of "friendship." This system is held together by a debt in the sense of a lack, which presents itself in the connection between cosmos and universe and equally as its personification between Humboldt and Arago. In this system, Humboldt's *Cosmos* becomes the figure of a large project that places the astrognosy of the universe in the service of terrestrial responsibilities. It is telling, writes Sloterdijk, that

> [. . .] in his world fresco, Humboldt, who has perhaps rightly been called the last cosmographer, no longer chose the earth as the vantage point from which to look out into the expansive space. Instead, in keeping with the spirit of his time and ours, he took up an arbitrary position in outer space from which to approach the earth like a visitor from a foreign planet.[24]

What Sloterdijk describes here is also known as the so-called Janeway syndrome: in the fictional universe of Star Trek, Captain Kathryn Janeway of the space shuttle *Voyager* ended up in the twenty-fourth century in the Delta-Quadrant of our galaxy, some 70,000 light years away from the earth. The mission of this Star Trek generation is for the first time not only the exploration of distant worlds ("to boldly go where no man has gone before"), but more so to return to earth. A Homeric seven years (that is, seven seasons) is how long their odyssey takes. A homecoming lies at the end. The goal of this exploration of the universe is the discovery of their own—but from now on foreign—planet as a home.

For the immense Humboldtian undertaking, the title "Universe" would have adequately fulfilled the devotion to exact research to which Humboldt had committed himself; nevertheless, he would thereby have neglected the direction and goal of this undertaking. Humboldt's cosmos concept connects to modern natural science, not in order to situate the earth in an infinite vacuum, but rather to shift it back, in a kind of neo-Ptolemaic perspective, to the center of the universe. The reference point of the earth, which Sloterdijk so emphatically invokes, is thereby neither absolute nor unified. As little as Janeway returns to earth as a whole world—the home of the Starfleet is in San Francisco and the universal language of the federation is English—it is as little possible on the real earth to ever steer from Europe towards a place that would not stand in relation to a meridian in Singapore or London or which would be possible to imagine outside of such a referential system. The effects of this referential system extend into Humboldt's concept of the cosmos. For the author of *Cosmos* bears this proper name, Alexander von Humboldt, which first of all identifies him as a human in the sense of a "terrestrial humanoid," in the language of sci-fi. At the same time, and to no lesser extent, this proper name inscribes him into a normative system, in which he becomes identifiable as a particular subject; this name stands for a certain provenance, a class, a gender, a belonging to a people, and so on. These considerably variable conditions contribute equally to the functioning of the proper name: on the one hand belonging to a common humanity, as a universal concept whose validity Humboldt sought to ensure through astronomical knowledge with his stargazer friend François Arago, and on the other hand the confinement of universality to a singular historical-political situation. Humboldt's cosmos concept, as naturalistic and panoramic as it appears, will not be able to remain untouched by both the universal and the particular, and, worse yet, it will not be able to avoid negotiating a relationship between these opposites: the World and the West. In what follows, I want to investigate *en miniature* which form this relation takes in Humboldt's writing about the journey to the Americas.

A star like a friend

To bring this conceptual differentiation—the cosmos as a humanitarian "compensation" (enrichment, supplement) to the concept "universe"—into focus, I want to look closer at two passages from Humboldt's *Relation historique du voyage aux régions équinoxiales du Nouveau Continent*, his report of the journey to the Americas. Humboldt began the journey in 1799, while Arago was still in school. The route took him from Spain, across the Canary Islands, and from there to South America: to Venezuela, along the course of the Orinoco river, and from there to Columbia via Cuba. On the crossing from Venezuela to Havana, in the twenty-seventh chapter, the report, which remains a fragment, abruptly breaks off.[25] It concludes with neither a conclusion nor any indication of the journey's further trajectory. Instead, it ends *in medias res* with a statistical survey of the racial, linguistic, and religious communities of the inhabitants of the new continent. These statistics give Humboldt the occasion for a remarkably long-sighted outlook: "There is something serious and prophetic in these inventories of the human race: in them the whole future destiny of the New World seems to be inscribed."[26] This sentence demonstrates very beautifully the program of the Humboldtian writing style: as a final coda and prelude alike, it marks the card index-like incompleteness and openness of this work. For Humboldt, what is at stake is no less than the "entire future," "the whole world," which he seeks to comprehend through critical investigations of the contemporary cultural and linguistic reality and in connection with economic, geographical, geological, astronomical, botanical, and zoological dimensions. Humboldt's South American work is dedicated to this all-encompassing connection. Just as later in *Cosmos*, here, too, he strives for a panorama of planetary relations, above and beyond all natural and disciplinary watersheds: the connection between demographic developments and the transmission of the mother tongue, between ocean currents and climate, earthquakes and magnetic declinations, finally between the Orinoco and the Amazon. This writing style is just as precise as it is concise, in equal measure obligation and mission as well as fragment and ruin. Actually, the *Relation historique* was supposed to encompass ten volumes in octavo, but effectively only three volumes were realized, in which only a third of the actual journey is presented.[27] Not without reason did Humboldt's friend Arago reprimand him once, "Humboldt, you do not know how a book is made, you write endlessly; but this is not a book, it is an unframed portrait."[28] Humboldt obviously wrote as he researched, according to Ottmar Ette: mobile and network-like, precisely in a rhizomatic form in line with a global epistemology, equally fragmentary as *sans fin*.[29]

Humboldt had composed and copy-edited the travel journal after his return to Paris, the world metropolis of science. He was in the scientific environment of the polytechnic school, whose correspondent he became, where in the first years he slept in an attic and where he also soon became acquainted with the meridian surveyor Arago.[30] As a polyglot cosmopolitan, Humboldt chose to write in his other, non-genuine mother tongue. This pertains not only for the *Relation historique* but also for the whole thirty-volume (or thirty-six in other editions) South American work which Humboldt published and to a large part financed under the title *Voyage aux régions équinoxiales du Nouveau Continent, fait en 1799, 1800, 1801, 1802, 1803, et 1804 par Alexandre de Humboldt et Aimé Bonpland*.[31] It required a German translation in order to make the writings accessible to his fellow countrymen.[32]

Let us take a closer look at a passage in this work. It comes from the third chapter of the first book of *The Travels to the Equinoctial Regions of the New*

Continent, in which Humboldt describes the crossing from Tenerife to the coast of South America in the summer of 1799. The ship's route leads from Santa Cruz to Cumaná across the Tropic of Cancer into the "torrid zone" and proceeds on the same route favored by the trade winds that since Columbus have driven ships to the Antilles.[33] During the journey, Humboldt oriented himself not only with the help of maritime maps and ship clocks; he also precisely observed every abnormality, and insofar as he finds them described in the journals of famous mariners, they serve him as nautical signposts: meteorological phenomena, strangely large masses of floating seaweed, flying fish, even the mysterious phosphorescence of the ocean. He knows to read all of these signs like the notifications of a global positioning system. The approach toward the equator and the entrance into the southern half of the globe are nevertheless experienced as a cosmic event, which dawns on him through his perception of celestial signs. To the traveler from the northern hemisphere, the spectacle of the southern night sky discloses another yet unseen strange world of stars: "Nothing awakens in the traveler a livelier remembrance of the immense distance by which he is separated from his country, than the aspect of an unknown firmament," so comments Humboldt on the transequatorial passage.[34] Humboldt knows in exact terms the dramatic apogee of the experience of the new sky; it happens on the transition when the traveler, from his point of observation in one hemisphere, looks out into the other one and beholds the familiar constellations of the northern sky setting on the horizon and, by contrast, the strange, uncanny constellations of the southern sky ascending, the most dominant and distinct of this other side being the Southern Cross.

In the night of July 4 to 5, 1799, Humboldt notes, "In the solitude of the seas, we hail a star as a friend, from whom we have long been separated."[35] In the solitude of the seas (*mers*), away from the homeland/the mothers (*mères*), the space-temporal reference points of the traveler's receive new dimensions. The vastness of the oceans stands for a new separation, which not only refers to his place of birth and his journey's destination, but rather and above all to a strange third place, which, though he has never been there, should be as familiar as an old friend to the traveler. After a long separation, the Southern Cross moves from the distance beyond the celestial equator into the visible realm of fixed stars. Now another time stands in contrast to the longtime of solitude, which is openly measured on the basis of the temporality of a human life: the eternal time of an astral friendship. While Dante in the *Divina Commedia* imagined the southern hemisphere as an uninhabited place, where the purgatorial fires break forth and the four stars at this other pole form a constellation "never seen before except by the first humans,"[36] for Humboldt the Southern Cross is the emblem of a heterotopia, as a site that, from the perspective of the north, is simultaneously an impossible place and the site of a homecoming. Humboldt's star friendship is based not only on closeness and intimacy; distance and foreignness contribute in equal measure to it and split it in—if you will—an unfamiliar familiarity. The view of the Southern Cross has the significance, for Humboldt, of a universal homecoming to an uncanny place, which inextricably links the foreign and the distant with a figure of the origin. The passage runs as follows:

> The pleasure we felt on discovering the Southern Cross was warmly shared by such of the crew as had lived in the colonies. In the solitude of the seas, we hail a star as a friend, from whom we have long been separated. Among the Portuguese and the Spaniards peculiar motives seem to increase this feeling; a religious sentiment attaches them to a constellation, the form of which recalls the sign of the faith planted by their ancestors in the deserts of the new world.[37]

These four stars, or, as Dante writes, "little flames," start a peculiar fire for the Europeans. For part of the crew, the joy at the sight of the Southern Cross stands for the return to a former homeland to which they are bound by a colonial relation. For another part, the Southern Cross is situated in a religious context, which is connected to the missionary activities of their ancestors and from which they assert a claim, grounded in genealogy, to a land known to them only as "the deserts of the New World." Humboldt observes these feelings of his fellow travelers with the same diligence with which he records meteorological atmospheres; he states them, even if he does not necessarily share them. Nevertheless, the entrance into the southern hemisphere has a special value for him, which is neither explicitly religious nor manifestly genealogically or colonially motivated.

The Southern Cross inspires the natural scientist Humboldt to a reflection that stands in relation first and foremost to astronomical observation, though it is not exhausted by this. The Southern Cross literally turns to an astro-cultural concept in which considerations of two distinct spheres converge: an exact astronomical one and a cultural-ideological one, which together elaborate an intricate concept of homeland. The Southern Cross serves him as a type of universal key which opens a cosmo-political space and allows the European to be simultaneously "in the world" and "at home." In this way, the cosmopolitan idea makes use of an astronomical model of knowledge; from the order (Greek *kosmos*) of a sky of fixed stars, there is derived an order of a different nature, namely a "cosmo"-political order. The European cosmopolitan, who turns his gaze up to the vault of stars, experiences, in the face of the Southern Cross, his expatriation from a national or European social order in order to transform— coming from the celestial bodies—his gaze from that of a citizen to that of a cosmopolitan

Certainly, the sky lends itself to be exceptionally fertile ground where feelings of home, religion, and belonging find especially favorable conditions. As a knowledgeable astronomer, Humboldt knows how to formulate speech acts about the sky in the form of declarative statements. That the universe harbors a unique rhetoric in the thought of globalization has been shown by Judith Butler. The gaze toward the stars presupposes a point of observation which is in truth idiosyncratic and particular but is equipped with universal features that suggest an extra-human standpoint and a general validity. This rhetoric makes use of a special mode of expression, a kind of "universal language," which asserts the general validity of cultural values and norms with the same grammar of which the universal natural laws are formulated. For Butler, it is a categorical imperative to set out the auto-referential structure of this universal rhetoric:

> I think that Zizek and I are in agreement on the point that we both make, in different ways, concerning how the exclusion of certain contents from any given version of universality is itself responsible for the production of universality in its empty and formal vein [...] [I]t is imperative to understand how specific mechanisms of exclusion produce, as it were, the effect of formalism at the level of universality.[38]

In the above-cited passage from Humboldt's travel report, it is in Butler's sense impossible that the religious feeling and sense of home that the sight of the Southern Cross provokes does not have a natural ground. Neither a constellation nor a genealogical order (the connection to ancestors) is capable of justifying the cosmopolitan experience, still less the universal idea of a "denaturalized homeland." For the "joy" at the sight of a constellation that one greets "as though a friend you have been separated from for a long time" presupposes an astro-cultural coding that can by no means be formalized or universalized. It belongs with the same right to all subjects who look up to the skies *beyond the equator* and who, in this liminal experience and in view of the new sky, become aware of the round shape of the earth. It cannot be emphasized enough that the estrangement of the stars cannot be experienced along a line of latitude in a movement from east to west but only in a northern or southern movement along the longitudinal axis. It is precisely here, on this axis, that Humboldt's cosmos concept calibrates itself.

Moon viewing in Cumaná

In a further passage—a further *Sternstunde* (historical moment)—we now want
to look at Humboldt's cosmos concept in connection with the critique of
universalism stemming from Judith Butler. In the fifth chapter of his American
travel journal, Humboldt reports on his stay in Cumaná in northeastern
Venezuela in 1798. The research society is extremely impressed by the diversity
of objects, but cannot get on with the arranged studies, because they themselves
had become an object of interest, with their instruments, microscopes, telescopes,
and electromotive apparatuses. Humboldt complains of the frequent visits by
curious inhabitants, who "seemed to be so pleased to see the spots of the moon
through Dollond's telescope," of the frequent "obscure questions" and of having
to repeat "for whole hours the same experiments."[39] The scenes seemed to him
"so much the more fatiguing, as the person who visited us had confused notions
of astronomy and physics."[40] In this way, he discerns a distinction between two
forms of astronomy. Characteristically, this difference does not lead back to a
heavenly truth but rather to a difference that goes back to national particularities:

> The curiosity excited respecting the phenomena of the heavens [...] takes a very
> different character among anciently civilized nations, and among those who
> have made but little progress in the unfolding of their intellectual faculties [...]
> [I]n the colonies, and among new people, curiosity, far from being idle or
> transient, arises from an ardent desire of instruction, and discovers itself with an
> ingenuousness and simplicity, which in Europe are the characteristics only of
> youth.[41]

For Humboldt, there are two ways of knowing the sky and the stars, two forms
of stellar knowledge, or, with reference to Hans Blumenberg, of "astronoetics." It
is notable that for Humboldt astral objects are not separated from one another
by the equatorial line, which separates perspectives situated in the northern
hemisphere from those in the southern. Humboldt draws much more a
distinction based on the particularities of "nations," which are either "anciently
civilized nations" or "new people" who "have made but little progress in the
unfolding of their intellectual faculties." This rhetorical figure, which founds a
cultural order on astronomical knowledge, echoes throughout Humboldt's travel
journal, continually insisting on this duality, which maintains itself with the very
cosmic authority that separates the planet into two hemispheres.

   Humboldt continues his report about Cumaná with a description of August
17, 1799. During the night, the sky above Cumaná offered a strange sight:

On the 17th of August a halo, or luminous circle, round the Moon, fixed the attention of the inhabitants, who considered it as the presage of some violent earthquake: for, according to the physical notions of the people, all extraordinary phenomena are immediately connected with each other.[42]

Humboldt continues, and explains, "Coloured circles around the Moon are much rarer in the countries of the North, than in Provence, Italy, and Spain," but in "the torrid zone beautiful prismatic colors appear almost every night."[43] Additionally, he explains that this optical phenomenon is also produced by strong humidity such as is found in Cumaná, where the moon rose after a thunderstorm:

As soon as she appeared on the horizon, we distinguished two circles; one large and whitish, forty-four degrees in diameter; the other a small circle of 1°43′, displaying all the colors of the rainbow. The space between the two circles was of the deepest azure. [...] This phenomenon had nothing extraordinary, except the great brilliancy of the colors, added to the circumstance that, according to the measures taken with Ramsden's sextant, the lunar disk was not exactly in the centre of the haloes. Without this actual measurement, we might have thought that the eccentricity was the effect of the projection of the circles on the apparent concavity of the sky.[44]

If in the second chapter of this book, in connection with Tiepolo's *Treppenhaus*, the discussion concerned the distortion of planetary projection; in Humboldt's commentary about optical phenomena, the apparatuses of observation play a decisive role. They correct the distortion of optical illusions. For the description of the halo indicates the same binary structure that we already observed in connection with the two forms of astronomy mentioned by Humboldt. Two circles can be distinguished, a large white one and a smaller one shining in all the colors of the rainbow. Moreover, the two circles could be observed in two ways: either with the gaze of the astronomer "from the north" who shows himself to be "knowledgeable," as he knows how to use the measuring instruments that correct the "naked" eye and reveal it to be erroneous; or alternatively, the halo around the moon can be observed with a gaze that corresponds to the inhabitant's knowledge of nature, according to which the halo is understood as an omen for a strong earthquake, that is, with a gaze that is through and through "ingenuous."

The two circles around the moon signify two forms of science, corresponding to the cultural codings of two hemispheres, each in their particular way, one with the naked, ingenuous eye, the other with a technical gaze, for which the ocular of the telescope or the sextant serves as a prosthetic sense. Yet only one of these two ways of looking claims for itself a universal validity. The occidental gaze is not only Eurocentric but rather also, as Sibylle Krämer writes, "ocularcentric."[45] The modern and an enlightened subject observes the stars with the technical gaze through the ocular of a telescope or sextant, which "sheathes" the naked eye, and to a certain extent separates the observer from himself, alienates him, or "denaturalizes" him.

Finally, there is another binary program worth pointing out, which arranges two distinct domains centripetally around a center of truth, like the haloes around the moon. In the passage about his stay in Cumaná, Humboldt twice mentions the large square. The first time is in connection with geographic measurement data:

> From the whole of the observations which I made in 1799 and 1800 it follows, that the latitude of the great square at Cumana is 10° 27' 52", and its longitude 66° 30' 2". This longitude is founded on the difference of time, on lunar distances, on the eclipse of the Sun on the 28th of October, 1799, and on ten immersions of Jupiter's satellites, compared with observations made in Europe.[46]

In this geo-astronomical terminology, the large square in Cumaná is measured with the coordinates that seem to be formalized in a universal system. After all, the latitude is a line that retraces the eclipse of the sun. Longitude as a line is in contrast determined over the course of negotiations between the great astronomical and nautical centers of Europe: Rome, Copenhagen, Jerusalem, St. Petersburg, Pisa. The meridian of Paris was, not coincidentally, determined by Humboldt's learned friend François Arago, until Greenwich was in 1884 named as the Prime Meridian of the world. In defining the coordinates of the great square, Humboldt not only situates it within the solar system; he also quantifies the distance of the great square in Cumaná to this very prime meridian of Europe. These coordinates are thus not exclusively determined by a universal system, but at the same time by this other hegemonic system that links up seafaring with colonization.

It is notable that, on the following page of the travel journal, the same great plaza is thematized in a completely different connection, one that carries out the ocular measurement of the "new world" with the occident's key measure of value:

> If the situation of our house in Cumana was highly favourable for the observation of the stars and meteorological phenomena, it obliged us to be sometimes the witnesses of afflicting scenes in the day. A part of the great square is surrounded with arcades, above which is one of those long wooden galleries, which are common in warm countries. This is the place where slaves, brought from the coast of Africa, were sold [...]. The slaves exposed to sale were young men from

fifteen to twenty years of age. Every morning coco-nut oil was distributed among them, with which they rubbed their bodies, to give their skin a black polish. The persons who came to purchase examined the teeth of these slaves, to judge of their age and health; forcing open their mouths as we do of those horses in a market.[47]

Let this denunciation of slavery serve as a textbook case of the humanism embedded in Humboldt's cosmic rhetoric.[48] The reflection about the celestial phenomena is immediately followed by an earthly observation: the observation of the slave trade. It is notable that the humanistic critique against the system of slavery stands in reciprocity with his astronomical knowledge, as though the one was a direct effect of the other. The scientific explorer Alexander von Humboldt shared this commitment against slavery with his friend François Arago.[49]

Cosmos, universe, globalization

Humboldt and Arago enjoyed a literally "celestial friendship." While Humboldt's astronoetic position is characterized in large measure by the *mobility* of the scientific *explorer* and the corresponding media of positioning, time measurement, and terrestrial cartography (the sextant and the telescope), Aragon's astronoetic activity in the observatory is founded on the *immobility* of the stationary observation and the celestial cartography (*carte du ciel*), whose central medium is astrophotography (daguerreotype and photometry).[50] Inquiry into the astronoetic structure of Humboldt's and Arago's concept of humanity is consequentially connected to a media-historical line of inquiry, namely the question regarding the function of telescope and observatory as "world media" in the era of the European late Enlightenment. The ideas of equality, freedom, and human rights prove to be, again, a universal idea, namely an idea that is literally derived from the order of the universe. For this reason, Butler and Zizek characterize the *Lumières* as a system offering in equal measure a critique of colonization and its vindication. Universalism amounts to speaking for the Other.

If under universalism one understands the formation of a remainder of European metaphysics, it takes a new form in the modern science of an ocular, post-Copernican astronomy. It purports to avail itself of a new, universal language in which the "truth" about optical illusions can be accounted for in precise measurement data. Its truth relates to astronomical truth as it does to the truth of human rights, and both truths are in equal measure derived from the stars. In this sense, Sloterdijk is right: Humboldt was probably "the last cosmographer." He comprehended the earth and everything earthly literally from the stars. And he did so in an eternally anachronistic sense, namely from today's point of view in the same way that the satellite view makes us experience the earth.

Well after Humboldt, in light of the first extraterrestrial images of the earth, Hans Blumenberg formulated this satellite perspective in an equally humanitarian expression, as Thomas Assheuer recalls some forty years later:

> The earth rising against a black sky, wrote the philosopher Hans Blumenberg well after Humboldt, seemed strangely deserted and inviolately alive, like an unpopulated improbability in cosmic space: "It looked as though humans, their works, and their waste did not exist." Humanity observed their own absence from the perspective of the moon; it saw the tranquility of a natural world devoid of humans, in order to then circumspectly project itself back onto the planet. This time not as an exploiter, but rather as a guest.[51]

Seen this way, Humboldt's cosmos concept remains in the realm of the questionable. On the one hand, he founds a universal imperative of planetary responsibility. On the other hand, he thereby confirms an ultimate Western and westward-oriented global order in whose name a contemporaneous globalization proceeds. Today, in a time when a new global reality is nascent, when electronic data streams switch the world to synchronous and humans to multi-site, Humboldtianism is enjoying a renaissance. This entails rethinking the conceptual pair cosmos/universe in this perspective, as well as newly triangulating the third concept, "globalization," in relation to its new high point. Humboldt posed this question in *Cosmos* without formulating it, let alone providing a decisive answer. It is our task to continue considering Humboldt's question, by first considering the openly anachronistic aspects of his work from a contemporary perspective and then asking ourselves what the concept of the cosmos means to *us* today, with regard to our place in the world (*mundus*), which, under the conditions of globalization (*globus*), requires a reconceptualization of its relationship to a superordinate world order (*kosmos*).

If there is one cosmos, and if, as for Humboldt, this one cosmos is coupled with a concept of humanity, then in this respect, this astronomical truth exhibits an irreparable blemish, for the earth's sky is a divided one. Precisely this division traverses the earth, taken cosmopolitically as an entire world and home planet of a cosmopolitan without regard for origin, race, gender, and so on. In distinction to the prime meridian, this division is non-negotiable. It is a law of nature. In this respect, the universal law of cosmopolitanism consists in recognizing this division and taking it into account as an infinite task or a debt that cannot be paid off.

6

Sublunar: Star Friendship in Orhan Pamuk's
The White Castle

The Venetian and Hoja

According to its etymology, "pair" (from the Latin *paria* or "equal things") means two individual things of the same kind, whereas today it also has the sense of "companions." In this rather literal interpretation, a complex structure can be discerned, one in which the pair is not automatically comprehended as a simple duality, a duality which is one or which would be unitary, but much more as two that belong together because they are bound to one another by something shared in common. What belongs together is, in principle, also divisible, and for this reason the behavior of pairs in literature and art has always been highly volatile. The charm of the pair lies less in their harmonic company and more in the many possible forms of divergence, in the tragedy of separation through external circumstance as well as through internal strife, in literature and arts as well as in life. This chapter is dedicated to the inner tension of the pair. It will entail observing difference in similarity and understanding the force—also and especially when it is a differential force—that holds the pair together.

An idiosyncratic literary pair can be found in Orhan Pamuk's novel *The White Castle*. It is composed of the novel's two protagonists: the first-person narrator, an educated young Venetian man, who is captured in 1650 by a Turkish fleet during a sea journey from Venice to Naples and abducted to Istanbul. In this foreign country, he becomes a slave of the local court scholar known as "Hoja," who appears as a narrated figure in the third person. Together the Venetian and Hoja form a dyad, literally a figuration full of tension. On the surface, they number two: the "I" (the Venetian) and the "he" (the Turk). The cultural contexts of the two protagonists are laid out in a likewise dual fashion: "I" and "he," slave and master, Christian and Muslim, Westerner and Easterner.

In the novel, though, there is also a level in which this opening symmetry shatters. The book starts in the genre of a historical adventure novel with the dazzling depiction of a naval battle:

> Our captain took heart when he saw the other two ships slip away from the Turkish vessels and disappear into the fog, and at last he dared to beat the oarsmen, but we were too late; even whips could not make the slaves obey once they had been aroused by the passion for freedom. Cutting the unnerving wall of fog into waves of color, more than ten Turkish galleys were upon us at once. Now at last our captain decided to fight, trying to overcome, I believe, not the enemy, but his own fear and shame; he had the slaves flogged mercilessly and ordered the cannons made ready, but the passion for battle late to flame, was also quick to burn out. We were caught in a violent broadside volley—our ship would surely sink if we did not give up at once—we decided to raise the flag of surrender.[1]

The motif of slavery is subtly introduced; the Muslim slaves on the Christian galley conceal themselves, so to speak, in the fog. They fall into the spotlight of the narrative in the instant that they change from the role of the victim to that of the perpetrator: freed by the Turkish privateers, the erstwhile slaves henceforth become slaveholders. The narrator is peculiarly involved in this complex and dynamic power relationship, which does not offer a simple victim-perpetrator or subject-object relationship, but rather which nests both in each other, in the manner of a set piece. And this relationship becomes even knottier. For while the captured Christians are consistently condemned to rowing by the Muslim privateers, the narrator draws the conquerors' attention to his unique education: in Florence and Venice, he studied science and art and knew something of astronomy, mathematics, physics, and painting. As this seems to make little impression on the barbaric Muslims, he rescues himself from the oarsmen's bench by then claiming to be a doctor.[2]

With these disclosures of his "identity" in the form of a commitment to a culture of science, one which contains a linguistic, cultural, and religious positioning to the world and the celestial bodies—indeed, to the stars themselves—that surround it, the Venetian paradoxically carries out the first alienation: he estranges himself from his fellow Christian captives, whose jealousy and hate he soon comes to feel. A second alienation follows the first almost immediately, as though the question of his "fellow people" inevitably raises the question of his fellow human beings, which is a more fundamental question, as it touches on the Other in itself, also and especially the absolute

Other, who speaks another language and follows other traditions and laws. This Other, the partner in the pair, enters by way of his "similar constitution" into the pact of the amalgamated duo. In the "ethics" of the Other, as Jacques Derrida discusses with reference to Emmanuel Lévinas, it remains undecidable who occupies the first and second positions in the pact of the pair. Phenomenologically, self and Other are not determinable, they are both a part of this twosome: Derrida characterizes the question of the ordinal number as the "question of the question," that is, the question that must itself be placed in question.

The narrator sees himself confronted with this "question of the question" at the end of the first chapter, as he comes face to face with "his Other" for the first time. This encounter is staged in a highly idiosyncratic fashion for literature: in Istanbul, the Venetian gained a reputation on the basis of his special abilities, and so he is regularly brought out of the dungeon to the Pasha in the palace, where he is used as a healer and consultant. In one of these visits, the following takes place:

> [T]hey took me to a room to wait, I sat down. After a few moments another door opened and someone five or six years older than myself came in. I looked up at his face in shock—immediately I was terrified. The resemblance between myself and the man who entered the room was incredible! It was *me* there [. . .] for that first instant this was what I thought. It was as if someone wanted to play a trick on me and had brought me in again by a door directly opposite the one I had first come through, saying, look, you really should have been like this, you should have come in the door like this, should have gestured with your hands like this, the other man sitting in the room should have looked at you like this.[3]

The setting of this scene is nothing remarkable. It is a normal room, with two opposing doors. But the manner and way in which the room is entered is thoroughly interesting. In its inspection, the static place transforms into a dynamic "space" of narrative, that is, into the subjectively experienced place that Michel de Certeau characterizes as "space." The principle of an uncanny repetition dominates in this space, a recursion of a regression that is absolutely unique (entering the room) and which, contrary to all spatial logic, nevertheless repeats. This space is staged in literature as a *mise en abyme*, a "setting-in-the-abyss," which conjures up the subject that enters it twice, as it were.

In the *mise en abyme* of the room in the Pasha's palace, the pair appears and with him the cultural encounter between East and West as a kaleidoscope of nested set pieces, a mosaic of ornamental motives, which in the further course of the novel is disassembled in a manifold way and then reassembled. This structure of the pair's organization in its "kaleidoscopic duality" will become the object of my investigation. Because the relation of the pair is mediated through shared astronomical activity, I would like to momentarily turn my gaze from *The White Castle* to the history of astronomical science, in order to discuss another pair that is likewise—as with the Venetian and Hoja—formed by a "star friendship."

"Sages" and "scholars"

Since antiquity, the light of the stars has inspired varying types of knowledge. Two fundamental forms are traced out by Hans Blumenberg in the second chapter of the Gospel of Matthew:

> From the East came the "Magi" (*magoi*), who turned their attention to the starry sky in such a way that nothing conspicuous could evade them; in Jerusalem, where they stopped to acquire a better understanding of the celestial sign, no one had noticed anything, because the "scholars" (*grammateis*) gathered around the Temple were completely engrossed in their books and the archpriests were wary of the stars, recalling how they had been idolized in Babylon.[4]

The Christmas story very nicely illustrates how one and the same celestial event informs two different forms of knowledge, the one sensual and observational, the other spiritual and reading, a division that corresponds to two cultural groups: an occidental one (Anatolian, *apo anatolōn*) and a Jewish-Pharisaic one.

The wise "magoi" from the Orient find their object of knowledge through pure intuition: to them, the conspicuous star, through its mere existence, signifies the birth of the Messiah: "for we have seen his star in the east, and are come to worship him" Matthew (2.2). Gazing at the star, they find their "orientation," for that is what "orient" literally means: to ascend or rise (*in oriente sole* means in the direction of the rising sun, eastwards).

It is then somewhat remarkable that orbital systems and the rotation of celestial bodies seem of secondary importance for the orientation of the magi. Hans Blumenberg calls attention to the fine distinction between having seen and having read something: "Those who had seen nothing nevertheless immediately knew which birthplace the prophet Mica had ordained for the shepherd of the people, for *that it how it is written*."[5] While the magi invoke the testimony of an extraordinary astronomical constellation, the scholarly *grammateis*, in accordance with the Jewish biblical and scriptural tradition, carry on with the art of prophecy, whose procedures rest on visionary knowledge through calculation, that is, on the knowledge of the world-nexus that the Greeks characterize as *kosmos*.

The differing types of celestial knowledge or *astronoetics*, as termed by Blumenberg, are observable time and again in the encounter between an Eastern and a Western history of cultural knowledge. Let us take a look at a pair of astronomers from the thirteenth century, during which southern Italy stood under the reign of the Hohenstaufen Emperor Friedrich II and a lively exchange between Western and Eastern astronomy took place.

Figure 6.1 shows the Persian astronomer Abu Ma'shar against the backdrop of the night sky in the iconography of the *grammateis*. He holds a book—like a monstrance, as a demonstration of an absolute and indisputable truth—and thereby takes on the appearance of a prophet, as Dieter Blume writes: "with the long, cascading white hair and the thick beard, turned toward the viewer in the

Figure 6.1 Abu Masar, in Georgius Fendulus, *Liber astrologiae*, Fol. 41v. Paris, Bibl. Nat. Ms. Lat. 7330, medieval image, also seen in Dieter Blume, *Regenten des Himmels: Astrologische Bilder in Mittelalter und Renaissance* (Berlin: Akademie Verlag, 2000), plate 17, 361.

gesture of a greeting, he corresponds to the type of a prophet or patriarch according to the Byzantine pictorial tradition."[6]

Figure 6.2 shows Georgius Fendulus himself, a rather unknown courtier, priest, and philosopher from the occident.[7] He is not holding and reciting the book; rather, he is writing it, and the process of writing itself is what his portrait shows. In his left hand, Fendulus is holding an astronomical instrument, always ready to gaze into the sky. When he writes, he is not only copying out but also translating Abu Ma'shar's book from Persian into Latin in the sense of a *translatio scientiae*; moreover, he seeks, in the observational measurement of the stars, to verify celestial knowledge by means of visual evidence, if not to augment and improve it.[8]

The staging of this pair of astronomers manifests a cultural semantics, one that has maintained itself across a long cultural-historical transmission to the

Figure 6.2 Image of the author, in Georgius Fendulus, *Liber astrologiae*, Fol. 1r. Paris, Bibl. Nat. Ms. Lat. 7330, medieval image, also seen in Dieter Blume, *Regenten des Himmels: Astrologische Bilder in Mittelalter und Renaissance* (Berlin: Akademie Verlag, 2000), plate 1, 315.

present day: namely the idea that Eastern astronomy is dogmatic, non-technical, and "astrological," while that of the West is progressive, technical, and truly "scientific." Nevertheless, there is a remainder from this partition in the form of a fascination for the Orient, which, beyond the stereotypical orientalism rightfully critiqued by Edward Said, has informed Western astronoetics.

It is no coincidence that the Star of Bethlehem is characterized as the Star of the Magi and not as the Star of Scholars. For the concept of a European history of science and history of faith, which insists today more than ever on a strict differentiation between astronomy and astrology as well as between West and East, this chiastic reversal of Eastern–Western lines of cultural transmission is highly remarkable. The wonder of Christmas, taken as the primal scene of a Judeo-Christian-Greek astronoetics, is decidedly ascribed to an Eastern astronoetics in the formulation of the "Star of the Magi." Of course, this is only an idiosyncrasy of language, only an idiom; the Star of the "Magi" does not conceal anything, except language itself. It is nothing further than language itself which does not cease to inspire inquiry again and again into the dichotomous program of this astronoetic pair and thereby to reorient and reoccident.

Orhan Pamuk's novel is made of nothing but language. So let us return to the text and investigate how Pamuk devises a cosmology that structures the relationship between the two protagonists and, with ever new surprises, drives a dynamic process of knowledge formation that produces a strange, even uncanny star friendship.

Pamuk's cosmology

Ever since their encounter in the palace, the Venetian and Hoja have formed an "intercultural" scientific duo, whose concept for innovation rests on the meeting of two scientific cultures. They predominantly undertake commissioned research for the palace: on the occasion of a royal marriage, they develop a fireworks display whose "violence and brightness of light and flame"[9] is so magnificent that it surpasses anything previously seen in Istanbul. In the course of the story, they construct the most outlandish models: a prayer clock with an intricate gear mechanism, a model of the universe with attached bells, and finally a monstrous war machine with which "the white castle" is to be stormed.[10]

Yet their actual research passion is reserved for astronomy. Already during their work on the fireworks display, the stars and their celestial order are exposed as a literary topos, which nourishes in equal measure encounter and conflict. In the process of mixing gunpowder, camphor, sulfur, and copper sulfate that comprised the firework powder, Hoja dreams, in a moment of intoxication, of a rocket that can fly to the moon. He asks the Venetian how he could be so sure that the moon is the nearest planet; perhaps they are only suffering from an optical illusion. The Venetian then reports on his astronomical studies and explains the basic principles of Ptolemaic cosmography. Hoja was not a stranger to this worldview, but he insisted on his assumption of a closer planet in a way as if he had proof of it.

> The next day he thrust a badly translated manuscript into my hand. In spite of my poor Turkish I was able to decipher it: I believe it was a second-hand summary of Almageist drawn up not from the original but from another summary; only the Arabic names of the planets interested me, and I was in no mood to get excited about them at that time. When Hoja saw I was unimpressed and soon put the book aside, he was angry. He'd paid seven gold pieces for this volume, it was only right that I should set aside my conceit, turn the pages and take a look at it. Like an obedient student, I opened the book again and while patiently turning its pages came across a primitive diagram. It showed the planets in crudely drawn spheres arranged in relation to the Earth. Although the positions of the spheres were correct the illustrator had no idea of the distances between them. Then my eye was caught by a tiny planet between the moon and the Earth; examining it a little more carefully, I could tell from the relative freshness of the ink that it had been added to the manuscript later. I went over the entire manuscript and gave it back to Hoja. He told me he was going to find that planet: he did not seem to be joking. I said nothing, and there was a silence that unnerved him as much as it did me.[11]

There is something to say regarding this dispute. Before observing its literary craftedness with the goal of arriving at a cultural critique, a few astronomical-historical contexts that touch on this dispute should be invoked.

First: Claudius Ptolemy

In second-century Alexandria, at that time the Roman province of Egypt, Ptolemy formulated a celestial theory. His theory was not groundbreaking for its time (in many regards it represented a step back from other cosmological theories). Rather, Ptolemy's merit consisted in exhaustively compiling and ordering the astronomical knowledge of antiquity. This theory became canonical for the worldview of late antiquity and Christianity, and it was superseded only in the early seventeenth century by the Copernican theses.

Second: *Almagest*

Almagest is Ptolemy's principal work of astronomy. Although it was originally composed in Greek, Latin translations were only completed relatively late (namely in the twelfth century), and then in part only from an Arabic translation. Already the title *Almagest* indicates the long path between antiquity and the European Middle Ages and to the important role of Arabic science as a mediator between the epochs. "Almagest": this is the Latinized form of the Arabic *al-Mid-schisti*, which in turn goes back to the Greek title *Megiste syntaxis* (Great arrangement).

Third: the Spheres

The Ptolemaic worldview assumes that the earth as a sphere rests motionless in the center of the cosmos. Invisible spheres, which support the celestial bodies, surround it. They are eight in number: the moon is closest to the earth, followed by Mercury, Venus, the Sun, Mars, Jupiter, and Saturn. These are the celestial bodies visible to the naked eye. While the planetary spheres are mobile, the outermost sphere is immobile. It contains the zodiac with the so-called "fixed stars."

*   *   *

In the above-cited scene, the dispute between Hoja and the Venetian revolves around this Ptolemaic worldview. In the further course of the novel, the dispute takes on new facets that extend beyond astronomical knowledge to touch on the relationship of the pair. Let us look more closely at this dispute, which binds these two literary characters, for better or worse, to two types of astronomy.

In Pamuk's literary staging, Hoja's worldview appears simply backward and naïve, a regression from the already regressive Ptolemy. Hoja wants to accept the existence of a star nearer than the moon. As proof, he provides a "primitive scheme" in a poorly-written version of the *Almagest*, in which the questionable celestial body was belatedly added "in fresh ink." A scientific proof could hardly be more dubious. The only argument that silences the Venetian lies in the power relations between master and servant. Pamuk stages Hoja's literal "weak power" with colorful literary means; the brutal naïvety of his way of thinking not only becomes visible in the selection and treatment of his scientific sources, but also in the interior design of the setting in which he carries out his studies: namely while "sitting on the low divans that lined the walls"[12] to which the Venetian is unaccustomed. Only years later was the slave capable of teaching his master what a table was by having a table made to measure. Hoja initially rejected it as inauspicious, as a four-legged funeral bier, but later got used to the table and chairs and credited them with helping him to think and write better.[13]

The pair relationship between Hoja and the Venetian seems to be determined this way: the allegedly superior first-person narrator, hailing from the Renaissance center of printing and science, has at his command the scholarly book-knowledge of the *Grammateis*. Hoja, by contrast, shows himself to be driven by a manic research impulse, while at the same time wholly absorbed by the fantastic-metaphysical mindset of a culture influenced by Islam; in the eyes of the narrator, Hoja "acted as if he had access to a knowledge that transcended what was in books."[14] The figures are laid out in this way and the pair relationship functions according to this binary program. But only on one level of the novel.

At a closer glance, the dispute over the small star in sublunar space reveals other, more subtle elements that structure the pair relationship. From the perspective of a history of science, it appears remarkable that the narrator, although having studied science in Venice and Florence in the first half of the seventeenth century, apparently is completely ignorant of the then heavily-debated *nova scientia astronomiae* along with the accompanying Copernican theory. In contrast to this dramatic *faux pas* is a remarkable deliberation by Hoja, who after all attempts to make novel inquiries into the magnitude of stars, against the backdrop of the possibility of optical illusions. In the course of the novel, Hoja develops these rather remarkable theses:

So we passed the first year, burying ourselves in astronomy, struggling to find proofs of the existence or nonexistence of the imaginary planet. But while he worked to design telescopes for the lenses he imported from Flanders at great expense, invented instruments and drew up tables, Hoja forgot the question of the planet; he had become involved in a more profound problem. He would dispute Ptolemy's system, he said, but we didn't engage in disputation; he talked while I listened: he said it was folly to believe that the planets hung from transparent spheres; there was something else that held them there, an invisible force, a force of attraction perhaps; then he proposed that the Earth might, like the sun, be revolving around something else, perhaps all of the stars turned around some other heavenly center of whose existence we had no knowledge. Later, claiming his ideas would be far more comprehensive than Ptolemy's, he included a number of new planets in his observations for a much wider cosmography, producing theories for a new system; perhaps the moon revolved around the Earth, and the Earth around the sun; perhaps the center was Venus; but he quickly grew tired of these theories.[15]

As audaciously and speculatively as Hoja puts forward his theses, at the same time they are far-sighted and innovative, for at base he intuitively anticipates the principles of the modern, heliocentric worldview, and with it the Keplerian laws and gravitation theory. He thereby makes use of astronomic devices and in particular the telescope. With his novel optical instrument, Galileo Galilei (1564–1642) had sparked a scientific revolution beyond the Mediterranean. By extending the range of vision to what had been previously invisible, coherences of larger orders such as the Copernican worldview are not only thinkable but from now on also visible. The telescopic view founded not only the new, ocular astronomy of observation, but brought the light of reason to the West.

The moment the telescope inaugurates the new theory of the description of the universe, it separates the new, ocular astronomy of the occident from the old, "naked" astronomy of observation, which had informed the sphere models of medieval astronomy in the course of the *translatio scientia*. This epistemic thrust took place temporally and spatially, so to speak, directly before the eyes of the Venetian. Instead of him, however, it is the Muslim astronomer who shows an (even if only intuitive) idea of the power of the telescope.

Optical methods have explosive potential. They revolutionize not only the seemingly eternal truth of astronomy. Rather, as medial *dispositifs* they are capable of overthrowing the classical order in the novel as well as the narrated relationship of the novel's figures. Ever since Gérard Genette, the literary medium of optics has been denominated as "focalization," whereby, in addition to a narrative approach, the organization of the gaze is included in narratological analysis. In the above-cited passage about the cosmological disputation, the focalization is organized complexly, as the following sentence demonstrates: "I saw that he listened with interest, but was reluctant to say anything that would reveal his curiosity."[16] The first-person narrator is here the subject of the gaze whose object is Hoja, but from a point of view that discloses something to the one seeing from which he can infer that it should remain concealed. This gaze discloses the Other to the same extent as the self. In their reciprocity, both positions function—as in an optical paradox—as reflection surfaces for the counterpart. According to the logic of the *mise en abyme*, the gaze produces an impossible space, similar to a room with two opposing doors, through which the subject—doubled—enters, in order to become aware of himself. The analysis of this focalization situation reveals the psychologization of a pair relationship whose complexity is in no way inferior to the well-known marriage dramas of Strindberg, Ibsen, or Flaubert in terms of pathological power. Behind its web of disdain, jealousy, rage, and mutual dependency lie hidden the tender nuances of an attentive curiosity, in which the search for the absolute truth of the cosmos discloses a search for the Other in the sense of an alter ego.

Mirror scenes

What the telescope does for astronomical research, the mirror does for the psychological exploration of the "I," and so it is no coincidence that the novel is full of mirror scenes. In the fourth chapter, Hoja finally poses the question that from this moment on dominates their common studies, even to the point of mania: "Why am I what I am?"[17] To the Venetian, the question seems to be quite familiar, for there, with the "others" (in renaissance Venice), one would have often made this inquiry with the help of mirrors: "Not only the palaces of kings, princes, and noblemen, but the homes of ordinary people as well were full of mirrors carefully framed and hung upon the walls."[18] The question of the I becomes the primary question, the question of the questions so to speak, the question of the I, as Other.

Under the threat of torture, Hoja seeks an answer; the servant, however, recognizes in this act of violence the vulnerability and dependency of his master to whom he becomes, in a new way, a tormentor. Day after day, they sit at the table, writing together in a way as "we also look at ourselves in the mirror,"[19] the one chained to his chair, the other to his anger and despair. These table scenes and mirror scenes are abyssal. They lead down into the depths of the abject, where Hoja, corroded by self-doubt, abandons his contempt for the Other. The Venetian in turn considers his newfound equality as a change of roles: in the future, not he, but rather Hoja would be the slave.[20]

The most dramatic mirror scene occurs during the period when the plague is running rampant in the city. The Venetian, who understands the danger of infection, regards the plague with angst and terror. Hoja, by contrast, regards it as deliverance from earthly chains and the final devotion to Allah. When they are alone in the room, Hoja suddenly undresses to examine his chest and abdomen while standing in front of the mirror. He discovers a pustule on himself. The Venetian feels uncomfortable in view of Hoja's nakedness. At the same time he is afraid of the pustule, which he identifies as a plague bubo, but without wanting to touch it. Hoja urges him to do so, because that is the only way he can arrive at a definite diagnosis. Then he confesses to being afraid of dying. He wants to check whether the Venetian is also infected and asks him to undress as well. As he does so, the Venetian feels a tingling of the flesh, which he attributes to a cool breeze in the room or the coldness of the mirror. Hoja examines him thoroughly, getting quite close to him, placing his fingers on his abdomen, examining his armpits, neck and the back of his ears, finally to determine that he has not been bitten by the insect.

> Squeezing the nape of my neck from both sides with his fingers, he pulled me towards him. "Come, let us look in this mirror together." I looked, and under the raw light of the lamp saw once more how much we resembled one another. I recalled how I'd been overwhelmed by this when I'd first seen him as I waited at Sadik Pasha's door. At that time I had seen someone I must be; and now I thought he too must be someone like me. The two of us were one person! This now seemed to me an obvious truth. It was as if I were bound fast, my hands tied, unable to budge. I made a movement to save myself, as if to verify that I was myself. I quickly ran my hands through my hair. But he imitated my gesture and did it perfectly, without disturbing the symmetry of the mirror image at all. He also imitated my look, the attitude of my head, he mimicked my terror I could not endure to see in the mirror but from which, transfixed by fear, I could not tear my eyes away.[21]

In the condensation of reciprocal and interlaced gazes, the mirror scene delivers the pair to the final intimacy. Naked, vulnerable, and mortal, the pair encounters itself. Its studious gaze attempts to fathom the symmetry of the mirror image, from the dermatological to the existential, as though the one was capable of being the Other, of thinking his thoughts, fearing his anxieties, seeing the world and the stars with his eyes, ultimately even dying his death. The ultimate encounter of the self turns out to be the encounter with the Other, with the Other as another self.

Star friendship

Cosmology and psychology are not an obvious pair. Nevertheless, Pamuk, by coupling the telescope and the mirror, knows how to create a literary *Doppelgänger* drama in which Eastern and Western modes of thought are exquisitely intertwined. The connection between the Venetian and Hoja is literally "abyssal," insofar as it touches on the stylistic means of the *mise en abyme* which creates impossible approaches and points of access to spaces that are not possible according to the traditional physics of space: worm holes, so to speak, science-fiction *avant la lettre*.

Nietzsche puts forward such a star friendship in an aphorism from his *Gay science*:

We were friends and have become estranged. [...] We are two ships each of which has its goal and course; our paths may cross and we may celebrate a feast together, as we did—and then the good ships rested so quietly in one harbor and one sunshine that it may have looked as if they had reached their goal and as if they had one goal. But then the almighty force of our tasks drove us apart again into different seas and sunny zones, and perhaps we shall never see each other again; perhaps we shall meet again but fail to recognize each other: our exposure to different seas and suns has changed us. That we have to become estranged is the law *above* us [...]. There is probably a tremendous but invisible stellar orbit in which our very different ways and goals may be *included* as small parts of this path; let us rise up to this thought. But our life is too short and our power of vision too small for us to be more than friends in the sense of this sublime possibility. – Let us then *believe* in our star friendship even if we should be compelled to be earth enemies.[22]

Nietzsche's star friendship is a matter of strangeness. The estrangement, however, does not arrive belatedly; rather, it reveals itself belatedly as something that was always intimate to friendship. In his *Politics of Friendship*, Derrida points out that strangeness is the basic structural condition for friendship.[23] The sublime possibility of a "star friendship" seems to be the demand of the pair. This holds true for the constellation of the Venetian and Hoja in Orhan Pamuk's *The White Castle*, but perhaps also for an ethics of the Other in the textual figure that we call the "world." Nietzsche's star friendship assumes the gesture of an ethics that is dedicated to the "politics" of the "cosmos" (thus, the "cosmopolitan") as the interminable task of elevating the question of "fellow people" to that of "fellow human beings."

7

In Earth Orbit: Constellation "Suitcase." Planetary Aesthetics in William Kentridge's *Felix in Exile*[1]

Those are the countless other worlds, the remote stars the man they burned spoke about. He never saw them, he just expected them to be there.
Galileo to Sagredo in Bertolt Brecht, Life of Galileo[2]

Remembrance and forgetting

The South African artist William Kentridge has been widely known in Europe since the 1990s, when his work was exhibited at the Venice Biennale and the Documenta.[3] His animated films are remarkably idiosyncratic. In these, Kentridge sketches out a unique aesthetics in an entirely inimitable handwriting, the many facets of which occupy contemporary art criticism.

What makes Kentridge's work special, as I would like to argue through an engagement with Kentridge's short film *Felix in Exile* (1994), is an aesthetic effect of globalization. With Kentridge, I will turn my gaze toward the "globe," taking its spherical form to be fruitful for the concept of a "planetary aesthetics." To this end, it will be necessary to look, on this globe of ours, from a vantage point in Central Europe towards the south, over the Alps, over the sea, and across the desert. We suspend the curvature of the earth, and our gaze travels along the line of longitude toward South Africa.

In 2010, we often looked in this way, when South Africa was the scene of a global event, a world party with vuvuzelas and Bofana Bofana, a world-game of countries and continents. From Europe, we watched "far away," watched the game in the Nelson-Mandela-Bay stadium in Port Elizabeth, which was transmitted by artificial satellites from the southern to the northern hemisphere of the planet.

South Africa today, after the World Cup. What, in our present distance, do we remember? What is memorable *today*, with present-day media technologies such as the artificial satellites which form, through an extraterrestrial hub, a worldwide space of information in which the division of north and south and even the spherical shape of the earth is annulled?

William Kentridge prophetically anticipated this moment. With foresight, he dedicated his series *Drawings for Projection* (1989–99) to exactly this, our present. In his films, he asks how the world and the global media will remember South Africa, in a future time (from his perspective) whose real actuality (at his time) was not knowable in any meaningful way, with one exception: with regard to the figure of forgetting, which equally takes place in and through global media, including the technologies of storage and archiving.

It has often been said that Kentridge has a serious interest in memory.[4] Taking Kentridge's video artwork *Felix in Exile* (1994) as my object of investigation, I too will argue that Kentridge deals with the visual dimension of memory and its counterpart, oblivion. Visualizing this forgetting is a far greater challenge than it is with memory. Forgetting is not simply equivalent to the invisible; in a film, a black screen would not be an appropriate visual equivalent of forgetting. It is precisely this problem that Kentridge faces in his video artwork: finding an inscription technique for what Martin Heidegger called the "uncanny structure of oblivion." Oblivion considers the visible to be there, but "concealed," as Heidegger puts it, by a "cloud of forgetting."[5] Forgetting is thus based on visibility as a possibility, as something that could be looked at but for some reason is not.

I will argue in this chapter that Kentridge's technique of filmmaking is devoted to the invention of a particular visual aesthetics, an aesthetics that explores visibility as a possibility that is defined by Heidegger's "cloud." This cloud structures the interplay of remembering and forgetting, it can take on various forms, and it encompasses all obstacles and resistances to a successful act of seeing. Insofar as looking (back) at South Africa takes place in a global context, the spherical shape of earth itself becomes one such obstacle that poses a challenge to the act of looking. Its basic problem resides in the limitation of the visual field, which results from the horizon as the line beyond which the visible surface of the earth hides, to refer to the literal meaning of *horizein* in Greek: "to border," derived from *hóros*: "boundary," understood as the apparent borderline that separates earth from sky. Crossing this border virtually requires the "tele-visual" potential of the so-called world media: the World Wide Web, artificial satellites, radio, and telegraph. It is through these technologies that events are perceived beyond the horizon and become global, or on the contrary that they are disregarded, not looked at, denied, or blocked out from memory. The focus of my analysis will be the question of how Kentridge's film deals with the curvature of the earth as the dispositive that decides what can be looked at and what cannot be looked at. In turn, I consider how the earth in Kentridge's film negotiates the geographic, medial, aesthetic, and political conditions of not looking.

A poetics of segregation

Felix in Exile is one of nine short animation films that together form the film series *Drawings for Projection*. At the center of Kentridge's stories is the film character Felix Teitlebaum, a self-portrait of Kentridge. The drama of this figure is loneliness as a special form of isolation; it concerns the abandonment of the beloved as well as the poetic loneliness of the artist as politically and aesthetically exiled. In the process, being separated in the sense of "apartheid" is inextricably intertwined with South Africa's historical politics of segregation.

In *Felix in Exile*, two spaces run in parallel, each accommodating one figure. First, there is Felix in a room (perhaps a hotel room in Paris) equipped with a bed, a washbasin with a mirror, and the icon of the migrant: the suitcase (see Figure 7.1). Second, there is the wide and open landscape, South Africa, the home country of the exiled, which is surveyed by a woman called Nandi, using a telescope and a theodolite (see Figure 7.2). The landscape of South Africa is the scene of the exploitation, control, and distribution of mineral resources and, ultimately, of bloody acts of violence.

Kentridge created *Felix in Exile* in 1994, on the eve of the first democratic, fully representative, supraracial election—as we remember—four years after Nelson Mandela was released from his twenty-seven-year detention and one year after being awarded, together with Frederik Willem de Klerk, the 1993 Nobel Peace Prize. At a moment long before the FIFA World Cup came to South Africa and before Mandela was elected president, Kentridge had already raised the question of how the apartheid regime and the many people who lost their lives in the battle for democracy would be remembered in the future. He thus recalled a time that had still to come, "a future for which APARTHEID will be the name of something finally abolished," as Jacques Derrida wrote, likewise some time beforehand.[6] This future is our present today. Kentridge's *Drawings for Projection* are memory traces in this grammatological sense: headings for a future to come to our memory.

Figure 7.1 Felix in a room; still from
Felix in Exile, directed by William
Kentridge. © William Kentridge 1994. All
rights reserved. The stills from William
Kentridge, *Felix in Exile*, 1994, 35mm,
copied onto DVD, were kindly made
available by Lisa Cloete, Johannesburg.

Figure 7.2 Nandi with telescope and
theodolite; still from *Felix in Exile*,
directed by William Kentridge.
© William Kentridge 1994.
All rights reserved.

For *Felix in Exile*, Kentridge created almost forty large-sized charcoal drawings on which he continually works: on one and the same sheet of paper, he draws with charcoal and occasionally uses some blue or orange pastel. Then he rubs out individual sections only to redraw them, leaving the erased traces behind like pale memories. He photographs the intermediary stages with a 35-mm camera using a stop-motion technique.[7] In this unconventional animation technique, two different aesthetic procedures are placed in a novel relation to one another, for it combines the gestural labor of the hand with the optical procedure of photography; in other words, the graphic movement of the line with the photographic print, the "trace" with the "imprint."[8]

In this way, the line travels past the edge of the paper or the frame and carves out its trail beyond spatial and temporal borders. Following the principle of adjacency or metonymy, a nomadic principle, the line strings together disparate places. Even within one and the same image, the line disregards the order of real codes and creates surreal connections. In the combination of drawing and photography (or trace and imprint), the surface of the earth is folded in such a way that distant places touch one another; intimate proximity and cosmic distance converge. This technical procedure draws together the pull of the line with the print of the photograph.

In the context of art criticism, Rosalind Krauss has described these space-time anomalies in terms of the concept of the palimpsest. She emphasizes that "the substance of the expression is charcoal, constantly modified by the application of the eraser."[9] The palimpsest is just such a practice in which the act of looking at a visible surface cannot be performed in a straightforward, affirmative manner but is always questioned by the other possibilities of imagination lying hidden in the depth of the image.

It is precisely this spatial paradox of two visible surfaces emerging at the same time that Mieke Bal is interested in when she focuses on the temporal counterpart of the palimpsest, that is "heterochrony," by which the real now-time is permeated with another time. Bal explores the specific aesthetic mode of cultural articulations originating in the context of contemporary migratory movements and finds it in the temporal asynchrony that unavoidably goes along with migration. The moving image and, more particularly, video art appear to her to be the ideal media of migratory culture in our age of globalization. Bal argues that the temporal texture of our cultural world resides in heterochrony as the aesthetic means of film that "can be seen as a form of foreshortening. Like its better known spatial counterpart, foreshortened time is distorted—made wider or thicker— and condensed."[10] In her analysis of *Felix in Exile*, Mieke Bal argues that "the tool he [Kentridge] uses to achieve heterochrony is the trace," and specifies that "this, of course, can be read as a metaphor of memory."[11]

It cannot be stressed enough, as I would like to add to Bal, that the concept of memory also includes oblivion, to touch on that most tender point of the trace as a heterochronic device. When Kentridge draws and redraws his objects by using the same sheet of paper again and again, he cannot avoid erasing an object in order to draw another one. For example, within one and the same shot, Kentridge turns the close-up image of a closed eye into a landscape, using the horizontal line of the eyelid as the horizon. Elsewhere in *Felix in Exile*, a constellation of stars is dissolved into a crumpled-up sheet of a newspaper, which is then modified into a burial shroud covering a face. This process is in principal infinite; it could go on at least until the paper decomposes.

The drawing technique that produces the palimpsest cannot satisfactorily explain the complexity of Kentridge's aesthetic procedure, nor does the heterochrony of film do so. The act of drawing, erasing, and redrawing as the basic condition of the palimpsest indeed relies on the presence of that which is looked at. It reveals the condition of presence as a possibility. It is by means of the photographic imprint that erasure becomes visible as that aspect of the drawing that withdraws itself from being looked at. Kentridge's palimpsests are not just traces; they are imprints of traces. They are concerned with drawing as much as with erasure, with appearance as much as with disappearance, with the possible as much as with the impossible.

Planetary aesthetics

In combining drawing and photography, or imprint and trace, the idiosyncratic aesthetic methods in *Felix in Exile* mix up the codes of time and space. They bring two separate spatiotemporal worlds into contact with each other: a time to be remembered and a time of remembering, a world hosting Felix and another world hosting Nandi, one in the northern, the other in the southern hemisphere of the globe. Although these two spaces along with their respective characters are "separate," or "apart" from one another, they come into contact in the interplay of imprint and trace.

Both spaces and figures (Felix and Nandi), who are diegetically held separate or "apart" from one another, are also cunningly placed in relation to one another throughout the film: water flows from a pool in the African steppe across the rim of the image and oozes out of the mirror in Felix's room, flooding it (see Figure 7.3). In its flood, the world turns into an "archipelago" in the sense of Édouard Glissant, in which nothing stays separate or apart, but everything becomes a part of the "*tout-monde*," engages in the poetics of relation and leads into "'planetary' influxes."[12] The water tap has become an interface that makes impossible connections possible, as has the telescope which makes distant things visible, objects in the starry sky as well as the "other" space in the other hemisphere of the planet. Sheets of drawings and newspapers drift across Africa and float from one shot to the next. These sheets of paper carry pieces of unspecific news about massacres in South Africa with them and spread the news across the world. As archival documents, they take the shape of waste paper encasing the globe: printed forgetting (see Figure 7.4).

Time and again, the starry sky serves Kentridge as a fantastic projection surface. As in the primal scenes of sci-fi cinema, the moon is not only imagined but also animated. With the help of a Georges Méliès-inspired "magic of cinema," the stars become protagonists. Their points connect to form a constellation, which then transforms into a crumpled newspaper, that then becomes a burial shroud, and so on.[13]

In this interweaving of sensorial processes arises a special aesthetics, a critical aesthetics in the sense of a planetary thought oriented against the segregation of space or against a system of apartheid. This planetary aesthetics translates the untranslatable, for it opposes "apartheid" as "racism's last word," as Jacques Derrida writes, which has always been "the archival record of the unnameable."

Figure 7.3 Water flooding Felix's room; still from *Felix in Exile*, directed by William Kentridge. © William Kentridge 1994. All rights reserved.

Figure 7.4 Sheets of paper drifted across Africa; still from *Felix in Exile*, directed by William Kentridge. © William Kentridge 1994. All rights reserved.

[N]o tongue has ever translated this name—as if all the parlances of the world were defending themselves, shutting their mouths against a sinister incorporation of the thing by means of the word, as if all tongues were refusing to give an equivalent, refusing to let themselves be contaminated through the contagious hospitality of the word-for-word. Here, then, is an immediate response to the obsessiveness of this racism, to the compulsive terror that above all forbids contact.[14]

According to Derrida, apartheid has thus always been infested by its own logic. Following its own principle of segregation, it has remained alone, isolated, and untranslatable, because, according to Derrida, language, with the help of apartheid, protects itself against apartheid. The video artwork *Felix in Exile* is about precisely this: the paradoxical idea of an isolation isolating itself. *Felix* is on the one hand a word that, taken as a common noun, can be translated as "happy." At the same time, *Felix* is a proper name and as such untranslatable, as Derrida emphasizes. *Felix* bears precisely this isolation or "exile" as an anagrammatic untranslatable remainder, a seclusion collapsed into itself, and ultimately also a forgetting that withdraws from memory.

Not far off is another aesthetic means that also functions as a procedure to expose apartheid to itself, namely the use of the self-portrait. Like the proper name, the self-portrait brings the play of a semiotic operation to the fore as a self-referential loop that cannot be escaped. The drawing appears to be a duplicate of the one drawn, or vice versa. This encapsulation of the self within the self as in the strictest isolation occurs also on the diegetic level of the film, when it finds a dramatic expression in the mirror scene. As an optical device, the mirror exposes

Figure 7.5 Felix and his mirror image; still from *Felix in Exile*, directed by William Kentridge. © William Kentridge 1994. All rights reserved.

Figure 7.6 Felix together with Nandi as his mirror image; still from: *Felix in Exile*, directed by William Kentridge. © William Kentridge 1994. All rights reserved.

Felix to himself by means of reflection. What the mirror reflects is Felix's mirror image in the sense of a repetition of the same (see Figure 7.5). This image is indeed identical with the self, but not quite. The uncanny of the mirror scene resides in the fact that the confrontation of the self with himself is not just pure repetition but rather the repetition of the same with a difference. Felix gazes in the mirror and faces the experience of loneliness that becomes visible as the impossible presence of Nandi (see Figure 7.6). The mirror scene is about the failure of the act of looking. At the same time, however, it brings to the fore the possibilities emerging from not looking, insofar as the intimate encounter of the self with the self in the mirror turns out to be the most forceful detachment of the self from the self. And yet, at the same time, it allows for an encounter with the Other.

Moon views

It is striking that the processes of observation in *Felix in Exile* are essentially an effect of optical instruments, which include the mirror and the devices for geodetic and celestial observation. When in the mirror scene Felix and Nandi look at each other as if through a window, there grows a remarkable telescope between their eyes, its two lenses located at both sides of the mirror so that the subject and the object of vision are indiscernible (see Figure 7.7). In other scenes, when Nandi surveys the land, her theodolite functions like a *laterna magica*, disclosing impossible images of past and future acts of violence to her. Actually, Nandi is a "seeress." Like a clairvoyant, she sees falling stars drawing lines that

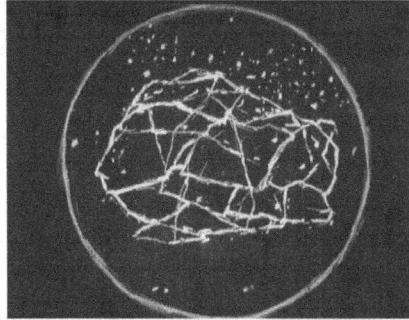

Figure 7.7 Felix and Nandi connected by a telescope; still from *Felix in Exile*, directed by William Kentridge. © William Kentridge 1994. All rights reserved.

Figure 7.8 Constellation "suitcase"; still from *Felix in Exile*, directed by William Kentridge. © William Kentridge 1994. All rights reserved.

do not disappear instantaneously into the night sky, but in blazing their trails delineate something that cannot be seen under normal circumstances. For example, they form a water tap on the moon, or they connect star points until the peculiar constellation of the constellation "suitcase" is created (see Figure 7.8).

Occasionally, sketches are made which, from the point of view of media history, remind us of that primal scene of modern astronomical painting that goes back to December 1609, when Galileo Galilei in Padua focused his telescope on the moon to perform the first ocular moon view in the history of humanity.[15] Galileo attempted to keep hold of the ephemeral sight of the moon by translating his look into a movement of the hand. The object of knowledge was not ascertained either by looking or touching, but rather by means of a "motoric intelligence" which is referred to as *disegno* in renaissance art theory, and which seeks the process of perception in a sensory feedback of eye and hand.[16]

With this aesthetic strategy of *disegno*, Galileo succeeded in creating images that were both scientifically and artistically felicitous. A new type of image was born; Horst Bredekamp calls it a "technical image," because the observer no longer encounters an object "naked" but rather "looks through" the eyepiece of the telescope.[17] With this technical prosthesis of the eye, the telescope performs perhaps the first "apartheid of the senses," whose physical detachment was then, however, bridged instantaneously in the motorics of the hand. Hand and eye enter into a voluntarily liaison, a connection in which the process of recognition materializes as a graphic line, in which the object of knowledge is equally "recognized" and "sensed." The graphic process of *Felix in Exile* is bound to precisely this visual-tactile form of thinking, which the untranslatable law of apartheid reproduces in the drama of the line. It captures the visible beyond "naked" visibility, the distant continent even beyond the horizon. It is no mere coincidence that astronomical instruments serve Kentridge as media of visualization.

The dilemma of the telescope

The telescope view sets a process in motion that can be understood as the primal scene of Western self-reflection. While the satellite orbiting the earth becomes a mirror of the earth, in this reciprocal gaze the earth loses its cosmic singularity and recognizes itself as a "star among stars."

A new, literally "cosmo-political" age enters. The telescope provides in equal measure the basic conditions for the sea journey and the discovery of the new world, as it attempts to "enlighten" the values and norms of the West in the darkest times of colonization. The light of stars makes the "world as a whole" into an object of experience, and in it, the question of the "fellow folk" becomes a question of the "fellow human." Not coincidentally, Kant takes up astronomical formulas of planetary orbits for his political theory of cosmopolitan law, and he bases the laws of friendship in mankind's "common ownership of the earth's surface; for since the earth is a globe, [it] cannot scatter [mankind] infinitely."[18] Even today, the charter of the UNO refers to this unconditional law, and even Felix's exile is committed to a "cosmopolitical" world order and the laws of friendship in this Kantian sense.

The telescope can be considered a critical device in yet another respect. In his study of early modern scientific culture, Hans Blumenberg speaks about the "dilemma of the telescope" as an instrument that operates from two ends. On the one hand, the telescope indeed allows augmentation of the range of the human gaze due to its magnifying effect. In Galileo's hands and with the Copernican theory in mind, it adduces visual evidence for the heliocentric world model. In so doing, according to Blumenberg, the telescope helps to abandon the ancient, Aristotelian thesis that the knowable would be limited to the visible. On the other hand, the epistemic shift caused by the telescope is based precisely on that rhetoric of an "eidetic reason" against which it admonishes. The new astronomy attaches itself to the visible as the ultimate instance of truth, as Blumenberg argues, and thus affirms precisely the Aristotelian tradition that it seeks to refute. After all, the subject of the telescopic gaze knows that more efficient telescopes will enhance the optical range further and allow for more precise observation.

The telescopic gaze is a critical gaze insofar as the subject of vision is aware of this technical condition of looking. It cannot avoid suspecting any new vision in its turn of being limited, preliminary, and thus able to be surpassed.[19] In sum, the dilemma of the telescope resides in the fact that it determines modern astronomical knowledge as a visual paradox that relies on overcoming the limitations of visibility as much as on recognizing them.

Let us take a closer look at Galileo's telescope. Galileo recognized that the moon has no perfect spherical shape but that its surface is serrated by calderas and mountain peaks, just like earth's! By optical analogy, he concluded that—just like the full moon—also the *full earth* glows (when it is full from the point of view of an extraterrestrial observer).[20] And finally, the discovery of Jupiter's moons provides incontrovertible evidence for the Copernican world system: when Galileo in *The Sidereal Messenger* reports the detection "of new celestial bodies," he means first of all the earth itself. Hans Blumenberg gets to the point, astronoetically speaking: Galileo "orients the telescope to the moon, and he sees the earth as a star in the cosmos."[21] Galileo's telescope looks—as with Kentridge— in two directions.

The moon and the starry sky come to function as a mirror in which the viewing subject encounters itself in the very moment of looking at the distance. Both Galileo and Kentridge, each in their specific historical frame, combine optical instruments with drawing technologies to actualize that global gaze that is by definition impossible because it is based on the impossibility of observing earth from a terrestrial point of view. In order to view earth as what it actually is—a globe of which the surface is serrated by calderas and mountain peaks, a globe that glows in the distance just like other celestial bodies—the gaze must overcome the horizon of vision while at the same time remaining aware of the conditions of the global gaze as a critical undertaking.

If already Galileo's telescope is marked by a dilemma, as Blumenberg argues, this double structure captures the world media in our contemporary age of accelerated globalization. Artificial satellites, along with other media of telecommunication, prompt us daily to rethink our place in the universe and to ask who we are as planetary subjects. And they also touch on the question of rethinking South Africa. When we speak today about South Africa, that is, after the system of apartheid has been abolished and even after South Africa has become the host of the FIFA World Cup 2010, we still have to renegotiate the relation between north and south. With the spherical shape of earth in mind, we must reconsider the concept of the globe and ask what world, planet, and globe mean in our age.

For our age, Gayatri Spivak demands a conceptual shift from "globe" to "planet," because other than the globe, the planet stands "in the sign of alterity": "If we imagine ourselves as planetary subjects rather than global agents [...], alterity remains underived from us [...], it contains us as much as it flings us away."[22] In *Felix in Exile*, Spivak's planetary imperative takes the form of a graphic line. The laws of hospitality are rewritten, in the course of this line, from a cosmopolitan ethics to a planetary aesthetics. This line, which engulfs the world, transforms "apartheid" into a poetics of "relation."

It is not categorical, however, that world events such as the World Cup are planetary events, and worldwide media are not necessarily planetary media, as Spivak points out in her distinction between the global and the planetary. The technology of artificial satellites is marked by a visual dilemma that is similar to the one that qualified Blumenberg's telescope. On the one hand, the satellites orbiting earth produce an encompassing and united information space by overcoming the globe's natural spherical shape. The same technology, on the other hand, divides the inhabitants of the globe into those connected to the information system and those who, due to technical, political, economic, religious, or sexual circumstances, stay "apart" from it. In this sense, we can today continue to interpret Kentridge's film as an imperative to act against this form of segregation in our globalized world, in that "future for which apartheid is," to echo Derrida, "the name of something finally abolished."[23]

Handwork and onanism

In his planetary aesthetics, Kentridge manifests the drama of the trace in yet another dimension. As a peculiar form of contact with oneself, the hand of the drawer repeatedly appears. The hand implements itself, and it does so even when it is itself invisible, for example when it, in the exile's lap under the blanket, adumbrates a movement that Derrida has called the work of the "supplement."

For Kentridge, the drawing is always also an act of self-dramatization. Not only that Felix encounters himself as an alter ego of the artist; rather, the film is full of scenes of self-exploration. This takes place in the realm of the visual as self-exhibition (for example in the mirror scenes), but also in the sensual realm of the tactile, self-experience through self-contact, for example in the staging of the hand that draws and thereby draws itself and discloses the body in its intimate and vulnerable manifestation, namely naked. In general, a sexual gesture of self-touching is occasionally intimated in the film. While viewing *Felix in Exile*, one should not lose track of Felix's hands, least of all when they are not visible in the image. In this way, the special organization of hand and eye can be understood as a critical aesthetic process, which structures the concept of "being-in-world" in a special way.

Let us remember that in *Of Grammatology*, Derrida uses Rousseau's *Confessions* to speak of onanism as that "dangerous supplement" that, in the face of a deficiency, becomes the epitome of surrogate in a chain of supplements. In an ideal way, onanism as a self-touching presence embodies the figure of difference as deferral. The "imaginary seductions" of self-affection are indeed performed with respect to an absent Other, by feeling its (his/her) trace as the touch of an absence.[24] This onanism, as Derrida writes, "permits one to be himself affected by providing himself with presences," by embracing and caressing the self as much as the Other.[25] Kentridge's drawing hand is in this sense bound to the logic of onanism. With it, Kentridge proposes an aesthetic procedure that (like onanism) is dedicated to apartness, one which intimately binds the sexual aloneness of the exile to political apartheid. The planetary aesthetics of *Felix in Exile* objects to the apartness, or more precisely, it directs—like onanism—this apartness against itself, in a self-affective caress, which has always already been a caress of the Other.

Behind the horizon

The horizon as the apparent borderline separating earth from sky cannot be situated in a definite way. It withdraws as one draws closer to it. It is always to come. It is precisely this horizon to come that Glissant addresses when focusing on "the realized horizon of the worlds."[26] It is remarkable that Glissant refers to the horizon by specifying it not just as an optical frontier, but rather as "*how* all [...] places circle the planet," thus as a mode or a manner to overcome the border of vision. It is as if Glissant had Spivak's planetary imperative in mind when he imagines a future for the humanity to come in the age of cultural globalization: "humanity is updating all over again, in a deplorable manner [...], by 'projecting' against yet unimaginable places, to the interplanetary horizon."[27] From Glissant we learn that we must think the globe as a whole, as a *tout-monde*. From Kentridge we learn about the aesthetic artifices to perform a global gaze by combining imprint and trace into an idiosyncratic film style that reinvents the earth-planet beyond the many manifestations of segregation and apartheid. Kentridge's idiosyncratic inscription technique induces an impossible look that abrogates the horizon as a limitation of vision and reinstalls it as a contact line where the northern and southern hemisphere come together. His horizon functions simultaneously as borderline and as interface. It reminds us that there might be something beyond the immediate reach of vision, something that is not looked at. This "Other," to echo Derrida, is not simply invisible. Rather, it is concealed by the visual obstruction caused by the spherical shape of the globe. This concealment does not just lead to visual skepticism. Rather, it becomes a forceful tool for a planetary aesthetics that reformulates Spivak's concept of planetarity in the domain of vision as the imperative to look. Look at what? Look at our planet when it arises like a distant star. This earth-up cannot be looked at in a realistic manner, indeed. But it can be drawn and photographed and enacted in a film, as a possibility.

Kentridge's aesthetic procedure makes possible an impossible view of the earth, one which cancels out the horizon's limit to the field of vision and, as in the satellite perspective, places the northern and southern hemisphere in relation. In the course of the line of the horizon, a sphere is formed which touches itself infinitely by virtue of its finite surface and recognizes itself as the planet of the Other.

8

Intergalactic: Universal Translation. Immanuel Kant, the Spaceship *Enterprise*, and the Circulation of the Planets

Cosmopolitanism

What is the significance of the figure of cosmopolitanism? And what does it mean to us today, that is, in an age in which the core values of the European Enlightenment have been deeply internalized: liberty-equality-fraternity, tolerance, human rights, and the right to general hospitality? The concept of cosmopolitanism appears so classically modern that it must come as a surprise to find, in the closing credits of postmodernity, that a peculiar actuality still inheres in it. As though it were eternal. For the question still poses itself what the concept means as categorical imperative and what it can mean today, that is, under the conditions of globalization, the recoding of national borders, the worldwide exchange of data and capital, and a medial interconnectedness that spans the globe. The concept of cosmopolitanism achieves a new and unprecedented relevance in the face of such varying global phenomena as climate change, the Mars Mission of the European Space Agency, global migration, and all such planetary developments that touch on the core values of cosmopolitanism. Therefore, it can hardly be concealed that the figure of cosmopolitanism couples the realm of the political directly to that of the cosmos. As though it were the stars themselves which dictated to us cosmopolitanism and planetary hospitality as celestial laws. Precisely this coupling of the cosmic and the political is the subject of this chapter.

First of all, it must be acknowledged that both cosmopolitical and cosmographic thought-figures require a medial form in order to be conceivable and knowable. Identifying stars and understanding the celestial laws both require the work of medial *dispositifs*. Methodically, it thus seems necessary to add another figure to the figure of cosmopolitanism, a concept or a theory which concerns the medial mediatedness of cosmopolitanism, and which accordingly takes an interest in how the infinite expanses of the cosmos can be shifted into the terrestrial realm of cognition. I would like to designate "television" as such a concept. Like the figure of cosmopolitanism, that—as we have seen—is actually two figures, so too is the concept of television in itself dichotomous. It first indicates a distance and second the sense of sight. I will elaborate on this concept of television with reference to some media-historical examples. As a beginning, the reference to the methodical conduit of these deliberations will suffice, deliberations according to which both concepts enter into dialogue with one another, in the form that the one is deployed as the analytical instrument for inquiry into the other, such that they shed light on one another in their mutual reflection.

Television

The literal meaning of "television" first of all points to that apparatus with which we look into the distance, and, since what follows concerns a television series (*Star Trek*), this meaning of "TV" must be recognized. As a *dispositif*, television also encompasses those apparatuses which function as instruments with which humans attempt to expand the range of the terrestrial gaze and to glance up at the cosmic celestial bodies. To know the stars and to interpret the universal laws are both based on the work of medial *dispositifs*, which reveal the universe to be mediated and make comprehensible how the infinite vastness of the cosmos is moved into the terrestrial realm of understanding, in order to form—in accordance with Blumenberg—a veritable "astronoetics," a knowledge of the world that stems from the stars.[1]

As instruments of knowledge, *dispositifs* in the sense of Michel Foucault can fall into very different realms, forming a "thoroughly heterogeneous ensemble" that encompasses "discourses, institutions, architectural forms, regulatory decisions, laws, administrative measures, scientific statements, philosophical, moral and philanthropic propositions."[2] The oldest known astronoetic *dispositifs* are the towers of Babel, those mythic buildings to which the Old Testament attributes the scattering of languages. From an archaeological perspective, the towers of Babel are supposed to serve not only as religious portals to the divine, but also as astronomical observatories. Seen this way, the first "television" was a work of architecture. And, not coincidentally, the political fate of the state was brought into direct connection with the cosmic course of celestial bodies.

From the ancient Near Eastern, Babylonian-Hellenistic, and biblical astronomers into antiquity and the Middle Ages, televisual *dispositifs* take the most varying forms: astronomical and philosophical theories, architectures of observation, procedures of celestial cartography, techniques of measurement and computation, and apparatuses like the astrolabe, armillary sphere, and celestial globe. A turning point in the history of television takes place in modernity. With the same force that the printing press impelled the circulation of knowledge, Galileo Galilei revolutionized the observation of the sky. Through his work with the Lipperhey telescope, he founded optical astronomy and secured an empirical basis for the Copernican worldview. His televisual *dispositif* is literally a seeing-machine that serves the earthly eye as a prosthesis, as an "extension" of the faculty of vision in the sense of Marshall McLuhan. Moreover, with the laws of gravitation Isaac Newton delivered the physical foundation for the heliocentric worldview. Together, the printing press, telescope, and gravitational theories provoked a revolution of the senses that fundamentally altered the understanding of cosmos and world.

In the age of industrialization, photography and spectroscopy offer the ability to record and break down light, thereby opening up new procedures of visualization, which have been improving since the 1980s through digital imaging processes and which culminate in the Very Large Telescope. More recently, there are instruments that are no longer bound to a terrestrial standpoint, since they can be shot into space with probes and rockets, where they bring us closer to the planets not only optically (Hubble Space Telescope) but also haptically (the Mars missions *Spirit* and *Aurora*). Space travel emphatically provokes further thinking and critical reflection on cosmopolitical models as utopias of a planetary humanity.

This brief media-historical overview of the apparatuses of television demonstrates that whenever man turns his gaze to the sky, he enters into a discursive order marked by a religious, philosophical, aesthetic, or natural-historical character, although these realms are never completely mutually exclusive. Images of the world are derived from the gaze in the sky, and these images—inevitably ideological and political—form the basis for systems of norms and values, such as the European Enlightenment with its cosmopolitical imperative.

I would like to dedicate special attention to these "*dispositifs* of television": first, to a philosophical proposition that the concept of cosmopolitanism literally refers back to a theory of heaven, namely Kant's political writings, those "originary writings" of occidental modernity on which the law of nations was founded when the League of Nations and the United Nations were established; and second, to the television, that optical device that brings the most removed into tangible proximity and that does not stop even at the cosmic distance of the universe. The most imposing *opus magnum* that since the 1960s has lastingly informed our perspective on the universe and the possible future of the planet is the television series *Star Trek*. The series offers rich intellectual provocation not only for spaceship engineers and astrophysicists but also and not least for a Cultural Studies that is interested in the processes of globalization and the fascination of the planetary.

The United Federation of Planets

From 2001 to 2005, Rick Berman and Brannon Braga produced the fifth *Star Trek* generation. It was conceived as a prequel of the narrative universe that had unfolded until then. Although produced later, it narrates earlier parts of the sci-fi history, namely the backstory of Kirk, Picard, and Janeway. The heroes of the fifth generation are Captain Jonathan Archer, chief engineer Commander Charles Tucker (Trip), communications officer Hoshi Sato, and the Vulcan science officer T'Pol.

The series deals with the first steps of humanity in interstellar encounters. It takes place in the twenty-second century, when a truly cosmic time descends on the earth. In this era, inner-planetary conflicts are finally resolved: threats of atomic and ecological catastrophes are averted, while war, poverty, and illness have been overcome. Slowly, hostile people and nations come together to form leagues of nations: the European Alliance, the African Confederation, the United States of America, and so on. Together, these form a world government: the so-called United Earth Government. Peoples and nations of all continents live henceforth in peace with one another; the conflictual adversary is from now on the "alien," the "Other" from another solar system.

Since earth year 2161, the earth, in the legal form of the United Earth, plays a leading role in the foundation of an interstellar federation of planets. The fifth generation of *Star Trek* deals with this peace process. At the very end of the series in the fourth and final season, the historical goal of an intergalactic peace is achieved, as a kind of teleological television (also known as a "happy end"). In Episode 96, entitled "Demons," Captain Archer is finally at the goal. Thanks to his heroic deeds, on January 19, 2155, for the first time in the history of the universe, representatives from eighteen worlds have gathered at a round table in order to lay the cornerstone for an interplanetary federation. The minister of the United Earth Government opens the conference with the following speech:

> Having endured a catastrophic world war, earth's governments came to this city for the purpose of creating a just and lasting peace among nations. Today, we have assembled here, again, representatives of numerous worlds to forge an unprecedented alliance. With this coalition of planets, we seek to strengthen our bonds of friendship, render permanent the peace that now exists among us.[3]

Long before *Star Trek*, a kind of screenplay for a "cosmic peace" had already been written. It conjured up a peace that was supposed to encompass all peoples and to endure for all times. This is the short but infamous text, *Perpetual Peace* (*Zum ewigen Frieden*), which in 1795 in his old age Immanuel Kant deduced from his critiques for a theory of justice and a theory of the state.[4] In the Europe of the Enlightenment, Kant's theory of cosmopolitanism is viewed as a political-philosophical innovation. For Kant is the first who places the enlightened citizen not only in relation to the domestic state but also on the scale of a "global citizen." Political action and political domination require, from a moral standpoint, not only national but also international protection. Kant not only distinguishes *ius civitatis* (civil law) from *ius gentium* (international law of nations in their relation to one another); above and beyond this, he defines a third and superior legal form: the *ius cosmopoliticum*, the cosmopolitan law. The conception of a "human right," which is held to secure the freedom and equality of all humans, is also based on this. Kant reformulates, based on a global political order that must be founded on institutions of justice, the idea of a European-Christian blueprint for peace, which up until this point was principally religious-based.[5]

For the fate of the planet and of mankind, Kant sees the compelling necessity of a union of states that encompasses all people of the earth and that will unite them in one idea, namely the "*idea of federalism* [that] should eventually include all nations and thus lead to perpetual peace."[6] The then actual behavior of European states finds itself a target of critique. For, as these states considered the recently discovered lands as if they were "belonging to no one,"[7] they colonized the earth and increased the inequality with respect to the foreigner.

Even today, Kant reveals himself in *Perpetual Peace* not only as a thinker of globalization *avant la lettre* but also as a pioneer in the critique of colonialism. It happens more than once that he grasps his philosophy of cosmopolitanism in a decidedly cosmological terminology. For example, Kant formulates the law of general hospitality as "the right of an alien not to be treated as an enemy upon his arrival in another's country."[8] Kant establishes this right as one to which all human beings have a claim "by virtue of their common ownership of the earth's surface; for since the earth is a globe, they cannot scatter themselves infinitely, but must, finally, tolerate living in close proximity."[9] For the colonization of the earth, this results in a general revision of the situation of humanity, because no political place on the globe is still independent of the political events of any other place.

Kant's "cosmopolitanism" is literally a cosmic concept. So too are the decidedly teleological expressions with which Kant describes the process "toward perpetual peace": "a universal cosmopolitan state [...] will at last come to be realized,"[10] "[f]inally," writes Kant again and again, thereby giving a reference to the time that is necessary until nations and citizens mature to this "cosmopolitan state." He compares the duration of this time with "the path of the sun and its entire host of satellites through the vast system of fixed stars."[11] The time taken to establish cosmopolitanism resembles, for Kant, the circulation of the planets whose "cycle appears to require so long a time to complete."[12]

In a closer reading of *Perpetual Peace*, a certain parallel rhetoric emerges, according to which Kant's concept of a "cosmic time" is conceived in teleological as well as televisual terms. Kant literally conjures up a *providence* which is intended for the course of the world "as the objective final end of the human species."[13] This "providence"—if you will, a literal "tele-vision"—will gradually bring forth the original grounds for the best world.

This astronomic mode of expression in Kant's late work is an ornamental as well as a cognitive metaphor. With it, Kant connects to the extensive natural scientific research with which he occupied himself in his youth and whose results he published in 1755 in an anonymous text: *Universal History and Theory of Heaven*. In this text, Kant formulates a cosmogony according to which the cosmos and solar system are comprehended in a never-ending process of emergence and dissipation. Solely based on the Newtonian law of gravity and without reference to celestial observation, Kant accounts for the emergence of celestial bodies from a rotating nebula of gas, which he conceives as distant galaxies, and with which he essentially anticipates the Laplacian theory.[14]

Kant's theory of heaven provides an explanation of the whole world-edifice (*Weltgebäude*) and the world-constitution (*Weltverfassung*), the development of the earth as well as the emergence of planetary life and humans endowed with reason. When Kant then—forty years later—speaks in his political writings of "world-citizenship," of the structure of the world and its divine endowment with meaning, of a theory of justice and the state, of perpetual peace, of the formation of virtue and the laws of hospitality, his concept of "cosmopolitanism" can be understood literally in connection with his astronomical theory of the world and the universe.

Kant was, if you will, "visionary" as an astrophysicist as well as a political philosopher. His instrument of television was, however, not an optical device. Unlike Galileo, Kant never looked at the stars through a telescope. And yet, so runs my thesis, it is worth taking a look at this enigmatic concept of television in the sense of a philosophical theory of heaven. To further sharpen this concept, we now look again at the other television of cosmopolitanism that *Star Trek: Enterprise* has in store.

The universal translator

The above-mentioned film sequence in Season 4, Episode 20 ("Demons") of *Star Trek: Enterprise* has as its subject a peculiar conference held on January 19, 2155 on earth in San Francisco. The conference participants—humans, Vulcans, Andorians, Denobulans, Tellarites, and other species—sit side by side in a large circle. Each has a peculiar appearance: a strange skin color, pointed ears, bulges in their face, or full-body armor. And each has his own value system, system of norms, and his own language. This linguistic difference is explicitly addressed, as it is otherwise rather seldom done in *Star Trek*; cultural otherness receives a treatment this way, and it presents that core problem that a successful political diplomacy must overcome. In keeping with the classical rhetoric of *Star Trek*, it is a highly developed technology that makes intergalactic conversation possible: small mobile phone-like devices that the conference participants carry in their shirt pockets (see Figure 8.1).

These devices function in a way that recalls the media technology of simultaneous translation, whereby a speech in a language is routed through microphone, transmitter, circuitry, and headphones to a physical and intelligent interpreter, who, with a minor delay, renders that speech for an addressee through another system of microphone, transmitter, circuitry, and headphones into another language.[15] Or when multiple interpreters are involved, this can happen in an unlimited number of parallel systems in a corresponding number of languages. The notorious noise in the glass booths of the European Parliament underscores how complex and risky interpreting is as a technical procedure.

If the technology of translation appears to be a miracle of communication, how much more miraculous is the interstellar conference of the United Federation of Planets. The earth minister delivers a speech about cosmic peace,

Figure 8.1 Tellarites at the conference of the interstellar Federation of Planets; still from *Star Trek: Enterprise* (created by Rick Berman and Brannon Braga), Season 4, Episode 096: "Demons," directed by LeVar Burton, written by Manny Coto. © Paramount Pictures 2005. All rights reserved.

and, as though by a miracle, he is understood by his audience irrespective of their cultural and linguistic identity. The (white, male) minister always speaks only in his own language, an earth language, that is, American English, or in the case of the dubbed film version: German or any other language that can be programmed into the digital storage device. The language of the host functions as a pure language of diplomacy, as a universal language in which universal peace is to be brought to its intended destination in the Kantian sense.

The staging of the inception of the intergalactic formation recalls the program of another mission, namely the biblical one recounted in Luke's story of Pentecost. The apostles are praying in Jerusalem before a polyglot people, and each speaks in his own language:

> How can each of us hear in our own language? Parthians and Medes and Elamites, as well as dwellers of Mesopotamia, Judea, and Cappadocia, Pontus and Asia, Phrygia and Pamphylia, Egypt and the parts of Libya belonging to Cyrene, and visitors from Rome, both Jews and proselytes, Cretans and Arabs: in our own languages we are hearing them speaking.[16]

Here it stands written that through a miracle, a miracle of translation, each will hear the other speaking in his own language on the Pentecost. As in the story of Pentecost, the aliens in *Star Trek: Enterprise* hear the words of the minister in their languages: Tellarites and Andorians, Denobulans and Vulcans, and all those who sit at the round table that is supposed to bring intergalactic peace. Source language and target language, speech and understanding are folded into one another in a strange simultaneity, the space between which is bridged by the miraculous technology of the universal translator.[17]

The process of translation itself remains invisible; what was said reaches— unmediated, lossless, and direct—the ear of the other through a Messianic determination, a determination that is cosmic in the sense that it plays at that point in the history of the universe where—with Kant—the world as a whole has been brought to its cosmopolitan destination. The television-cosmos appears for a moment as "televisual" in the sense of Kant's "cosmic providence," as the fulfillment of fate, after which a mature humanity develops its "original abilities" and scales the last step where the earth—"finally"—reaches a paradisiacal final condition. This is literally the moment when the orbit of the planets closes.

While Kant formulates the miracle of this cosmic final goal in the realm of a theoretical teleology, in the case of the television it is based in a technical process. The universal translator's mode of operation draws on a filmic procedure that, like the Pentecostal miracle, makes the abyss between languages invisible: synchronization. Through this procedure, the viewer hears Andorians and Tellarites, Denobulans and Klingons speaking in their language and understands them without loss and without the resistances of foreignness; he hears them in their own monolingualism, one which excludes the monolingualism of the Other.[18]

While all communicative gaps are smoothed over in the process of universal translation, visual inconsistencies become prominent in the televised film. At one point, the television image sets its sights on its own technical *dispositif*: the camera. For one shot, the *narrating* camera takes the point of view of a *narrated* video camera that is worn on one of the characters' foreheads (see Figure 8.2). In the next shot, the video image of this narrated camera itself takes the place of the television image (see Figure 8.3).

However, this video setting does not take over the narrative position without reflection, but the film in the film becomes visible: the frame of the body camera appears on the edges of the screen, the image quality is poorer, and the sound duller. The television screen becomes a literal *mise en abyme*: the viewer looks into it as though into an abyss that opens up through the view of the diegetic viewer. The television image arranges the positions of the gaze according to a visual logic that makes the viewer, as an object of seeing, into a subject. Through this staging of the camera gaze, the fixed positions of subject and object of

Figure 8.2 Cut: Conference observers with cameras at the conference of the interstellar Federation of Planets; still from *Star Trek: Enterprise* (created by Rick Berman and Brannon Braga), Season 4, Episode 096: "Demons," directed by LeVar Burton, written by Manny Coto. © Paramount Pictures 2005. All rights reserved.

Figure 8.3 Counter-cut: the view of the conference participants through the narrated video camera; still from *Star Trek: Enterprise* (created by Rick Berman and Brannon Braga), Season 4, Episode 096: "Demons," directed by LeVar Burton, written by Manny Coto. © Paramount Pictures 2005. All rights reserved.

observation are destabilized. For one shot, the voyeuristic appearance of the conference attendees becomes the focus of the gaze. But characteristically, their position also dissolves in the eye of the camera. In this eye, the visibility of the gaze is itself withdrawn. The act of seeing is, on the one hand, dismantled in its voyeuristic economy (that is always also a colonizing one).[19] On the other hand, in the dismantling itself a direct and unhindered view of the Other is granted, literally of the "alien" that takes part in the cosmic becoming, insofar as he televisually "alienates," that is to say, divests himself of his in/visible otherness.

Babylonian conference

In the fifth generation of *Star Trek*, the universal translator is once again a source of tension in the intergalactic exchange. It does so in a prominent way in Episode 74, "The Council." This episode takes place a year before the large peace conference, at a time in which the war between the species still continues. At one point, there is a development in which Captain Archer gets the opportunity to establish contact with the aliens known as the Xindi. He takes a spaceship to an ancient council chamber on the planet of the Xindi (see Figure 8.4), in order to

Figure 8.4 Captain Archer and his companion on a landing approach to the Xindi Council Chamber; still from *Star Trek: Enterprise* (created by Rick Berman and Brannon Braga), Season 3, Episode 074: "The Council," directed by David Livingston, written by Manny Coto. © Paramount Pictures 2004. All rights reserved.

convince the antagonistic alliance of humanity's receptivity to peace, and in this way to prevent a final destructive blow to the earth. Accompanying him is a mediator and Hoshi Sato, communication officer of the starship *Enterprise* and inventor of the universal translator.[20]

The staging of the universal translator is here quite different from the minister's speech on peace. If the one was held in a single, uniform language that leads the species of the universe to world peace, in the council chamber the rifts between the different species break open. Arboreals and Reptiles, two of the five existing Xindi species, make threats of war and annihilation in rasping voices. The monstrous and the uncanny aspects of foreignness become visible when, during the conference, a representative of a third Xindi species, an Insectoid, suddenly gets on his front antennae and stands up threateningly. He does not speak Archer's language—his voice chirps and buzzes (see Figure 8.5). In the next shot, the sonar noises of the Aquatics, a fourth Xindi species that lives underwater, sound equally strange.

This time, the universal translator does not normalize the foreign. Not sophisticated enough, it organizes the process of translation into a phase of speaking in a source language and a phase of understanding in a target language. The actual act of translation lies in between, namely at the point when the device registers what was said. Hoshi Sato presses the keys of her translation machine,

Figure 8.5 Captain Archer in conversation with an Insectoid, Communications Officer Sato in the background; still from *Star Trek: Enterprise* (created by Rick Berman and Brannon Braga), Season 3, Episode 074: "The Council," directed by David Livingston, written by Manny Coto. © Paramount Pictures 2004. All rights reserved.

and in the display there appears a transcript that transfers the meaning of the speech from the one language into the other. In the space *between* source and target language, the constitutive condition of translation becomes visible: the disparity of languages. Cinematically, the medial procedure of translation is staged not by using the technique of dubbing to erase the foreignness of languages but rather by using another technique to undertake the translation and thereby to reveal it as a transcription in a double sense, translating from one language to another as well as from speech to script: subtitles.

It is no coincidence that the motif of the council chamber takes up, in an image of that 4,000-year-old fort, a cultural-historical topos that could hardly be more prominently depicted. Framed in the window of the spaceship, a brown-tinted image appears, with cotton clouds, a dramatic depiction of the horizon as a seam between earth and sky: in between them, as a vital link, the tower looms imposingly (see Figure 8.4 above).

For a moment, Pieter Breughel's famous image of *The Tower of Babel* flashes up, and with it the myth of the loss of universal communication.[21] Babel, so sacred scripture indicates, inflicts a wound that is only healed in the Pentecost miracle of the unifying spirit of the church. From time immemorial, the tower has stood as the epitome of misunderstanding and disharmony between languages and peoples, who once, as it is written in Genesis, had as "the whole earth one language and the same words," until the sons of Sem "migrated from the east" and settled "in the land of Shinar," built themselves a "city" and a "tower with its top in the heavens," and promised to "make a name for ourselves" in order to avoid being "scattered abroad upon the face of the whole earth." Then, however, it is written, Yahweh descended to view the city and tower, and he confused their languages "so that they will not understand one another's speech," and he "scattered them abroad from there over the face of all the earth." "Therefore, it was called Babel, because there the LORD confused the language of all the earth; and from there the LORD scattered them abroad over the face of all the earth."[22] In Genesis, the scattering of languages marks the end of the paradisiac original condition of the world as a whole world, as a whole earth that has one language and one common vocabulary. With the confusion of languages comes the destruction of cosmic peace, in which humanity had been unified in God's name.

Speaking another language emerges as a condition of foreignness in which the Other splits into the double figure of the "Hostis": in Latin, *hostis* means both "guest" and "enemy." The hostility of the Other bases itself on its otherness: its appearance, manners, and habits, its norms and values, and ultimately its language, which identifies the Other as a final stranger. The inherent contradiction in the concept of cosmopolitanism becomes apparent in the figure of the Other. Fatally, the legitimation of colonization, against which cosmopolitanism asserts itself, is based on otherness, for whenever the values of the European Enlightenment—world peace, hospitality, and cosmopolitanism— are seen as universal, they must be asserted on other continents no less than in foreign galaxies. Thus, the law of cosmopolitanism necessarily contravenes its own imperative. Cosmopolitanism unifies humanity in a universalistic whole, but at the same time problematizes the variety of languages and cultures.

The problem of otherness is that it can only come to light in those untranslatable and resistant moments that defy direct visualization. It is no coincidence that the universal translator functions according to the principle of a medium "without inter-space," that is, much more a non-medium that bridges the source and target language in a fully accessible universal language, thereby founding the very utopian and a-topian space in which the species of the universe approach a cosmopolitical universal peace.

From a Cultural Studies perspective, a problem looms over the claim of a universal translation, for the essential difference and uniqueness of languages and cultures threaten, in view of such a universalistic center of truth, to fade away. Alterity requires this very intermediary space where what constitutes translation comes to light: the difference and the confusing Babylonian diversity of languages. The Tower of Babel makes clear, in a nearly ideal way, the significance of the medial *dispositif* for the cosmos as a world-political construction. Babel stands on the one hand emblematically for linguistic and cultural diversity, but at the same time the towers have served as astronomical observatories; they were—as I have already mentioned—the first televisual apparatuses. It is no coincidence that Arno Borst characterizes ancient Babylon as a "well-ordered cosmic state," believed to be dedicated to the "divinity of the cosmos": "one attempted to approach the god Marduk through these temple towers," which, as astronomical observatories, should "perhaps produce the connection between heaven and earth or even [be] something like a ladder reaching to Heaven."[23] Already in the original biblical text, polyglotism and multiculturalism turn out to be astronoetic concepts. The language of the planets is seen—in the Pentecostal story and in Genesis just as in the starship *Enterprise*—in a holy universal language; the "foreign language" and in general the "task of translation" function as the suspenseful obstacles on the path to eternal peace.

Planetary *dispositifs*

In Kant's writings, there are numerous references to the otherness of the Other: to the Turks as well as to the racial distinctions of Africans and of the inhabitants of other continents. Concerning the object of the current consideration, the reciprocal relation between television and cosmopolitanism, one of Kant's reflections is particularly remarkable, namely his consideration of an otherness of "the third kind." In his astronomical writing on the *Theory of the Heavens*, there is a peculiar addendum: the "third part." It bears the title "Appendix: Comparison between the Inhabitants of the Stars," and in many regards, it comes across as a comment on the wondrous sci-fi fairy tales of the starship *Enterprise*:

> Should the immortal soul remain forever attached to this point in space, to our Earth for the whole infinity of its future duration [...]? Who knows whether it is not intended to get to know at close quarters those distant spheres of the solar system [...]? Perhaps some further spheres of the planetary system will form around them in order to prepare new places for us to reside in other heavens, after the completed passage of time prescribed for our stay here. Who knows, perhaps the satellites orbiting around Jupiter will light our way in the future?[24]

It is remarkable that Kant had always already accounted for the Other in his theory of cosmopolitanism. And even the Other from the other planet plays a role in his system of a universal cosmic structure. However, it is equally remarkable that Kant never recognized the mediation of the universe: neither the technologies of the construction of otherness nor the constructedness of the standpoint from which universal hospitality can be preserved. Kant's cosmos is eternally unmediated. This explains the mistrust that Kant reserves for images as *dispositifs* of television: "imaginary pictures" appear to him as "uncertain," and while they might serve as entertainment, they cannot serve as a *dispositif* of an astronoetics.

Repeatedly, *Star Trek* has autoreflexively taken its televisual logic into consideration: through film-in-a-film sequences, through clever mirror constructions, through the figure of the universal translator who provides the translation in the film as well as the synchronization settings in the DVD menu. Kant's concept of cosmopolitanism remains skeptical of the televisual *dispositif* as a medium's autoreflexive praxis. His writings repeatedly speak of images with a mistrust that borders on iconoclasm. It is no coincidence that Kant the astronomer managed to get by without a telescope or any optical media. If we interpret these "uncertain imaginary images" literally as images in the sense of a televisual *dispositif*, then the concept of "cosmopolitanism" can be thought anew. The techniques of medial construction would come into focus together with the political strategies of the mediation of a standpoint from which universality could be claimed as a center of truth, from which also the question of hospitality could be decided.

If hospitality is a universal law, as Kant writes in the third definitive article on perpetual peace, then this poses an unbridgeable difficulty: if each person on account of the roundness of the earth has the same right of residence, how should we ever decide to whom the right and to whom the duty of hospitality is assigned? With what right will anyone ever be able to pose the first question, the question of the otherness of the Other? Derrida calls the law of absolute hospitality a "perversion and pervertability of the law," insofar as it must necessarily contravene its own pretension of universality and unavoidably come across to the Other as an act of violence.[25] For the identity of the guest must be clarified before hospitality (or asylum) can be granted. The question of the proper name is always the "first" question on which the conditions for cultural and linguistic "identity" base themselves and in turn the conditions for constitutional and international law, on which the laws of hospitality depend. Through this necessary and indispensable "first question," hospitality, as the universal law that is constitutive for eternal peace, becomes impossible. Absolute hospitality both requires this first question and forbids it. For absolute hospitality requires, as Derrida specifies,

> [...] that I open up my home and that I give not only to the foreigner [...], but to the absolute, unknown, anonymous other, and that I *give place* to them, that I let them come, [...] without asking of them either reciprocity (entering into a pact) or even their names.[26]

The law of hospitality declares the proper name to be untranslatable, because every question in one language would ineluctably present an act of violence toward the idiom of the foreign one.[27] As soon as the proper name of the guest comes into play, the chance of a "true," absolute" or "universal" hospitality is already lost, and with it everything cosmic and the whole aim of an eternal peace, toward which the path of the planets in the solar system is directed.

Hospitality in *Star Trek*'s television is first and foremost an effect of aesthetic strategies produced by camera work. The inextricable structure of hospitality becomes visible precisely in the abyss (or in the *mise en abyme*) where the gaze itself becomes an object of the gaze. Where the television image destabilizes the fixed positions of seeing subject and seen objects, it also loosens the initial moment of first contact from its fixed frame. Not only is the seeing subject dislodged from his originary and privileged position; rather, the very claim of an allegedly originary Other, the very emblem of otherness, becomes problematic.

In this respect, it must be recognized that cosmopolitanism and television form a conceptual pair, in whose entwinement the problematic of alterity only first becomes visible. In the long term—that is, in the time that it takes for a planetary orbit to be completed—the development of better devices alone will not suffice to improve the view of the stars. What is much more crucial, following the cosmopolitical imperative, is to consider the gaze itself as a planetary *dispositif*.

9

Heaven on Earth: Paul, a Cosmopolitan?[1]

For "everyone who calls on the name of the Lord will be saved".

Romans 10.13

[...] in every place [...] both theirs and ours

1 Corinthians 1.2

Why Paul?

"Why St. Paul?" asks Alain Badiou. "Why solicit this 'apostle'?"[2] Badiou is interested in the foundational power of a beginning that Paul initiates, not with regard to the founding history of the Church as an institution, but rather as the founding moment of a universal figure which tolerates no exception, at no time and in no place. For Badiou, Paul is our "contemporary," not only because he touches on the political question of how the contemporary state (the parliamentary democracy), as asylum and host, makes judgements according to the principle of difference (French vs. non-French), but rather because with Paul we can designate a point that stands outside the order of state and law. Badiou understands the Pauline "gospel" (εὐαγγέλιον) as a radical universality: as a pure affirmation that abolishes differences in a way that cannot be dialectically recuperated. It is a pure "yes": an "unqualified affirmation of life" that enters beyond the "power of death" (not as its "negation" but rather as "extraction"), and it founds the "equality within humanity itself."[3]

Just as Badiou, who freely confesses that he is not an ecclesiastic, does not keep Paul in his "original" epistemic framework, in this chapter Badiou's reading of Paul will be deliberated in a setting that at first glance does not seem suited for cultural analysis, which is both related to philosophy and foreign to it, and which in any case is no closer to it than to religious studies. This chapter inquires into what Badiou's concept of universalism can mean for cultural analysis and how we can abide his polemical attack on so-called "cultural and historical relativism." Badiou insistently warns against the "progressive reduction of the question of truth [. . .] to the linguistic form of judgement":[4]

> All access to the universal, which neither tolerates assignation to the particular, nor maintains any direct relation with the status—whether it be that of dominator or victim-of the *sites* from which its proposition emerges, collapses when confronted with this intersection between culturalist ideology and the "victimist" [*victimaire*] conception of man.[5]

To those critical theories which, in varying contexts (that of language, nation, race, gender, or religion), are based on a critique of dominance and hegemony and which pursue emancipatory interests of the diverse forms (subset, supplementarity, secondarity, and so on), Badiou imputes a deficiency that consists in their lack of a sense for the very remainder that is elevated above the singular here and now of the Pauline truth. Badiou is provocative. At this point, however, he leaves open exactly which works he is against; his provocation remains anonymous. In the reception of Badiou, this openness is not infrequently regarded as a plea against a philosophy of difference—prematurely, in my opinion.[6] The figure of *différance* as difference and deferral has inspired whole schools to undertake a philosophical and Derrida-educated critique of metaphysics. For cultural analysis, this offers a central analytical instrument for a critique of the processes of alterization in the sense of *différance* (Derrida) or *othering* (Spivak). Repeatedly, the rhetoric of universalism is placed under suspicion of claiming universal validity in a given syntax, but in truth is underlain by the normative conditions of a bourgeois value system of the European Enlightenment that can be traced back to Kant and Hegel. Universal statements thus factor in an implicit recognition and denial of difference.

More interesting than the question about who in particular Badiou's anonymous provocation is directed against seems the question of what exactly it calls forth (*pro-vocare*). What is its effect? And what uses can Badiou's polemic against cultural historicism and the "status of the sites" have for cultural analysis, whose main interest consists precisely in the dismantling of the Eurocentric rhetoric of place? Let us accept this provocation. Let us read Badiou's reading of Paul in regard to the question of how Badiou conceives of Paul as a founding figure, by which name he calls Paul (alias Saul), and what, for Badiou, the quotation marks mean that he uses when he speaks of Paul as an "apostle." What, therefore, happens to the concept of site or place when Badiou of Rabat speaks of Paul of Tarsus?

The event (the subsets)

For Badiou, Paul is a "poet-thinker of the event."[7] The incident or intervention that Badiou characterizes as the Christian event forms the Archimedean point from which he discloses the universal power of Paul's founding act. Basically, it concerns the following: Paul was born at the beginning of the common era, in Tarsus in Cilicia, in modern-day southeastern Turkey, and was educated in Jerusalem according to the Pharisaic principles. His mission consisted in ensuring that Mosaic Law was observed among the Jewish diaspora. When he, "zealous [...] for the traditions of [his] fathers" (Galatians 1.14), sometime between the years 25 and 30, went to Damascus to persecute Christians, the resurrected Christ suddenly appeared to Paul and commanded him to preach as an apostle the Gospel to the people. Badiou wants to see the event understood decidedly not in the sense of a cultural historical relativism. Instead, he demands a differentiation between "Christ" as a living historical figure and Messiah and "Jesus" as "'someone' devoid of predicative traits, entirely absorbed by his resurrection."[8] When Badiou makes reference to how Paul "reduces Christianity to a single statement: Jesus is resurrected,"[9] then for him the Christ event consists not in this historically datable, localizable, and "fabulous" moment of resurrection. Rather, Badiou is interested in distinguishing the event from the "fable" (the linguistic, readable form) as that which goes beyond history, which remains when the fable-like content disappears and when one disregards the question of the historical authenticity of the resurrection.[10] By separating the two parts of a name, Jesus and Christ, Badiou abstracts the event from every single particularity; the event reveals itself first and foremost as metaphysical, as "that invisible and indirectly accessible residue."[11]

Badiou's conception of the event is intimately interrelated with the concept of the subset. Badiou follows an established understanding when he acknowledges that for Paul the foundation of universalism rests on the overcoming of difference. The great Pauline achievement is commonly seen in the fact that Christianity, which was seen in the eyes of the Greco-Roman world as an obscure Jewish sect, received the status of a universal religion, a religion "for all people." Paul's merit is that he, from 40 to 60 CE, as early Christianity began to spread beyond Palestine, called for freeing the so-called "gentiles" from Jewish Law. If Paul is characterized, ever since the Jerusalem Apostle Council, by the epithet "Apostle of the People," then it is because he, in his programmatic verses in Romans, made a then-significant distinction obsolete: "it is the power of God for salvation to every one who has faith, to the Jew first and also to the Greek" (Romans 1.16–17).

For Badiou, it is extremely important to accurately understand the founding communitarianism of these subsets, "to the Jew first, and also to the Greek." In his introduction, he polemicizes against a way of thinking that renounces "the concrete universality of truths in order to affirm the rights of 'minorities', be they racial, religious, national, or sexual."[12] What he thereby places in question is the "real unifying factor behind this attempt to promote the cultural virtue of oppressed subsets, this invocation of language in order to extol communitarian particularisms."[13] Badiou hastens to emphasize that he does not want Paul's so-called "Jew" and "Greek" to be understood as religious groupings (with regard to the opposition between monotheism and polytheism) or as a "nation" in the sense of an "objective human set grasped in terms of its beliefs, customs, language, territory, and so forth."[14] Instead, for Badiou the subsets are characterized through the topic of the discourses:

1. "The Jew first": They are chosen and await the prophet who gives signs. Their discourse is the discourse of letters and laws; for them the path toward salvation leads through the "deciphering of signs (Jewish ritualism and prophecy)."[15] In short, "Jews are looking for signs and 'demanding miracles.'"[16]

2. "And also the Greek": "[T]he Greeks are 'looking for wisdom' and asking questions."[17] Their discourse constitutes itself through philosophy and wisdom as an adoption of the "fixed order of the world." What seems essential in this formulation—and later I will treat this in more detail—is that Badiou literally makes use of an astronomical terminology. In antiquity, order was called "cosmos" and world, "geo-" or "mundus," and not coincidentally the term "universalism" also belongs to this lexical field. As a matter of fact, Badiou adds, "Greek discourse is *cosmic*, deploying the subject within the reason of a natural totality."[18]

For Badiou, what is decisive for both of these opposed discursive regimes is that they are destined to found a third discourse, that of Christianity, which is neither Judeo-Christian/prophetic nor Greco-Christian/philosophical, nor consisting of a synthesis of both, but rather a totally new discursive order. Its universal message forbids any further thinking about the subsets in their difference: "Only the third [Christian] discourse holds to its division as a guarantee of universality."[19]

Next to (1) the prophet and (2) the philosopher, Badiou introduces (3) the apostle whose concern is neither (i) the decipherment of signs nor (ii) the apprehension of the total order; rather, his mission as a messenger (ἀπόστολος) is said to consist solely in the announcement of the Christ-event. Badiou specifies that the apostle is neither a witness of the event nor a memory of it. For Badiou, the Christ-event does not belong to "the order of fact, falsifiable or demonstrable," and it is not of interest "as a particular, or miraculous, fact"; rather, the resurrection of Christ is said to be a "pure event, [the] opening of an epoch, [the] transformation of the relations between the possible and the impossible."[20]

The Christ-event operates, according to Badiou, under a fully other regime than the (1) Jewish or (2) Greek discourse: it is (i) "illegal" and (ii) "a-cosmic," (a) "signaling nothing" and (b) "refusing integration into any totality."[21] In other words, it does not represent or confirm a law nor does it establish a total world order; instead, it adopts a completely other form of discourse. Not coincidentally, Badiou vehemently contradicts Nietzsche, who in *The Antichrist* characterizes the Pauline gospel of the Christ-event as "a lie" and a "deliberate falsification" of a "counterfeiter."[22] For Badiou, the great revolution of Christianity consists not in the genuine or fake actions of miracle workers, but solely in the declaration of universal grace as a discursive order in which the difference between the Jew and the Greek becomes obsolete. Beyond this opposition, "the subject as division" can be founded:

> To *confess* the nondifference between Jew and Greek establishes Christianity's potential universality; to *found* the subject as division, rather than as perpetuation of a tradition, renders the subjective element adequate to this universality by terminating the predicative particularity of cultural subjects.
>
> If the event is able to enter into the constitution of the subject *declaring* it, it is precisely because through it, and irrespective of the particularity of persons, it ceaselessly re-divides the two paths, distributing the "not [...] but" which, through an endless process, sets aside the law *to enter into grace*.[23]

Badiou does not cease emphasizing that the Christ-event stands beyond the opposition of "Jew" and "Greek" and that he furthermore wants to see "Jew" and "Greek" above the particularizing thinking of ethnic, religious, cultural, and linguistic difference; of sole significance for him is the event's function as possible recipient of the grace of God. Within Badiou's theoretical frame, his ontology of the multiple, the figure of difference seems to have no place, or more specifically, difference serves the apostle only to overcome each and every mark of otherness and thus as an evangelic springboard into the universal realm of Christianity: "For God judges without regard of the person" (Romans 2.11).

"Confessing," "founding," "proclaiming," "entering into grace"—those are the central verbal operations in which, for Badiou, the discursive regime of the divided subject takes place. As speech acts, these verbs correspond to a certain model whereby the verb "does" what it "says." The Christ-event *fulfills itself* not as a historical particularity—it is neither (1) the *confirmation* (in Austin's terms, "the constative") of a prophetical fulfillment nor (2) the establishment of truth—but rather something completely different, as Badiou formulates it: "Christians confess the crucified Christ."[24] And with the expression, "I here confess," they formulate a classic performative, which Austin has taught us can be neither true nor false (and thus not a "lie," structurally speaking). Performatives can nevertheless succeed or fail, namely in the case when they are not intended seriously (e.g. if Paul was only a poet) or when they conflict with contextual discourse conditions (e.g. if Paul was not authorized as a prophet).[25]

When Badiou places the self-declared "apostle" in quotation marks, he draws attention to how Paul sees himself confronted with the problem that he, unlike Peter, the "genuine apostle," did not know Christ during his lifetime. Paul must therefore declare himself an apostle. With quotation marks, Badiou calls into action the work of citation as a performative praxis. The quotation marks indicate that the figure of the apostle makes use of a context, that is, a system of cultural values and norms. Further, the simple quotation marks indicate a form of improper speaking; they show that a certain irony is at play, that the "self-declared apostle" is not authorized in the system of true apostledom, which is based on witness and memory. The self-declaration develops its immense power as an event because it breaks with the traditional context. The founding break takes place in the confrontation between the self-declared and the genuine apostles, that is, in the citation of the apostle as "apostle"; it emerges, because the "apostle," as a singular figure, cites, repeats, or iterates the context.

As Jacques Derrida has elaborated, *itera* means "repeatable" as well as "again, other."[26] Within the scope of Derrida's theory of performativity, the "pure event," which for Badiou founds universalism, unfolds its foundational force by making use of a "total context" that is citable, repeatable, or iterable in all places and at all times, and by breaking with this context at the same time. According to Derrida, the work of the event is based on precisely this "power to break with the context," whose iterability in the sense of the possibility of repetition and "becoming different" provides the indispensable condition for its universal functioning.[27] This break forms the link between the universality and the singularity of the event. Even Badiou admits that a "truth procedure is only universal insofar as it is supported, at that point through which it indexes the real, by an immediate subjective recognition of its singularity," and he repeatedly emphasizes the paradoxical nature of "truth as universal singularity," albeit in a certain order, namely with the universal as a direction or goal: "For if it is true that every truth erupts as singular, its singularity is immediately universalizable."[28] If one can also ask how this paradoxical constellation is reversible and which effect a "singular universality" would have for a truth procedure, it suffices here to point out that Badiou involves the concept of universality as a final "affirmation" in a paradoxical turn whose force of rupture is owed to no other figure than difference as repetition and otherness.

Being-gentile (ἔθνος)

Badiou's interest in subsets is concentrated on what remains whenever "real unifying factors" are disregarded, that is, what of the discourse of the Jew and the Greek remains in light of the "pure event." For him, the "universalizable singularity" of the subject must be distinguished from its "identitarian singularity."[29] It is nevertheless necessary for his philosophy to speak of Paul as an "apostle of the people." And Badiou does this with philological care. He not only mentions the literal description *ethnē* but also points to how it is "rather inaccurately translated" in French as "nations."[30] If Badiou regards this term's connotation of "the open multiple of peoples and customs" as irrelevant for the Pauline gospel, his philosophical procedure is nevertheless based on a philological excursus on the term *ἔθνος*. With his multilingual parlance of "people" [*peuples*], *ethnē*, and "nations," Badiou involuntarily recalls the cultural bandwidth of the addressees of the Pauline epistle: the inhabitants of Rome, Corinth, Galatea, and so on. In his formulation, all of these linguistic or ethnic "communitarian particularisms" resonate, particularisms on which the Tower of Babel once faltered and which were said to be overcome only in the unification of the Pentecostal miracle, bringing together "Parthians and Medes and Elamites and residents of Mesopotamia, Judea, and Cappadocia [...] visitors from Rome [...] Jews [...] and Arabs" and so on (Acts 2.9–11). To take Paul as the "apostle of the people" is to concern all of these groups. Badiou, however, is interested exclusively in "these two entities": "the Jew and the Greek."[31] But what exactly does *ἔθνος* mean for Paul's universal gospel and how, for Badiou, is this term, apart from this misappropriated linguistic and ethnic difference, related to "being a gentile"?

Let us turn our philological gaze, like Badiou, to the passage where Paul announces his visit to the Roman community.

I have often intended to come to you [...] in order that I may reap some harvest among you as well as among the rest of the Gentiles [τοῖς λοιποῖς ἔθνεσιν]. I am under obligation both to Greeks and to barbarians ['Έλλησίν τε καὶ Βαρβάροις], both to the wise and to the foolish.

Romans 1.13–14

In the parallel between "Greeks and Non-Greeks" and "the wise and the foolish," the Greeks are ascribed with the discursive regime, as Badiou would say, of education and wisdom, while the "Non-Greeks" (*barbaroi*) are ascribed with the regime of foolishness. This address is provocative for multiple reasons. Badiou sees not only an equivalence between "Greek" and "gentile" but above all the dissolution of the binary of Greek-Jew. What interests him is neither the "straightforward opposition between Jewish monotheism and official polytheism" nor a "national" coding. For the Pauline concept of ἔθνος, for Badiou, has nothing to do with what we "spontaneously understand by means of the word 'nation.'"[32] Instead, everything turns on the regimes of Jewish versus Greek discourses; they mark the site at which differences become obsolete.

On closer examination of these verses, however, the founding universal force of this opposition (Jew-Greek) is not exhausted in the discourse of "education" described by Badiou; it requires other codes. In this connection, the complexity of the concept of ἔθνος appears extraordinarily productive: in it, Paul understands not only the "Greek" as gentile, as Badiou correctly diagnoses, but also the "Non-Greek" as gentile ('Έλλησίν τε καὶ Βαρβάροις). What is notable above all is that Paul describes the subset that is translated—also "quite imprecisely"—as "non-Greeks," literally as *barbaroi*. With this designation, a political and juridical order enters into the religious one that Badiou had qualified as irrelevant. For as Emile Benveniste has shown, in antiquity institutions had differentiated the non-Greeks into different subsets according to lineage, language, and economic power, whereby the foreigners (*xenoi*), according to the prevailing law, were not granted citizenship, but hospitality: "*xenos* indicates relations of the same type between men linked by a pact which implies precise obligations also extending to their descendants."[33] The *barbaroi*, instead, stood entirely outside of the law. The rule of Antidotos once characterized the *barbaros* as "nothing, a son of nothing."[34] In his essay on hospitality, Derrida characterizes the *barbaros* as the "absolute other, [...] the savage absolutely excluded and heterogeneous."[35] Even in Paul's time and still in ours, such distinctions—between the German and the non-German, the European and the non-European, and ultimately between the identifiable foreigner and those without identification papers—remain significant. This juridical distinction remains in no way external to Badiou's concept of universalism; rather, it makes a decisive difference, especially if it is brought into connection with an ethics of hospitality as an absolute law, a point about which I will go into more detail later.

For now, let us follow the common translation of *ethnoi* as "gentiles," which is imprecise but widespread and which Badiou follows too: the apostle of the "people" is the apostle of the "gentiles," of the "gentile people." This weaving together of the ethnic and the religious, which appears irrelevant given Badiou's strict rejection of every particular attribution of the subject, runs throughout all of Paul's writings and will become all the more urgent in a following reading of Romans.

In this regard, the verses are especially noteworthy where Paul denounces the sins of the gentiles and speaks of those humans that "knew God" but "did not honor him as God or give thanks to him." "Claiming to be wise, they became fools" (Romans 1.21–2). This gentile subset is not treated further in the discursive regime of wisdom and philosophy that Badiou thematizes; rather, it bears quite different stigma:

> Therefore God gave them up in the lusts of their hearts to impurity, to the dishonoring of their bodies among themselves, because they [...] worshiped and served the creature rather than the Creator [...] Their women exchanged natural relations for unnatural, and the men likewise gave up natural relations with women and were consumed with passion for one another.
>
> Romans 1.24–7

Did Badiou overlook this passage in Romans? Certainly not. When Badiou demands of us that we tackle the concept of the *ethnos* by overlooking these sub-subsets and ignoring this stigmatization, it is in no way a matter of making a case for a program of discrimination. Even if Badiou polemicizes against a cultural historicism that is committed to the marginalization and the "eternal victim status" of certain subsets (above all, this seems to be an eternal program in Western thinking: those who practice fornication or worship idols), what is at stake for him is solely the affirmation of universal truth as *the* program for the possibility of the impossible, which would be superior to all historicization and all laws, including the segregation laws of certain dictators as well as the immigration laws of our democracies. In view of this truth, the stigmas described above simply do not fit into Badiou's reading of the Pauline gospel: they neither add anything to it, nor do they take anything away from it, nor do they question their invariability.

If Badiou also insists that the thinking of difference is obsolete in the system of universalism and that every claim of otherness is inevitably accounted for and taken apart by the third discourse, it should be observed that the sacrilegious behavior of idolatry and certain sexual practices—Paul later makes mention of circumcision and many food taboos—are not simply external to the Pauline gospel. The treatment of iconolatry as a deviant cultural practice and of homosexuality as an unnatural one does not emerge spontaneously and independently of the gospel; rather, they are its very effect, as a result of a *denial of a confession*: "And since they did not see fit to acknowledge God, God gave them up to a base mind and to improper conduct" (Romans 1.28). The cultural, religious, and sexual coding of the diverse subsets of the godless is treated not under the figure of the law but rather under that of grace; that is, in precisely the system that for Badiou constitutes universality. Taking sacrilegious behavior as a visible stigma stands in the service of the revelation of God, and in this regard it is not a *sign for* something (constative, which can be true or false) but rather an event (performative). In this constellation, the stigmas of otherness form the indispensable structural conditions for the possibility of "receiving grace," as an event that can succeed (or fail). In this sense, the stigmatization is not incidental to the system of universalism, but rather is produced by it as both a visible effect and necessary condition for the success of grace as a performative. Being gentile prevails as something not external to the "pure event" but rather as a co-operator, particularly in its religious, cultural, and sexual particularity. The system of the Christ-event produces otherness to the same degree that it challenges it.

Sonhood (lineage)

Let us take a closer look at the particular concept of the subject that Badiou's reading of Paul demands: in requiring the renunciation of conventional differences, universalism cultivates a subject "divided in itself by the challenge of having nothing but the vanished event to face up to."[36] The subject who declares a confession experiences this division. It needs neither (1) a "miraculous guarantee" nor (2) "arguments or proofs"; declaration does not attest to "any lack and remains withdrawn from its fulfillment by the figure of the master [who could furnish signs or answers]"[37] and thereby does not enter into the logic of the master. Therefore, according to Badiou, the subject takes the place of the son, namely the son "who does not attest to any lack" and whose evidence is universal:

To declare an event is to become the son of that event. That Christ is Son is emblematic of the way in which the evental declaration filiates the declarant. [...] It is by consenting to the figure of the son [...] that the Father causes us ourselves to come forth universally as sons.[38]

Through the power of declaration, the subject emerges from the serfdom of the master and into the "equality of sons": "The resurrected Son filiates all of humanity."[39]

It is hardly surprising that for Badiou the sexual difference of father and son, like the ethnic, cultural, and linguistic differences between Jew and gentile, Greek and non-Greek, is meaningless. Badiou does not once attempt to even acknowledge that this makes no difference for the universal of the Pauline system. In view of the refinement of his argumentation, it appears almost banal to draw attention to how Badiou's theory self-evidently demands that we understand "the son" as a genderless, grammatical category, like "hostage," "member," "assistant," all of which are words whose natural gender [*Geschlecht*] cannot be inferred from grammatical gender [*Genus*]. Badiou has providently foreclosed every critique of the rhetoric of otherness in his polemic against "cultural relativism."[40]

If we then ask what, for Paul, sonhood means for the founding of universalism, according to Badiou every sexual contingency would be without influence on the universality of his gospel. The figure of the apostle needs no authorization from outside, neither an origin (Tarsus) nor a lineage (the line of Benjamin, *natio*); for Badiou's concept of the subject, the force of the event, with which Paul declares himself an "apostle," suffices. Paul draws the power to break with the context of apostledom from the Damascus event, which, like the Christ-event, needs no basis outside of itself, (1) no legitimation through the law and (2) no bond to the fixed order of the world; the pure event is, as Badiou writes, (i) "illegal" and (ii) "a-cosmic." Let us look, then, at the Damascus event and inquire once again into this unprecedented performative of self-naming, which contravenes the basal discursive conditions of naming, with a particular focus on the question of gender.

The anonymous author of the Acts of the Apostles mentions the Damascus event three times. Although the narratives differ in terms of the narrative position and scope, each time it is reported that Paul hears how Jesus calls his name in Hebrew, that is, in the language of the Pharisees and the Jewish diaspora: "Saul, Saul, why do you persecute me [*Scha'ul*, לואש]?"[41] Not coincidentally, he hears the name twice each time, as an echo or repetition, with the only difference being the temporal delay. Derrida has discussed, in varying contexts, that repeatability forms the basic condition for the functioning of the proper name, particularly when the subject does not exist before naming but only belatedly "gives birth to itself" in the act of naming or signing; the name can only function from then on in the course of this deferral.[42]

Saul, however, is also called Paul (Παῦλος). The enigmatic change, colloquially referenced in German in the dictum *vom Saulus zum Paulus* (lit. "from Saul to Paul"; "to make an about-face"), takes place in the book of Acts rather incidentally, neither on the road to Damascus nor at the following baptism, but only four chapters later, belatedly, in a subordinate clause: "But Saul, who was also called Paul" (Acts 13.9). Not once in his letters does Paul call himself by this other name. It seems at best to be embarrassing to him, or perhaps he is only indifferent. If the double name in the "fabulous" or "anecdotal" story of the apostle stands for anything, then it is for the multilingualism of the apostle and for, as one would say today, multiculturalism, which was self-evident in the multi-ethnic city Jerusalem as well as in the Mediterranean. Finally, the Jewish-Greek double name stands in a series with the third, Latinized form "Saulus," in the language of the Roman colonizers, who designate the apostle by his identity as a legal person under Roman law.

These indifferent proper names, which are there from birth on and whose "identitary singularity" render them meaningless for Badiou, prove to be, upon closer inspection, foundational for precisely that overcoming of difference that Badiou characterizes as the "division of the subject." The confessing subject enters into grace in the very act of appealing to the son as a universal category. Its "division," however, takes place in precisely this logic of the proper name, which is contained in the play of difference in the minimal pair Saul/Paul. The self-proclaimed "apostle" bears this condition of being a son first of all, as I would like to claim, in his proper name, which is, undecidable between Jewish and Greek, always both and which possesses a third, Roman dimension.

The proper name necessarily calls up all of those features of "identity" that Badiou excludes from the Pauline gospel as a contingent, "unifying factor": the father, genealogy, family (lineage), origin, birth (*natio*), mother tongue, and so on. These "identitary" qualities of the proper name produce the very connections between the universal and singular son that are at stake for Badiou. The universal sonhood emerges insofar as the proper name is untranslatable, insofar as it expresses (as the proper name Babel does) the inappropriate and unbalanced in the self-relationship of language and at the same time refers to "the impossibility of finishing" of a "'true' translation" in a universal or pure language for the "worldly totality."[43] The singular sonhood cannot be separated from this, however; it is necessarily also communicated when saying the proper name, insofar as the proper name "Paul" has a translatable meaning in Greek: Παῦλος means "small" and thereby refers to a common noun. Every time that the apostle calls himself and appoints himself, he performs this double operation of proclaiming the untranslatable, universal message by stating that he descends from a family from Tarsus from the house of Benjamin, the "smallest" of the twelve tribes of Israel. "Paul" is a patronym in this double sense: it refers at the same time and with the same authority to the name of the patriarch and to God the Father. This variation on the genealogical line in the proper name proves itself to be constitutive for the universal program for which Paul vouches with his name.

Paul, a cosmopolitan?

Only much later than his letters has Paul himself arrived in the metropolis, Rome, as a prisoner, in order to be judged for his gospel. Admittedly, he cannot himself witness his demise *at this place*. In the epistles, however, it is reported in his name how Paul does not stop referring to his sonhood as a rhetoric of the place until his death. At his arrest in Jerusalem, he reproaches the high priests: "Brothers, I am a Pharisee, a son of Pharisees. It is with respect to the hope and the resurrection of the dead that I am on trial" (Acts 23.6). To the Romans, on the other hand, he calls upon his Roman citizenship: "I am a citizen by birth" (Acts 22.28). Both times, he states, in effect, "I am from Tarsus, and I am a Roman; I am one of you, your brother and your son, and you surely cannot kill your own son."

However, being a Pharisee in this place also characterizes that "identitary singular" Jewish subset which in the time of the second Jewish Temple is at odds with the Sadducees. In his defense speech, Paul therefore establishes the universal community precisely by sowing discord among the high priests and by trying in his distress to win the Pharisees to his side. And with this other dictum, *civis romanus sum*, he appeals to his Roman citizenship by birth, which protects the uncondemned from being flogged. With this, he appeals to the duties that bind the Roman colonizer to a pact, "which implies precise obligations also extending to their descendants," as Benveniste describes the laws of conditional hospitality.[44] Paul thus refers to the fact that he is not *barbarous* and must not be treated like a barbarian. He thus breaks with the universal law which would bestow a just treatment not only on the foreigner with certain special rights but also on the barbarian, this "absolute other," "who has neither name, nor patronym, nor family, nor social status," as Derrida writes.[45] This break with the universal law is for Derrida structurally unavoidable, for the law of absolute hospitality is unconditional; it requires

> [. . .] that I open up my home and that I give not only to the foreigner (provided with a family name, with the social status of being a foreigner), but to the absolute, unknown, anonymous other, and that I *give place* to them, [. . .] without asking of them either reciprocity (entering into a pact) or even their names.[46]

Paul as an "urban cosmopolitan," as Badiou writes,[47] enters into this very conflict, when he announces the universal sonhood of humanity, for whose truth he stands in and for which he will be condemned. With this very announcement, he appeals at the same time to the conditional law that appertains to him by virtue of his singular sonhood.[48] In this sense, Badiou's conception of a final and unavoidable affirmation, an "affirmation without preliminary negation,"[49] which is carried out in the grace of the pure event, remains not untouched from that structural untranslatability of universal truth, as an "unending mission," that, as Derrida writes, remains interminable and aporetic. For the unconditional non-identification of the one who pleads for protection or asylum is not inevitably "lovelier" than his identification that binds him to a contract. "Is it more just and more loving to question or not to question?" asks Derrida, and concludes that it follows that, "the question of the foreigner" be taken "as the question of the question."[50]

Paul was very likely called by his name: Saul, Paul, Saulus. All these addresses as an apostle of Jews and Greeks are involved equally in his sonhood. The singular proper name and hence the related status as a citizen of Rome form the necessary conditions for the becoming-universal of his gospel. With every naming, he enters into this conflict anew, of becoming a subject accountable both to the universal and the singular law, whereby the one demands a necessary break with the other, without simply being its adversary. Unlike Badiou, for Derrida the absolute law never takes the form of a pure affirmation, but it can very likely, in the sense of an aporia, lead to "perpetually progressive movement."[51]

If Badiou addresses Paul as a contemporary and cosmopolitan and makes the universal message for civil rights, immigration policy and asylum law his concern in our times, what figure does he then stand up for? To let the foreigner come unconditionally, regardless of nation, language, religion, and so on, also means receiving him *as the Other*, in the persistence of his otherness, in his identitary singularity, that is, in invocation of his name, in his foreign language with its customs and traditions and in recognition of the special status of places.

Cosmic singularity

Universalism and cosmopolitanism hang closely together insofar as both concepts make use of a certain astronomical terminology that upon closer observation also structures the three accounts of the Damascus event. Each time, the story is supplied with other details, but two observations above all are of interest for the analysis of Badiou's reading of Paul.

First, the light: all three narratives speak of a type of cosmic singularity in the form of an unusual light, which grows in intensity with each further account. In the first version, Paul is suddenly surrounded "by a light from heaven" (Acts 9.3). In the second version—the anonymous narrator here cites in direct speech Paul's defense speech in the Temple of Jerusalem—the location of the sun is precisely fixed: "about noon a great light from heaven suddenly shone around me" (Acts 22.6). In the third version, which presents Paul's defense speech before Agrippa in Rome in the first person, it reads, "At midday [...] I saw on the way a light from heaven, brighter than the sun that shone around me and those who journeyed with me" (Acts 26.13). The pure event that founds universalism belongs, according to Badiou, to no existing discursive order: it is "a-cosmic" and "illegal." Although it requires no authorization from outside, it draws its universality literally from the inexplicable, heavenly or cosmic light that provides the discursive regime of Greek cosmology delineated by Badiou with another scientific-historical meaning.[52] This light is "brighter than the sun," that is, brighter than the brightest visible star from the earth, a kind of supernova.[53] As an astronomical anomaly, this light is viable only because it deviates from the "normal" phenomena of light, because it is, in the contemporaneous discourse of the cosmos, new and *other*, if not unexpected. When Badiou claims that with Paul "we notice a complete absence of the theme of mediation. Christ is not a mediation,"[54] I would like to counter that the three accounts of the Damascus event stage Jesus precisely as a "mediation," literally a "pure medium."

Second, the media of revelation: the actual recognition of revelation, which makes the apostle a divided subject, in Badiou's sense, does not take place on the road to Damascus, as Badiou flippantly writes, nor does the voice that Paul hears reveal to him "both the truth and his vocation."[55] The great light stands for nothing and mediates nothing; it merely blinds. In order to reveal his divine message, a whole series of mediations are needed: first, Paul *sees* the light, then he *hears* a voice. Depending on the version, his companions share this sensual experience. While the visual experience is arranged as an intensification (bright, brighter, brighter than the sun), the sensual experiences of his companions are organized chiastically (they hear but do not see, or see but do not hear). In any case, these phenomena stand in opposition to a process of communication, more so than conveying anything: Paul is blinded "because of the brightness of the light" (Acts 22.11), and his companions become speechless. Only three days later, in Damascus, does the revelation take place, and here again not abruptly but through the intervention of the disciple Ananias, who, like a switch point in a telecommunications network, receives in a vision the divine mission of Paul and discloses this vision to his addressee by means of a laying of hands and a verbal appeal, until finally "the scales fall" from Paul's eyes. In no way can it be said that the event takes place "unmediated," but rather by a complex telecommunications system with visual, auditory, and tactile transcriptions. Its reality is revealed to be the reality of the medium itself, together with its technical conditions and disruptions.

The claim of unmediatedness is the actual crux of every claim to universal truth[56] and it is no coincidence that it is related to the universe itself, in order to found not only a supra-European or global standpoint, but even an extra-human or divine one beyond the particularity of the positions. In occidental thought, this program always appears whenever particular concepts of the human are supposed to be made valid "for all humans," in movements of Christianization, colonization, globalization, and so on. In the New Testament, this astronoetic rhetoric can be found not initially in Paul; rather, the birth of the Holy Land is announced through a star that is regarded as a universal event both by the wise men (*magoi*) from the Orient and the scholars (*grammateis*) from the occident.[57] The light of the stars shines in the crown of stars of the Immaculate Conception statue, just as it does in the European Flag.[58] Kant grounded his "cosmo-political" idea literally on an astronomical theory, when he grounds the law of general hospitality in the spherical form of the earth, on whose surface humans "cannot scatter themselves infinitely."[59] The heavenly light illuminates the discourse of *Lumiére* and grounds the "equality of sons" and brothers in the political program of the Enlightenment just as in the post-Enlightenment program of Badiou,[60] and it legitimizes human rights as a "universal" right of nature, as Butler and Spivak, among others, have extensively elaborated.[61] And even Badiou implicitly makes use of this rhetoric, when he divests a cultural category like universal ethics of its identitary particularity and its specific rhetoric of place, speaking of it as though of a mathematical truth. Overall, the rhetorics of the universal tend to misappropriate the work of media as *dispositifs* of revelation.

Spivak, not coincidentally, demands a conceptual rethinking of the "universal" in terms of the "planetary." Planetary thought, and here Spivak is in full agreement with Badiou, steers attention from the "global" in the sense of a "transnationalization of global capital" and toward the "planet" in the sense of our earth as the "human habitation in community."[62] Spivak's planetary, though, reformulates the form of possibility—that is the conjunctive, which Badiou situates *beyond* difference—as a "planetary imperative to responsibility, seen as a right precomprehending becoming-human."[63] At no point, however, does planetary thought validate universal statements; Spivak reveals every "universalization" to be a "re-territorialization,"[64] that is, a new emplacement of what is supposedly placeless. Instead, the planet stands for Spivak in the sign of alterity, and its imperative is first of all an ethics of alterity: "We must think our individual home as written on the planet as planet, what we learn in school astronomy. In this refracted view of ethics, Space may be the name of alterity."[65]

Planetary thought is a thought of place. It does not only know of latitudes and longitudes as lines encompassing the globe, but also recognizes in this unifying system the different views of the starry sky in the northern and southern hemispheres, the impossibility of viewing the Southern Cross and the Northern Star simultaneously. The planetary subject carries out its division precisely in light of this broken view, in recognition of its particular standpoint for every universal statement, that is, in the figure of difference.

Even though Badiou does not cease to emphasize that for Paul the "Christ-event [...] is precisely what indicates the vanity of places,"[66] his universalism is not simply the antagonist of planetary thought. His ontology of the multiple is not suitable as a simple opposite to the thought of difference. And in this respect, he also does not provide the exact counter-program to "cultural relativism," which he polemically announces, nor to cultural analysis, for that matter. For everything that interests Badiou in Paul is dedicated to precisely this imperative to reimagine the planet.

10

Finally: East Pole and West Pole

With the coordinate system emerges not only a geodetic survey network in which every position on the planet becomes localizable, but it also provides an instrument for the projection of the spherical form of the globe onto a two-dimensional surface. In other words, it is a method of translation. No matter what technology the cartographers adopt, they consistently see themselves confronted with the problem that the reality of the world must adapt to the materiality of their data storage devices. In the case of the *mappa mundi*, the frameless and decentered sphere must adapt to a framed and centered surface.

The cartographic approaches are known. The Mercator projection from 1569 proceeds in an isogonic way, with the result that equatorial countries are proportionally correct while the surfaces near the poles are blown up to the point of unrecognizability. By contrast, the Gall-Peters projection (1972) offers an equal area representation, which, by mapping all areas so that they have the correct sizes relative to one another, valorizes equatorial areas with respect to the so-called rich industrial lands in the north, and as such is considered politically correct by the UNO and other organizations. Alternatively, the Wagner IV projection (1949) mediates between equal-area and isogonic projection and endeavors to reduce angular distortion.[1]

Each of these world models undertakes a visual manipulation with which they attempt to reduce the Gaussian curvature, through stretching, distorting, splitting or folding the spherical surface. As a result, they deliver a translation that—as in the myth of the abduction of Europe—is based on deception and seduction. Only with digital world maps like *Google Earth* can the earth begin to be experienced by an observer as a spherical surface, because the rotary axis (of the so-called azimuthal projection) is calculated anew for every position and so the distortion on the margins is adjusted correspondingly.

Maps are translations of the world into signs, and the coordinate system provides the axes along which translation takes place. As signs, however, the world becomes tangible in other ways. Not only do maps communicate, with the same authority as writing—where is up and where is down—but above all they define center and periphery. By affording overviews and insights, maps expand the horizon of the known world, whose global connectedness now becomes tangible, and they make distant places accessible, as markets, as providers of raw materials, as cultivated, missionary, cultural, or linguistic territory. And insofar as maps are foldable, they produce surprising and impossible connections between remote areas, and in this way they hand their users over to a "poetics of Relation."[2] Seen this way, the experience of the distorted world of paper maps or of the constantly newly and differently distorted world on the screens of our computers is also an experience of encountering a cartographically mediatized Other.

Critical cultural theories, not the natural sciences, have taught us that the prime meridian is not a celestial line but rather the work of a seafaring policy of globalization of the nineteenth century. In this connection, it seems necessary, proceeding from this critical reflection on the prime meridian, to consider an "East Pole" and a "West Pole" as impossible places. If one wanted to inscribe these unnatural poles on a globe, the East Pole would lie where the equator intersects the 90th meridian east (in the Gulf of Bengal), while the West Pole would lie at the opposite side where the equator intersects the 90th meridian west (in the Galapagos Islands).[3] The idea of such an East Pole and West Pole cannot be justified, neither by the orbit of the sun nor by the axis or rotation of the earth; like the prime meridian, they are pure geodetic entities, coolly calculated ideas that lack all earthly passion and cosmic grandeur.

With this knowledge of the impossibility of these places, the world and the whole world context in the solar system are to be taken seriously in a way that is both very old and highly contemporary. In view of an East Pole and a West Pole, the whole system of longitudes will now appear far-fetched, and instead on the routes of colonization or globalization that proceeded westwards and eastwards from Europe, the focus will now be on a north-south division of the globe, which is in no way arbitrary but determined by the great cosmic movements of planetary orbit and rotation. With this "re-polarization," climatic zones rather than trade zones will be the focus of attention.

If in this sense the Europe of the present meets Atlas, it will again be confronted with undiminished topicality with its ancient, mythical mission: the task of translation. Even and especially in the present age of global "flows," Europe will not live up to this task or this responsibility by retreating to a "fortress" from where world affairs can be measured and dominated. For in the relationship of the world as a whole, the ecological, economic, financial, social, cultural, linguistic, and other movements, whenever they emanate from Europe, will in one way or another also return to it. It will therefore be important that Europe recalls her name, which reminds her of her role as a translator. In particular, she once carried over (or "trans-lated") herself, and was never quite with herself, but she always stands in relation to a distance in which she looks and from which she is looked at. In brief, Europe should remain aware of her relation to the Mediterranean and the regions that lie behind it.

Afterword

The original German version of this book, *Der babylonische Planet: Kultur, Übersetzung, Dekonstruktion unter den Bedingungen der Globalisierung*, was published in October 2013 by Winter Publisher in Heidelberg (Germany). The book started with a foreword that I wrote shortly after the death of its author, my wife Sonja Neef (1968-2013). It begins as follows:

> Babylonian projects tend to remain unfinished. This also holds for this book, only about half of which is a work of last hand, otherwise a work of penultimate hand. This collection of essays was conceived over many years. At times, the engagement with these topics was the focus of her work; at other times, it ran in the background. Some chapters were pre-published in other versions at different places. A serious illness forced itself into the phase of completing the book version, which reduced Sonja's strength for the last, condensing revision and finally [...] took away her mind, so that further work on the book was no longer possible.[1]

It has now taken eight years to complete an English translation of this text. I would like to thank the people without whom such a publication would not have been possible. First and foremost, I thank Sonja's doctoral advisor, Prof. Dr. Mieke Bal from the Amsterdam School for Cultural Analysis (ASCA). Right after Sonja's funeral, she gave the impetus to publish an English version of the *Babylonian Planet*, even before the German version was completed. Over the years, she has always motivated and supported me in this project. Without her, the contact to Bloomsbury Publishing would not have been possible. Over the last year, she has invested a lot of time in helping to check the translation and to prepare the documents for the publisher.

I would equally like to thank Prof. Dr. Henry Sussman (Yale University), who has been a committed supporter of the translation project from the beginning. It is thanks to him that I have been able to establish contact with the translator. Also, he has been a factor of motivation (for me as well as for the translator) and he supported me with the task of checking the translation and preparing the documents for Bloomsbury Publishing, just as Mieke did. It is wonderful to see that Sonja had such great friends in science (and in real life), who keep her memory alive until today.

A big debt of gratitude goes to Jason Groves, who has devoted himself to the translation work with great enthusiasm and commitment. Over the years, we have been in close contact with each other and we have witnessed how our lives have changed. In the end, together we have been able to successfully master this great task of translation. Thanks also to Carlos Gasperi Labbee, who was on board when the translation work began. I would also like to emphasize my thanks to DeepL as a support tool, whose progress has made our translation work easier. Sonja, who worked as a translator in her early years, would have been delighted with these technological advances towards a "universal translator." Very likely, she would have made this the subject of her own research, as starting points in this book indicate.

I would further like to thank Andreas Barth and Winter Publisher, who supported Sonja's book with great help and now made possible the publication of the English translation at Bloomsbury Publishing; Günter Blamberger and the Morphomata International Center for Advanced Studies in Cologne, a think tank and meeting venue, where Sonja felt very much at home in the last phase of her healthy life; and finally the staff at Bloomsbury Publishing, who supported me reliably, particularly Lisa Goodrum, Lucy Russell, and Liza Thompson.

There is no reason to bemoan the fact that it took quite a long time until the English version was ready for publication. I am sure that Sonja's thinking is still highly relevant today—especially in times of migration and the coronavirus pandemic. This is also shown by another publication from last year: Hedwig Wagner, then Sonja's successor as Junior Professor of European Media Culture at the Bauhaus-Universität Weimar and now Professor of European Media Studies at the Europa-Universität Flensburg, recently published what is, according to the blurb, "the first German-language publication on European Media Studies." Sonja's programmatic text "Was ist europäische Medienkultur?" ("What is European media culture?")[2] was included in this anthology, which is dedicated to Sonja. This text was written in 2004, when Sonja had just taken over the junior professorship in Weimar and had to think about how this then new subject of European media culture should be conceived. This essay is also the basis for the second chapter of the *Babylonian Planet* and thus the nucleus of the entire book, which can be understood as a legacy of how Sonja envisioned the subject of a European media culture. Incidentally, it was Hedwig who organized a commemoration event for Sonja in December 2013 in Weimar on the occasion of the publication of the German version of the *Babylonian Planet*. In this way, I can thank her once again.

It is a reassuring thought for me to know that still in the twenties of the twenty-first century texts by Sonja get published, so that she is still alive as a scientist. Sonja would be very grateful for that.

Martin Neef

Braunschweig, April 2021

Notes

1 The Babylonian Planet

1 Édouard Glissant, *Introduction to a Poetics of Diversity*, trans. Celia Britton (Liverpool: Liverpool University Press, 2020), 24.

2 For further reference, cf. Moritz Wullen, "Mythos Babylon," in *Babylon: Mythos*, ed. Moritz Wullen and Günther Schauerte (Munich: Hirmer, 2008), 17–20, as well as the section "Turm" (84–102).

3 Dietmar Steiner, "Die Hure Babylon und One Mile High," in *Der Turmbau zu Babel. Ursprung und Vielfalt von Sprache und Schrift, vol. 1: Der Babylonische Turm in der historischen Überlieferung der Archäologie und der Kunst*, ed. Wilfried Seipel (Graz: Kunsthistorisches Museum, 2003). In order to facilitate understanding, all quotations that originally came from French and German and for which no published English version was available were translated into English by Jason Groves.

4 Patricia Pisters, "The Mosaic Film: Nomadic Style and Politics in Transnational Media Culture," in *Art and Visibility in Migratory Culture: Conflict, Resistance, and Agency*, ed. Mieke Bal and Miguel Á. Hernández-Navarro (Amsterdam: Rodopi, 2012).

5 Cf. also the section "Sprachverwirrung" in Wullen and Schauerte, eds., *Mythos Babylon*, 127–42, especially 130–7.

6 Manuel Castells, *Local and Global: Management of Cities in the Information Age* (London: Earthscan, 1997), 44.

7 Arjun Appadurai, *Modernity at Large: Cultural Dimensions of Globalization* (Minneapolis: University of Minnesota Press, 1996), 33.

8 Martin Heidegger, "Building Dwelling Thinking," in Martin Heidegger, *Poetry, Language, Thought*, trans. Albert Hofstadter (New York: Harper & Row, [1951] 1971), 144–5.

9 Heidegger, "Building Dwelling Thinking," 146.

10 Karsten Harries, "Unterwegs zur Heimat," ed. Eduard Führ, *Bauen und Wohnen/ Building and Dwelling. Martin Heidegger's Foundation of a Phenomenology of Architecture* (Münster: Waxmann, 2000), 101–20. Cf. also with respect to modern building under the conditions of globalization Sonja Neef, *An Bord der Bauhaus: Zur Heimatlosigkeit der Moderne. Einleitung*, in *An Bord der Bauhaus: Zur Heimatlosigkeit der Moderne*, ed. Sonja Neef (Bielefeld: Transcript, 2009), 21–4.

11 Félix Guattari, "Pratiques écosophiques et restauration de la cité subjective," in *Qu'est-ce que l'écosophie?*, ed. Stéphane Nadaud (Paris: Lignes, 2013), 33.

12 Here and henceforth, King James Bible translation.

13 Cf. here to the 2008 exhibition, *Babylon: Myth and Truth*, staged in Paris, Berlin, and London, in cooperation with the so-called "Universal Museums" of Europe, the Musée du Louvre, the Staatliche Museen zu Berlin, and the British Museum. The central ambition of the exhibition was to distinguish between the "historical" Babylon and the "mythical" one (Peter-Klaus Schuster, "Vorwort," in *Babylon: Wahrheit*, ed. Joachim Marzahn and Günther Schauerte (Munich: Hirmer, 2008), 7) and to correct the mythical notion of the hotbed of sin deformed by the "distorted picture of the Hebrew tradition" (Beate Salje, "Vorwort," in *Babylon: Wahrheit*, ed. Marzahn and Schauerte (Munich: Hirmer, 2008), 10). With this distinction in mind, a topographical division was made in the museum itself, with the "historical" Babylon being presented in the south wing of the Pergamon, and the "mythical" one in the north wing, respectively, accompanied by a cataloged publication divided-up similarly.

14 Jacques Derrida, "Des Tours de Babel," in Jacques Derrida, *Psyche: Inventions of the Other*, trans. Joseph Graham (Stanford, CA: Stanford University Press, [1987] 2007), 192.

15 For a historical study of Ancient Babylonian cuneiform writing, cf. Jerrold S. Cooper, "Sumerian and Accadian," in *The World's Writing Systems*, ed. Peter T. Daniels and William Bright (New York: Oxford University Press, 1996). A discussion of the principle of consonant and vowel distribution can be found on p. 47. Cf. here also Eric Havelock, *The Literate Revolution in Greece and its Cultural Consequences* (Princeton, NJ: Princeton University Press, 1982). In the discussion of the example "Jak and Jil" (beginning with p. 78), Havelock provides an inventory of various possibilities for reading and enunciating ancient oriental cuneiform: absent vowels often force the reader to fill in gaps based on context. These allow a "guessing-room," thereby creating ambiguities, what has led Havelock and philology to classify these as "less than efficient reading-instruments" (Havelock, *The Literate Revolution*, 70). For a euro-, logocentric critique of this approach, cf. Aleida and Jan Assmann, "Einleitung: Schrift—Kognition—Evolution. Eric A. Havelock und die Technologie kultureller Kommunikation," in Eric A. Havelock, *Schriftlichkeit: Das griechische Alphabet und die kulturelle Revolution*, ed. Aleida and Jan Assmann (Weinheim: VCH, 1990), 7–10, 23–5; cf. also Sonja Neef, *Imprint and Trace: Handwriting in the Age of Technology*, trans. Anthony Matthews (London: Reaktion Books, 2011), 312–13, n. 23.

16 Van Dale, *Etymologisch Woordenboek: De herkomst van onze woorden*, ed. P. A. F. van Veen (Utrecht: Van Dale Lexicografie, 1989), 80. The following supplement is provided there: Akkadian: *bâb ili*: the door of God (*bâbu*: door); Arabic: *bâbu, ilu*

(God), *ilâhu*; Hebraic: *êl*; the Greek form of Babel refers back to the Akkadian *bâb ilâni*: "door of the gods." Cf. further Arno Borst, *Der Turmbau von Babel: Geschichte der Meinungen über Ursprung und Vielfalt der Sprachen und Völker* (Munich: dtv, [1957] 1995), 80, n. 65, 83–4; 116–17; as well as Petra Eisele, *Babylon: Götterpforte oder große Hure* (Bern: Scherz, 1980), 149.

17 Borst, *Turmbau*, 80–1.

18 Cf. Eisele, *Babylon*, 148.

19 Borst, *Turmbau*, 76, 82, 114.

20 Gen. 11.1.

21 Derrida, *Tours de Babel*, 192.

22 Derrida, *Tours de Babel*, 192.

23 Voltaire, *Philosophical dictionary (A–I)*, trans. Peter Gay (New York: Basic Books, [1764] 1962), 106–7.

24 Derrida, *Tours de Babel*, 193; Derrida plays on words here: *Gift* means "poison" in German (translator's note).

25 Derrida, *Tours de Babel*, 207.

26 Cf. Derrida, *Tours de Babel* , 192.

27 Reiner Luyken, "Der Banausen-Bau zu Babel," *Die Zeit*, July 23, 2009.

28 Borst, *Turmbau*, 80; compare with Eisele, *Babylon*, 145–6.

29 Mathieu Ossendrijver, "Astronomie und Astrologie in Babylonien," in *Babylon. Wahrheit*, ed. Joachim Marzahn and Günther Schauerte (Munich: Hirmer, 2008), 373–4, 379, 382. Further, cf. Eisele, *Babylon*, 153–4, 275–7.

30 Borst, *Turmbau*, 79.

31 Borst, *Turmbau*, 78–9.

32 Borst, *Turmbau*, 78–9.

33 Borst, *Turmbau*, 3, 6.

34 Borst, *Turmbau*, 224.

35 Derrida, *Tours de Babel*, 195.

36 Walter Benjamin, "The Task of the Translator," in Walter Benjamin, *Selected Writings*, vol. 1: *1913–1926*, ed. Marcus Bullock and Michael W. Jennings, trans. Harry Zohn (Cambridge, MA, London: Belknap Press, [1923] 1996), 259. See also Derrida, *Tours de Babel*, 202, 207. To name a few excellent studies on Benjamin that have examined this point in greater detail, cf. Alfred Hirsch, *Der Dialog der Sprachen. Studien zum Sprach- und Übersetzungsdenken Walter Benjamins und Jacques Derridas* (Munich: Fink, 1995), as well as *Übersetzung und Dekonstruktion* (Frankfurt am Main: Suhrkamp, 1997); Christian Hart-Nibbrig, ed., *Übersetzen: Walter Benjamin* (Frankfurt am Main: Suhrkamp, 2001); and Michael Wetzel, "Unter Sprachen—Unter Kulturen: Walter Benjamins 'Interlinearversion' des Übersetzens als Inframedialität," in *Medien in Medien*, ed. Claudia Liebrand and Irmela Schneider (Cologne: DuMont, 2002).

37 Derrida, *Tours de Babel*, 222.

38 Derrida, *Tours de Babel*, 205.

39 Derrida's concept of cosmopolitanism is further elaborated on in Sonja Neef, "Planetarische Ästhetik: Kosmopolitismus bei Jacques Derrida und Ingo Günther," in *Astroculture: Figurations of Cosmology in Media and Arts*, ed. Sonja Neef, Henry Sussman, and Dietrich Boschung (Munich: Fink, 2014), 143–4.

40 Gayatri Chakravorty Spivak, *Imperative zur Neuerfindung des Planeten / Imperatives to Re-Imagine the Planet* (Vienna: Passagen, 1999), 44.

41 Spivak, *Imperative zur Neuerfindung des Planeten*, 60.

42 Spivak, *Imperative zur Neuerfindung des Planeten*, 56.

43 Spivak, *Imperative zur Neuerfindung des Planeten*, 76.

2 Europe: Myth and Translation

1 An earlier version of this chapter appeared as "M/Othering Europe. Or: how Europe and Atlas are Balancing Hand in Hand on the Prime Meridian—she Carrying the Alphabet, he Shouldering the Globe they are Walking on," *Journal of Visual Culture* 6, no. 1 (2007).

2 Gayatri Chakravorty Spivak, "Translation as Culture," *Parallax* 6, no. 1 (2000): 14; publisher: Taylor & Francis, reprinted by permission of the publisher (Taylor & Francis Ltd, http://www.tandfonline.com).

3 Glissant, *Introduction*, 5.

4 Glissant, *Introduction*, 11.

5 Glissant, *Introduction*, 20.

6 Georg Wilhelm Friedrich Hegel, *Aesthetics: Lectures on Fine Arts*, vol. 2, trans. Thomas Malcolm Knox (Oxford: Clarendon Press, [1835] 1975), 1040. Compare Glissant, *Introduction*, 20-1.

7 Glissant, *Introduction*, 22, 26.

8 Literary formulations of Europe from early antiquity to the present are collected in Almut-Barbara Renger, ed., *Mythos Europa: Texte von Ovid bis Heiner Müller* (Leipzig: Reclam, 2003), while visual interpretations are in the exhibition catalogue by Siegfried Salzmann, ed., *Mythos Europa: Europa und der Stier im Zeitalter der industriellen Zivilisation* (Bonn: Arbeitskreis selbständiger Kulturinstitute e.V., 1988).

9 Derrida, *Tours de Babel*, 192.

10 Berger, "Europe," in *Paulys Real-Encyclopädie der Classischen Altertumswissenschaft*, vol. 6/I, ed. Georg Wissowa (Stuttgart: J. B. Metzler, 1907), col. 1287, 1298.

11 Wikipedia.org, "*Europe*," https://en.wikipedia.org/wiki/Europe#Name.

12 Berger, "Europe," col. 1287; cf. Van Dale, *Etymologisch Woordenboek*, 249.

13 Herodotus, *Histories*, ed. James Romm, trans. Pamela Mensch (Indianapolis: Hackett, 2014), 4.45. Whereas in German, the proper name "Europa" encompasses both mythological figure and continent, in English it is possible to distinguish between the two, as seen in this translation of Herodotus. Nevertheless, following the German, we have elected to refer to both the myth and continent by a single name: "Europe" (translator's note).

14 See Berger, "Europe"; cf. Winfried Bühler, *Die Europa des Moschos: Text, Übersetzung und Kommentar* (Wiesbaden: Steiner, 1960), 18–27.

15 For details, see Emile Benveniste, *Indo-European Language and Society*, trans. Elizabeth Palmer (Miami: University of Miami Press, [1969] 1973); Julia Kristeva, *Strangers to Ourselves*, trans. Leon S. Roudiez (New York: Columbia University Press, [1988] 1991), and the chapter therein "The Greeks Among Barbarian, Suppliants, and Metics," 41–64.

16 Bühler, *Die Europa des Moschos*, 17–19.

17 Gustav Schwab, *Die schönsten Sagen des klassischen Alterthums: Nach seinen Dichtern und Erzählern* (Gütersloh: Bertelsmann, [1877] 1974), 26–33; Eduard Mörike, *Werke und Briefe*, vol. 8.1: *Übersetzungen*, ed. Ulrich Hötzer (Stuttgart: Klett, 1976), 158–62.

18 Bühler, *Die Europa des Moschos*, preface.

19 Benjamin, "Task of the Translator," 260. Benjamin here complains about Hölderlin's translations of Sophocles.

20 Benjamin, "Task of the Translator," 259.

21 Bühler, *Die Europa des Moschos*, preface.

22 For the English translation by J. M. Edmonds used in this chapter (Moschos, "Europa," in *Greek Bucolic Poets*, trans. J. M. Edmonds. Cambridge, MA: Harvard University Press, 1912), it is remarkable how the translator imitates an old-fashioned language. In doing so, he obviously projects the otherness of antiquity onto another otherness: that of some faraway nostalgic English past (translator's note).

23 See Benjamin, "Task of the Translator," 253.

24 See Jacques Derrida, *Monolingualism of the Other or the Prosthesis of the Origin*, trans. Patrick Mensah (Stanford, CA: Stanford University Press, [1996] 1998), 22–3, 25.

25 Gayatri Chakravorty Spivak, *Outside in the Teaching Machine* (London: Routledge, 1993), 114.

26 Moschos, "Europa," vv. 102–7, 437.

27 Benjamin, "Task of the Translator," 257.

28 Herodotus, *Histories*, 5:58–9; cf. Harald Haarmann, *Universalgeschichte der Schrift* (Frankfurt am Main: Campus, 1991), 271.

29 Haarmann, *Universalgeschichte*, 284.

30 See Florian Coulmas, *Writing Systems of the World* (Oxford: Basil Blackwell, 1989), 141; Haarmann, *Universalgeschichte*, 278–82; Neef, *Imprint and Trace*, 9–13.

31 This strict classification of letters into two parallel writing systems is, of course, pseudo-mythographically exaggerated here. For a detailed investigation into the relationship between Phoenician and Semitic script, cf. Haarmann, *Universalgeschichte*, 278, 288. The development of the letter signs mentioned here is systematically discussed in Marc-Alain Ouaknin, *Mysteries of the Alphabet: The Origins of Writing*, trans. Josephine Bacon (New York: Abbeville Press, [1997] 1999), *Heh*, 158; *Vav*, 170; *Resh*, 299; *Ayin*, 264–7; *Peh*, 277–8; *Het*, 192.

32 Havelock, *Literate Revolution*. Havelock argues that only the writing of vowels in the new full alphabet made possible the disintegration of oral ways of thinking—based as they were on rhythm and repetition—and it also made possible an epistemic impetus in the direction of abstract, even arithmetic forms of thinking. For a cultural-critical account of this—diachronic as well as synchronic—chauvinistic claim, cf. footnote 15 in Chapter 1 of this book.

33 Klaus Zimmermann, "Eratosthenes' Chlamys-Shaped World: a Misunderstood Metaphor," in *The Hellenistic World: New Perspectives*, ed. Daniel Ogden (London: Duckworth; Swansea: Classical Press of Wales, 2002).

34 See Hans Treidler, "Europa," in *Der kleine Pauly: Lexikon der Antike*, ed. Konrad Ziegler and Walter Sontheimer (Munich: J. B. Metzler, 1979), 448–9.

35 Berger, "Europe," col. 1300, 21–43.

36 A striking panorama of the history of atlases from the early forms to those of satellite images can be found in the volume Hans Wolff, ed., *Vierhundert Jahre Mercator, vierhundert Jahre Atlas: "Die ganze Welt zwischen zwei Buchdeckeln." Eine Geschichte der Atlanten* (Weißenhorn: Anton H. Konrad Verlag, 1995).

37 Dava Sobel and William J. H. Andrewes, *The Illustrated Longitude: The True Story of a Lone Genius Who Solved the Greatest Scientific Problem of His Time* (London: Walker, 1995), 3–4, 167–8.

38 Christine Buci-Glucksmann, "Der kartographische Blick der Kunst. Beschreibung und Allegorie," in *Atlas Mapping: Künstler als Kartographen. Kartographie als Kunst*, ed. Paolo Bianchi and Sabine Folie (Vienna: Turia & Kant, 1997), 59.

39 Svetlana Alpers and Michael Baxandall, *Tiepolo and the Pictorial Intelligence* (New Haven, CT: Yale University Press, 1996).

40 Alpers and Baxandall, *Tiepolo*, 154.

41 Alpers and Baxandall, *Tiepolo*, 115–17. On the concept of a "pictorial intelligence" and on the claim of Alpers and Baxandall that Tiepolo's images are non-narrative, cf. Mieke Bal, "Preisgabe der Autorität oder Pläydoyer gegen den Begriff der Intention," in Mieke Bal, *Kulturanalyse*, ed. Thomas Fechner-Smarsly and Sonja Neef, trans. Joachim Schulte (Frankfurt am Main: Suhrkamp, 2002), 322–7.

42 Alpers and Baxandall, *Tiepolo*, 154.

43 Alpers and Baxandall, *Tiepolo*, 110.

44 Moschos, "Europa," vv. 8–15, 429.

45 Moschos, "Europa," vv. 24–26, 431.

46 Michael Wetzel, "Alienationen: Jacques Derridas Dekonstruktion der
    Muttersprache," in Jacques Derrida, *Die Einsprachigkeit des Anderen oder die
    ursprüngliche Prothese*, trans. Michael Wetzel (Munich: Fink, 2003), 147.

47 Derrida, *Monolingualism*.

48 Derrida, *Monolingualism*, 25.

49 Gen. 11.1–9.

50 Derrida, *Monolingualism*, 22.

51 Derrida, *Monolingualism*, 40.

52 Wetzel, "Alienationen," 154.

3 On the Shores of the *Cité nationale de l'histoire de l'immigration* in Paris

1   An earlier version of this chapter appeared as "À la plage du musée: la Cité nationale
    de l'histoire de l'immigration," trans. Cathérine Rogister, *Les Cahiers du GEPE* 3
    (2011), and "Au bord de la langue de la Cité nationale de l'histoire de l'immigration,"
    trans. Cathérine Rogister, *Multitudes* 46 (2011).

2   Sophie Wahnich, *L'impossible citoyen: L'étranger dans le discours de la Révolution
    française* (Paris: © Editions Albin Michel, 1997), 13. Translated and reproduced with
    kind permission of Editions Albin Michel, Paris.

3   Paul Valéry, "Présence de Paris," in Paul Valéry, *Œuvres complètes*, vol. 2, ed. Jean
    Hytier (Paris: Gallimard, [1937] 1960), 1012.

4   Michael Bakhtin, *Rabelais and his World*, trans. Helene Iswolsky (Bloomington:
    Indiana University Press, [1965] 1984), 17.

5   Cf. Mary Stevens, "Designing Diversity: The Visual Identity of the 'Cité nationale de
    l'histoire de l'immigration,'" *Eurodiv* 56 (2007).

6   Marie Treps, *Les mots voyageurs: Petite histoire du français venu d'ailleurs* (Paris:
    Seuil, 2003), 224.

7   For a discourse/analytical deconstruction of the "universal language" of the republic
    around 1798, cf. Wahnich, *L'impossible citoyen*; additionally, cf. Kristeva, *Strangers to
    Ourselves*, especially "On Foreigners and the Enlightenment" (127–68) and the
    discussion of Rousseau, in particular 174–6.

8   Derrida, *Monolingualism*, 2.

9   Derrida, *Monolingualism*, 23.

10 Michael Bakhtin, "Discourse in the Novel," in Michael Bakhtin, *The Dialogic
    Imagination: Four Essays*, ed. Michael Holquist, trans. Caryl Emerson and Michael
    Holquist (Austin and London: University of Texas Press, [1975] 1981), 314–15.
    Bakhtin's concept of heteroglossia refers to the voices in the polyphonic novel that

brings the voices of narrator, a fictive author, or one of the characters into relationship with one another.

11 Bakhtin, "Discourse in the Novel," 324–5.

12 Luce Irigaray, *This Sex Which Is Not One*, trans. Catherine Porter and Carolyn Burke (Ithaca, NY: Cornell University Press, [1977] 1985), 17.

13 On the history of the Parisian "hemispheres," cf. Maurice Agulhon, "Paris: Durchquerung von Ost nach West," in *Erinnerungsorte Frankreichs*, ed. Pierre Nora (Munich: C. H. Beck, 2005).

14 Guy Le Hallé, *Histoire des fortifications de Paris et leur extension en Ile-de-France* (Lyon: Horvath, 1995), 266–75.

15 Eugène Atget, "Zonier de Paris," in *Paris: Eugène Atget (1857–1927)*, ed. Hans Christian Adam (Cologne: Taschen, 2000), 194–9.

16 Maureen Murphy, *Un Palais pour une Cité: Du musée des colonies à la Cité nationale de l'histoire de l'immigration* (Paris: Réunion des musées nationaux, 2007), 27.

17 Such was the message on an advertisement for the world fair; compare Murphy, *Un Palais pour une Cité* , 92–3.

18 See Eric Deroo, *L'illusion coloniale* (Paris: Tallandier, 2005), 104–45; cf. Dominique Taffin, "Les avatars du musée des arts d'Afrique et d'Oceanie," in *Le palais des colonies: Histoire du musée des arts d'Afrique et d'Océanie*, ed. Dominique François (Paris: Réunion des musées nationaux, 2002), 184–6.

19 Dominique Jarrasse, "Le décor du palais des colonies," in *Le palais des colonies: Histoire du musée des arts d'Afrique et d'Océanie*, ed. Dominique François (Paris: Réunion des musées nationaux, 2002), 88–90.

20 Jarrasse, "Le décor du palais des colonies," 104–10.

21 Jacques Toubon, "Editorial: Changer le regard contemporain sur l'immigration," in *Ouverture de la Cité nationale de l'histoire de'l immigration* (exhibition brochure) (Paris: CNHI, 2007), 4.

22 Mieke Bal, *Double Exposures: The Subject of Cultural Analysis* (New York: Routledge, 1996), 3–4.

23 On the double ground of museum authenticity, cf. my analysis of the exposition strategies of the Anne Frank museum in Neef, *Imprint and Trace*, 191–235, in particular 196–205, 211–14, 225–35.

24 https://www.ina.fr/video/I04082365.

25 The museum devotes a further installation to the migrant bag in the section *Nouveaux objets, nouvelles pratiques* (New objects, new practices).

26 See the volume by Olivier Jobard and Florence Saugues, *Kingsley, carnet de route d'un immigrant clandestin* (Paris: Édititons Marval, 2006), 104, 108–9.

27 Jacques Chirac, "Retrouvez l'intégralité du discours de Jacques Chirac prononcé le 30 janvier 2006 lors d'une réception en l'honneur du Comité pour la mémoire de l'esclavage au Palais de l'Elysée." https://www.lefigaro.fr/politique/le-scan/2014/03/

27/25001-20140327ARTFIG00102-le-discours-de-jacques-chirac-sur-l-esclavage.php.

28 Chirac's suggestion drew a flood of criticism, because the May 10 memorial day recalls less the injustice of slavery and instead foregrounds the justice of the republic that on May 10, 2001, per senate resolution, declared slavery a crime against humanity.

29 http://www.frontex.europa.eu.

30 See Joseph Hanimann, "Unerwünscht. Ungeliebt: Die *Cité de l'immigration* in Paris öffnet ihr Museum," *Frankfurter Allgemeine Zeitung*, October 12, 2007, 43.

31 Chirac, "Retrouvez."

32 Toubon, "Editorial."

33 Jacques Derrida, *Of Hospitality: Anne Dufourmantelle Invites Jacques Derrida to Respond*, trans. Rachel Bowlby (Stanford, CA: Stanford University Press, [1997] 2000), 23.

34 See Mireille Rosello, *Postcolonial Hospitality: The Immigrant as Guest* (Stanford, CA: Stanford University Press, 2001), 2.

35 Glissant, *Introduction*, 5.

36 Derrida, *Hospitality*, 15.

37 Cited in Wahnich, *L'impossible citoyen*, 10; see also 23–5.

38 Derrida, *Monolingualism*, 2.

39 Glissant, *Introduction*, 12.

4 *Outre Mèr(e)*: Jacques Derrida and the Mediterranean

1 An earlier English version of this chapter appeared as "Outre mèr(e): Jacques Derrida and the Language of the M/Other," in *(M)Other Tongues: Literary Reflexions on a Difficult Distinction*, ed. Juliane Prade (Newcastle upon Tyne: Cambridge Scholars, 2013).

2 Here one could certainly add another chapter on Derrida and the Atlantic, given how decisively North American relations shaped his academic career.

3 Jacques Derrida, *The Other Heading: Reflections on Today's Europe*, trans. Pascale-Anne Brault and Michael B. Naas (Bloomington: Indiana University Press, [1991] 1992), 120. Derrida here cites Paul Valéry, "Fonction de Paris," in Paul Valéry, *Œuvres completes*, vol. 1, ed. Jean Hytier (Paris: Gallimard, [1927] 1960), 1008.

4 Derrida, *Other Heading*, 120.

5 Compare with Judith Butler, Ernesto Laclau, and Slavoj Žižek, *Contingency, Hegemony, Universality* (London: Verso, 2000); and also Spivak, *Imperatives*.

6 Derrida, *Other Heading*, 15.

7 Compare with Karl-Wilhelm Welwei, *Die griechische Polis* (Stuttgart: Steiner, 1998), 15. I thank Eva Koczizsky for the critical discussion of the historical aspects of this chapter.

8   See Geoffrey Bennington and Jacques Derrida, *Jacques Derrida*, trans. Geoffrey Bennington (Chicago and London: University of Chicago Press, 1993), 5.

9   Bennington and Derrida, *Jacques Derrida*, 19.

10 Again and again, Derrida made the latent absence of the mother philosophically "fruitful": to a certain extent, it became a breeding ground for his concept of *différance*. In another context, Rousseau's mother made this absence uncannily renowned; in *Of Grammatology*, trans. Gayatri Chakravorty Spivak (Baltimore, MD: Johns Hopkins University Press, [1967] 1976), Jacques Derrida situates her death at the beginning of a "chain of supplements." To briefly recall, Rousseau's mother died after childbirth and was replaced by Madame de Warren, who first became a surrogate mother and later a lover. Her unavailability, in turn, was substituted by onanism, a "dangerous supplement," and then by countless fetishes. Derrida only overlooks Thérèse, the unknown Parisian laundress and the mother of five illegitimate children with Rousseau; at the most, he mentions her in passing, while her children, who grew up in a foundling hospital, remain nameless. This seems to be their contribution to Derrida's conception of difference: not calling them by name and certainly not by the paternal name.

11 Bennington and Derrida, *Jacques Derrida*, 5.

12 Yōko Tawada, *Überseezungen* (Tübingen: Konkursbuchverlag, 2002). The title of the book is a pun. The neologism *Überseezungen* is a compound from *Übersee*, "overseas," and *Zungen*, "tongues." Phonetically, it resembles the lexicalized word *Übersetzungen*, "translations."

13 Tawada, *Überseezungen*, 101.

14 Bennington and Derrida, *Jacques Derrida*, 129–30.

15 On the politics of writing direction, cf. Neef, *Imprint and Trace*, 66–71, 144–7.

16 Derrida, *Monolingualism*, 44.

17 Derrida, *Monolingualism*, 33

18 Derrida, *Monolingualism*, 1.

19 Derrida, *Monolingualism*, 42.

20 Derrida, *Monolingualism*, 37–8. Algerian women still occupy a special position in this school system; cf. the report by Sid Ahmed Dendane, school inspector in colonial Algeria, on "le souvernir de l'univers féminin" (54–6) and "l'artinasat masculin" (65–7), in Sid Ahmed Dendane, *Algerie intérieure: De 1936 à 1996* (Algiers: ENAG, 2008).

21 Derrida, *Monolingualism*, 37.

22 Derrida, *Monolingualism*, 37; for the echo from Walter Benjamin's artwork essay, see Neef, *Imprint and Trace*, 153–7.

23 Régine Robin, "Autobiographie et judéité chez Jacques Derrida," *Études françaises* 38, no. 1–2 (2002): 207–18.

24 Derrida, *Monolingualism*, 14.

25 Derrida, *Monolingualism*, 16.

26 Derrida, *Monolingualism*, 16.

27 Derrida, *Monolingualism*, 15–16.

28 Derrida, *Monolingualism*, 1.

29 Derrida, *Monolingualism*, 34.

30 Derrida, *Monolingualism*, 28.

31 Derrida, *Monolingualism*, 2.

32 Derrida, *Monolingualism*, 37.

33 Derrida, *Monolingualism*, 37.

34 Sigmund Freud, "The Uncanny" [1919], in *The Standard Edition of the Complete Psychological Works of Sigmund Freud*, vol. 17, trans. James Strachey et al. (London: Hogarth Press, 1971), 220; cf. Kristeva, *Strangers*, 183.

35 Spivak, "Translation," 14–15.

36 Spivak, "Translation," 15.

5 The Southern Cross: The Planetarism of Alexander von Humboldt and François Arago

1 Dante, "Purgatorio," Canto I, 28–34, in Dante Alighieri, *The Divine Comedy. In three volumes, Vol. II.—Purgatory*, trans. Charles Eliot Norton (Cambridge: Riverside Press, [1472] 1892), 2. Georg Peter Landmann explicates this passage in his German Dante edition as follows: "Dante imagined the southern hemisphere, where Purgatory Mountain rises up, to be uninhabited; only Adam and Eve could have seen these four stars. Did Dante have knowledge of the Southern Cross, perhaps through Marco Polo? It is possible; more important is the allegorical significance: the four stars are the four Pagan cardinal virtues: Justice, Prudence, Fortitude, and Temperance." Dante, *Divina Commedia*, trans. Georg Peter Landmann (Würzburg: Königshausen und Neumann, [1472] 1997), 104.

2 Louis Sala-Molins, *Le Code Noir ou le calvaire de Canaan* (Paris: Presses Universitaires de France, 1987), ix–x; more detailed 221–61.

3 See François Arago, *History of My Youth: An Autobiography*, trans. W. H. Smyth, Baden Powell, and Robert Grant (Boston: Ticknor and Fields, 1859), 8–14.

4 Theresa Levitt, "'I thought this might be of interest . . .': The Observatory as Public Enterprise," in *The Heavens of Earth: Observatories and Astronomy in Nineteenth-Century Science and Culture*, ed. David Aubin, Charlotte Bigg, and H. Otto Sibum (Durham, NC: Duke University Press, 2010), 300–2.

5 Arago, *History*, 18–40.

6 Arago, *History*, 43–90. Douglas Botting provides a distorted version of Arago's autobiography in *Alexander von Humboldt: Biographie eines großen*

Forschungsreisenden (Munich: Prestel, 2001), 230. "He [Arago] starved for two years in a dungeon, before he was transferred to a concentration camp in Algeria."

7   See Alexander von Humboldt, "Einleitung," in Franz Arago, *Sämmtliche Werke*, vol. 1, ed. W. G. Hankel (Leipzig: Otto Wigand, 1854), 4; vii–xxi.

8   See Levitt, *Observatory*, 289–300.

9   On the encounter of Arago and Hugo in 1834, cf. Sonja Neef and Henry Sussman, "The Glorious Moment of Astroculture: Introduction," in Neef, Sussman, and Boschung, eds., *Astroculture*, 9–12.

10 Neef, Sussman, and Boschung, eds., *Astroculture*, 287–8; cf. Petra Werner, *Himmel und Erde: Alexander von Humboldt und sein Kosmos* (Berlin: Akademie Verlag, 2004), 130.

11 See letter from Humboldt to Arago on May 16, 1845; cf. Werner, *Himmel und Erde*, 127, 130.

12 Arago, *History*, 77; compare with Humboldt, "Einleitung," III; cf. also Werner, *Himmel und Erde*, 124–5.

13 See Alexander von Humboldt and François Arago, *Correspondance d'Alexandre de Humboldt avec François Arago (1809–1853)*, ed. Ernest-Théodore Hamy (Paris: Guilmoto, 1907).

14 Werner, *Himmel und Erde*, 125–8.

15 Humboldt, "Einleitung," xxii.

16 Werner, *Himmel und Erde*, 127, 134.

17 See Ottmar Ette, *Alexander von Humboldt und die Globalisierung: Das Mobile des Wissens* (Frankfurt am Main: Insel, 2009), 403–4.

18 Ette, *Humboldt*, 14, 16.

19 For a textual genesis perspective, cf. Werner, *Himmel und Erde*, 28–31; in debate with Arago, Humboldt mentioned "Physique du monde" as a working title (30).

20 For example, in the three-volume monumental work by Hans Blumenberg, *The Genesis of the Copernican World*, trans. Robert M. Wallace (Cambridge, MA: MIT Press, [1975] 1987). In reference to the telescope as a medium of epistemic change, cf. also Hans Blumenberg, "Das Fernrohr und die Ohnmacht der Wahrheit," in Galileo Galilei, *Sidereus Nuncius*, ed. Hans Blumenberg (Frankfurt am Main: Insel, 1965).

21 See Alexandre Koyré, *Von der geschlossenen Welt zum unendlichen Universum*, trans. Rolf Dornbacher (Frankfurt am Main: Suhrkamp, 1969), 2.

22 See David Aubin, Charlotte Bigg, and H. Otto Sibum, "Introduction: Observatory Techniques in Nineteenth-Century Science and Society," in Aubin, Bigg, and Sibum, eds., *Heavens of Earth*, 1–3.

23 Peter Sloterdijk, *In the World Interior of Capital*, trans. Wieland Hoban (Cambridge: Polity Press, [2005] 2013), 22.

24 Sloterdijk, *In the World Interior of Capital*, 22.

25 Two prominent German editions of Alexander von Humboldt's travel report coexist today: *Die Forschungsreise in den Tropen Amerikas*, 3 vols., ed. Hanno Beck (Darmstadt: Wissenschaftliche Buchgesellschaft, [1807–34] 1987–97); and *Reise in die Äquinoktial-Gegenden des neuen Kontinents*, 2 vols., ed. Ottmar Ette (Frankfurt am Main: Insel, [1807–34] 1991–9). Here and in the following, page references are given to the Insel edition, which follows the abridged version, *Reise in die Aequinoktial-Gegenden des neuen Kontinents*, 4 vols., ed. Hermann Hauff (Stuttgart: J. G. Cotta, [1807–34] 1859–60). In contrast, the Darmstadt edition contains two further chapters and breaks off equally abruptly. For a comparison of the different editions, cf. Hanno Beck, "Zu dieser Ausgabe des amerikanischen Reiseberichts," in Alexander von Humboldt, *Die Forschungsreise in den Tropen Amerikas*, vol. 3, ed. Hanno Beck (Darmstadt: Wissenschaftliche Buchgesellschaft, 1997), especially 387–96. The English references are taken from the English translation: Alexander de Humboldt, *Personal Narrative of Travels to the Equinoctial Regions of the New Continent, During the Years 1799–1804*, 7 vols., trans. Helen Maria Williams (London: Longman, Hurst, Rees, Orme, and Brown, [1807–34] 1814–29).

26 Humboldt, *Personal Narrative*, vol. 6 (1826), 845.

27 See Ette, *Humboldt*, 403–4.

28 Cited after Alexandre de Humboldt, *Correspondance scientifique et litteraire*, vol. 1, ed. J. B. de la Roquette (Paris: E. Ducrocq, 1865), xxxv. The reprimand referred to Humboldt's *Examin critique*, which likewise was dedicated to Arago, a component of the American travel work.

29 Ette, *Humboldt*, 404–5.

30 Compare Ernest-Théodore Hamy, "Préface," in Humboldt and Arago, *Correspondance*. The French edition is accessible in the digital library Gallica of the Bibliothèque Nationale de France. Compare relatedly Botting, *Humboldt*, 224–35; Ottmar Ette, "Der Blick auf die neue Welt," in Humboldt, *Äquinoktial-Gegenden*, 1565–6.

31 See Ette, "Blick," 1565; Botting, *Humboldt*, 236–7.

32 For a survey of the history of the translations and their publication, see, for example, Beck, "Ausgabe," 371–93; and also Ottmar Ette, "Zu dieser Ausgabe," in Humboldt, *Äquinoktial-Gegenden*.

33 Humboldt, *Personal Narrative*, vol. 2 (1814), 2.

34 Humboldt, *Personal Narrative*, vol. 2 (1814), 19.

35 Humboldt, *Personal Narrative*, vol. 2 (1814), 371.

36 Dante, *Purgatorio*, Canto I, 23–4.

37 Humboldt, *Personal Narrative*, vol. 2 (1814), 371–2.

38 Butler, Laclau, and Žižek, *Contingency*, 137.

39 Humboldt, *Personal Narrative*, vol. 2 (1814), 232.

40 Humboldt, *Personal Narrative*, vol. 2 (1814), 233.

41 Humboldt, *Personal Narrative*, vol. 2 (1814), 233–4.

42 Humboldt, *Personal Narrative*, vol. 2 (1814), 236.

43 Humboldt, *Personal Narrative*, vol. 2 (1814), 236.

44 Humboldt, *Personal Narrative*, vol. 2 (1814), 237. Humboldt writes about the phenomenon of twinkling stars, a theory of Arago's: "I remember with pride that excerpts from this beautiful theory of the scintillation of stars were first, in the year 1814, made known in the fourth book of my work 'Voyage aux regions équinoxiales du nouveau continent.' This treatise itself [...] is one of the crowning adornments in this collection of the works of my renowned friend. Other excerpts, touching on the same object, but borrowed from newer manuscripts from 1847, are gathered in the astronomic parts of *Kosmos*." Humboldt, "Einleitung," ix.

45 Sibylle Krämer, "Kann das 'geistige Auge' sehen? Visualisierung und die Konstitution epistemischer Gegenstände," in *Mit dem Auge denken. Strategien der Sichtbarmachung in wissenschaftlichen und virtuellen Welten*, ed. Bettina Heintz and Jörg Huber (Zurich: Edition Voldemeer; New York: Springer, 2001), 349.

46 Humboldt, *Personal Narrative*, vol. 2 (1814), 235.

47 Humboldt, *Personal Narrative*, vol. 2 (1814), 238–9.

48 Michael Zeuske makes an important differentiation with reference to Humboldt's "Political Essay on the Island of Cuba": "Humboldt was a reformer and advocated, despite fiery accusation, not the immediate abolishment of slavery, but instead to override the local elites through 'philanthropic legislation and wise institutions' and moreover 'soon' and with 'vigorous measures' [Alexander von Humboldt, *Cuba-Werk*, ed. Hanno Beck (Darmstadt: Wissenschaftliche Buchgesellschaft, [1829] 1992), 179]. If his denunciations show him to be an enlightened advocate of natural law, in his analysis and prognosis he showed himself to be a positivist historicist, a 'good student' of the German Historical School. For the reforms recognized to be necessary, he wagered on existing institutions rather than revolutionary rupture of these very interests and structures." Michael Zeuske, "Humboldt, Historismus, Humboldteanisierung: Der 'Geschichtsschreiber von Amerika,' die Massensklaverei und die Globalisierungen der Welt," *Alexander von Humboldt im Netz* 3, no. 4 (2002). See also Michael Zeuske, *Schwarze Karibik: Sklaven, Sklavereikulturen und Emanzipation* (Zurich: Rotpunktverlag, 2004).

49 Werner, *Himmel und Erde*, 124–36.

50 See Aubin, Bigg, and Sibum, "Introduction," 7.

51 Thomas Assheuer, "Die Erdflüchtlinge," *Die Zeit*, July 16, 2009, 40.

6 Sublunar: Star Friendship in Orhan Pamuk's *The White Castle*

1 Orhan Pamuk, *The White Castle*, trans. Victoria Holbrook (New York: Vintage Books, [1985] 1998), 13–14.

2 Pamuk, *White Castle*, 15.
3 Pamuk, *White Castle*, 21–2.
4 Hans Blumenberg, *Die Vollzähligkeit der Sterne* (Frankfurt am Main: Suhrkamp, 1997), 27.
5 Blumenberg, *Die Vollzähligkeit der Sterne*, 27.
6 Blumenberg, *Die Vollzähligkeit der Sterne*, 35.
7 See Blumenberg, *Die Vollzähligkeit der Sterne*, 34.
8 Blumenberg, *Die Vollzähligkeit der Sterne*, 361, 315, 23–35.
9 Pamuk, *White Castle*, 26.
10 Pamuk, *White Castle*, 8.
11 Pamuk, *White Castle*, 25–6.
12 Pamuk, *White Castle*, 24.
13 Pamuk, *White Castle*, 34.
14 Pamuk, *White Castle*, 33.
15 Pamuk, *White Castle*, 34.
16 Pamuk, *White Castle*, 25.
17 Pamuk, *White Castle*, 58.
18 Pamuk, *White Castle*, 60.
19 Pamuk, *White Castle*, 62.
20 Pamuk, *White Castle*, 69.
21 Pamuk, *White Castle*, 81–82.
22 Friedrich Nietzsche, "Star Friendship," in Friedrich Nietzsche, *The Gay Science*, ed. and trans. Walter Kaufmann (New York: Vintage Books, [1882] 1974), 225–6.
23 Jacques Derrida, *Politics of Friendship*, trans. George Collins (London: Verso, [1994] 1997).

7 In Earth Orbit: Constellation "Suitcase." Planetary Aesthetics in William Kentridge's *Felix in Exile*

1 Other versions of this chapter, with varying focal points, have been published as "The horizon to come: Planetary aesthetics in William Kentridge's *Felix in Exile* and Galileo Galilei's moon drawings," in *On not Looking: The Paradox of Contemporary Visual Culture*, ed. Frances Guerin (New York: Routledge, 2015); and "'Video-Graphie' und die Ästhetik der Apartheid," *Rheinsprung* 11 (2012).
2 Bertolt Brecht, *Life of Galileo*, ed. John Willett and Ralph Manheim, trans. John Willett (London: Bloomsbury, [1939] 1995), 25: As is well known, Brecht is referring to Giordano Bruno as "the man they burned."
3 In 1993 and 2005, Kentridge took part in the Venice Biennale; in 1997 and 2002 in the documenta.

4   See, for example, Sue Williamson and Ashraf Jamal, *Art in South Africa: The Future Present* (Cape Town: David Phillip, 1996); Judith Hecker, *William Kentridge: Trace* (New York: Museum of Modern Art, 2010), 9–15.

5   Martin Heidegger, *Parmenides*, trans. André Schuwer and Richard Roicewicz (Bloomington: Indiana University Press, [1943] 1992), 82.

6   See Jacques Derrida, "Racism's Last Word," in Jacques Derrida, *Psyche: Inventions of the Other*, vol. 1, ed. Peggy Kamuf and Elizabeth Rottenberg (Stanford, CA: Stanford University Press, [1987] 2007), 377. Derrida wrote his essay for the opening of the exhibition of artworks of the association of "Artists of the World Against Apartheid" in November 1983 in Paris at the Rothschild Foundation. There were no works by William Kentridge included in this collection.

7   See Staci Boris, "The Process of Change: Landscape, Memory, Animation, and *Felix in Exile*," in *William Kentridge: Exhibition catalogue*, ed. Neal Benezra, Staci Boris, and Dan Cameron (Chicago: Museum of Contemporary Art; New York: New Museum of Contemporary Art, 2001).

8   For a detailed analysis of the relation of "imprint" and "trace," the first related to the art theory of Georges Didi-Huberman, the second to the work of Jacques Derrida; cf. Neef, *Imprint and Trace*.

9   Rosalind Krauss, "'The Rock': William Kentridge's *Drawings for Projection*," *October* 92 (2000). For the concepts of "substance" and "expression," Krauss refers to Louis Hjelmslev's structuralist system.

10 Mieke Bal, "Heterochrony in the Act: The Migratory Politics of Time," in Bal and Hernandez-Navarro, eds., *Art and Visibility*, 224.

11 Bal, "Heterochrony in the Act," 224.

12 Glissant, *Introduction*, 12.

13 Not coincidentally, in 2003 Kentridge dedicated to *Méliès* his series *Seven Fragments for Georges Méliès*, which contained among others the animated film *Journey to the Moon*.

14 Derrida, "Racism," 378.

15 Cf. also Neef and Sussman, "Glorious Moment," 12–15.

16 Horst Bredekamp, "Gazing Hands and Blind Spots: Galileo as Draughtsman," in *Galileo in Context*, ed. Jürgen Renn (Cambridge: Cambridge University Press, 2002); Samuel Y. Edgerton Jr., "Galileo, Florentine 'Disegno,' and the 'Strange Spottedness' of the Moon," *Art Journal* 44 (1984).

17 Horst Bredekamp, Birgit Schneider, and Vera Dünkel, "Editorial: Das technische Bild," in *Das Technische Bild: Kompendium zu einer Stilgeschichte wissenschaftlicher Bilder*, ed. Horst Bredekamp, Birgit Schneider, and Vera Dünkel (Berlin: Akademie Verlag, 2008).

18 Immanuel Kant, "Perpetual Peace: A Philosophical Sketch," in Immanuel Kant, *Perpetual Peace and Other Essays on Politics, History, and Morals*, trans. Ted Humphrey (Indianapolis and Cambridge: Hackett [1795] 1983), 118.

19 Blumenberg, "Fernrohr," 12–19.

20 Blumenberg, "Fernrohr," 22.

21 Blumenberg, "Fernrohr," 20.

22 Spivak, *Imperative*, 46.

23 Compare with note 6 above.

24 Derrida, *Grammatology*, 150.

25 Derrida, *Grammatology*, 153.

26 Édouard Glissant, *Poetics of Relation*, trans. Betsy Wing (Ann Arbor: University of Michigan Press, [1990] 1997), 195.

27 Glissant, *Poetics of Relation*, 195.

8 Intergalactic: Universal Translation. Immanuel Kant, the Spaceship *Enterprise*, and the Circulation of the Planets

1   Blumenberg, *Vollzähligkeit*, 547–9. In the last chapter of this book, Blumenberg sketches the object of astronoetics, in an ironically modest gesture, as "exploration of the dark side of the moon through pure thought" (that is, in the absence of satellites), and he describes its methods as "orbiting around the concept of theory following an instrumental blackout and the dissipation of the spectacular" (Blumenberg, *Vollzähligkeit*, 548). In truth, Blumenberg produces, with his astronoetic glosses, an effective procedure for the critical analysis of Western astrocultural thought. Cf. further Neef, Sussman, and Boschung, eds., *Astroculture*.

2   Michel Foucault, "The Confession of the Flesh" [1977], in Michel Foucault, *Power/ Knowledge: Selected Interviews and Other Writings 1972–1977*, ed. and trans. Colin Gordon (New York: Pantheon Books, 1980), 195.

3   *Star Trek Enterprise*, 5th Generation, narrated time 2151–2155, 2161; "Demons," Season 4, Episode 096, 02:14–04:31. Directed by LeVar Burton, written by Manny Coto. © Paramount Pictures 2005.

4   Cf. Neef, "Planetarische Ästhetik," 151–4.

5   Volker Gerhardt, *Immanuel Kants Entwurf "Zum ewigen Frieden": Eine Theorie der Politik* (Darmstadt: Wissenschaftliche Buchgesellschaft, 1995).

6   Kant, "Perpetual Peace," 117.

7   Kant, "Perpetual Peace," 119.

8   Kant, "Perpetual Peace," 118.

9   Kant, "Perpetual Peace," 118.

10 Immanuel Kant, "Idea for a Universal History with a Cosmopolitan Intent," in Kant, *Perpetual Peace*, 38.

11 Kant, "Idea for a Universal History," 37.

12 Kant, "Idea for a Universal History," 36. See Kristeva, *Strangers*, 171.

13 Kant, "Perpetual Peace," 120.

14 Immanuel Kant, "Universal Natural History and Theory Of The Heavens" [1755], trans. Olaf Reinhardt, in Immanuel Kant, *Natural Science*, ed. Eric Watkins (Cambridge: Cambridge University Press, 2012). See also Fritz Krafft, "Wissenschaftshistorische Einführung in Kants Kosmogonie," in Immanuel Kant, *Allgemeine Naturgeschichte und Theorie des Himmels*, ed. Fritz Krafft (Munich: Kindler, 1971).

15 This technical process of simultaneous translation had its own baptism of fire at the Nuremburg Trials. For a critical demolition of the utopia of a "pure language of law," cf. Cornelia Vismann, "Sprachbrüche im Nürnberger Kriegsverbrecherprozess," in *Rechenschaften. Juristischer und literarischer Diskurs in der Auseinandersetzung mit den NS-Massenverbrechen*, ed. Stephan Braese (Göttingen: Wallstein, 2004); on the technical history of simultaneous translation, cf. 49–51.

16 Acts 2.1–13.

17 See Sonja Neef, "Interstellar Hospitality: Missions of Star House Enterprise," in Bal and Hernandez-Navarro, eds., *Art and Visibility*, 288–93.

18 This is in opposition to the model of monolingualism that Derrida formulates as the monolingualism that "would always have preceded me" as "the language of the other," from which language comes and to which it returns; Derrida, *Monolingualism*, 1, 42. For Derrida (as for Heidegger), language remains "unassimilable": "my 'own' language is, for me, a language that cannot be assimilated. My language, the only one I hear myself speak and agree to speak, is the language of the other." Derrida, *Monolingualism*, 25–6.

19 On the differentiation of two types of gaze, namely "glance" (the fleeting but communicative gaze) and "gaze" (the contemplative but also penetrating, fixating, and even colonizing and voyeuristic gaze), cf. Norman Bryson, *Vision and Painting: The Logic of the Gaze* (New Haven, CT: Yale University Press, 1987), 87–9; as well as its further elaborations in feminist film theory.

20 Star Trek Enterprise, "The Council," Season 3, Episode 074, 14:00–17:32. Directed by David Livingston, written by Manny Coto. © Paramount Pictures 2004.

21 For an analysis, informed by Benjamin's translation essay, of the visual dialectic of this image, cf. Joanne Morra, "Utopia Lost: Allegory, Ruins and Pieter Bruegel's *Towers of Babel*," *Art History* 30, no. 2 (2007).

22 Gen. 11.1–9.

23 Borst, *Turmbau*, 79. Compare Derrida, "Tours de Babel."

24 Kant, "Universal Natural History," 307.

25 Derrida, *Hospitality*, 53.

26 Derrida, *Hospitality*, 25.

27 On the untranslatability of the proper name, cf. Derrida, "Tours de Babel," 197; and the section "BBL" in chapter 1 of this book.

9 Heaven on Earth: Paul, a Cosmopolitan?

1   An earlier version of this chapter appeared as "Badiou von Rabat über Paulus von
    Tarsus: Universalismus, Kosmopolitanismus und das Denken des Planetarischen," in
    Treue zur Wahrheit. Die Begründung der Philosophie Alain Badious, ed. Jens Kipp
    and Frank Meier (Münster, Unrast, 2010).

2   Alain Badiou, *Saint Paul: The Foundation of Universalism*, trans. Ray Brassier (Palo
    Alto, CA: Stanford University Press, [1997] 2003), 3.

3   Badiou, *Saint Paul*, 69–73.

4   Badiou, *Saint Paul*, 6.

5   Badiou, *Saint Paul*, 6.

6   See Dominik Finkelde, *Politische Eschatologie nach Paulus: Badiou—Agamben—
    Žižek—Santner* (Vienna: Turia & Kant, 2009), 12–13. Finkelde differentiates between
    an interpretive tradition of "difference-philosophy, alterity, and deconstruction," to
    which Agamben and Santner stand in close proximity, and an allegedly "new"
    interpretive tradition in Badiou and Žižek. There is no direct Badiou-Derrida
    debate. The present contribution can be assessed to a certain extent as an attempt to
    simulate such a debate. Antonia Calcagno has undertaken a similar comparison in
    Badiou and Derrida: Politics, Events and their Time (London: Continuum, 2007). In
    contrast to me, Calcagno settles the question of who pushes the question of the
    aporia further in favor of Badiou.

7   Badiou, *Saint Paul*, 2.

8   Badiou, *Saint Paul*, 63.

9   Badiou, *Saint Paul*, 4.

10 Badiou, *Saint Paul*, 6.

11 Badiou, *Saint Paul*, 6.

12 Badiou, *Saint Paul*, 7. For the explosive material that can reside in small numbers in
    a society fixated on normativity, cf. Arjun Appadurai, *Fear of Small Numbers: An
    Essay on the Geography of Anger* (Durham, NC: Duke University Press, 2006), 8–11.

13 Badiou, *Saint Paul*, 6.

14 Badiou, *Saint Paul*, 40–1.

15 Badiou, *Saint Paul*, 42.

16 Badiou, *Saint Paul*, 58.

17 Badiou, *Saint Paul*, 58.

18 Badiou, *Saint Paul*, 41.

19 Badiou, *Saint Paul*, 64.

20 Badiou, *Saint Paul*, 45.

21 Badiou, *Saint Paul*, 42.

22 Badiou, *Saint Paul*, 60–1. Badiou here cites Friedrich Nietzsche, *The Antichrist*, trans.
    Henry Louis Mencken (New York: Cosimo, [1895] 2005), § 42.

23 Badiou, *Saint Paul*, 57, 64.

24 Badiou, *Saint Paul*, 58.

25 See John L. Austin, *How To Do Things With Words* (Oxford: Clarendon Press, 1962), 21–2; as well as Derrida's critique of the inauthentic, so-called non-serious or "parasitic" speech acts, cf. Jacques Derrida, "Signature, Event, Context" [1972], in Jacques Derrida, *Limited Inc*, trans. Samuel Weber and Jeffrey Mehlman (Evanston, IL: Northwestern University Press, 1988), 16–17.

26 Derrida, *Limited Inc*, 7.

27 Derrida, *Limited Inc*, 14–20; cf. also Neef, *Imprint and* Trace, 149–53.

28 Badiou, *Saint Paul*, 22, 13, 11.

29 Badiou, *Saint Paul*, 11.

30 Badiou, *Saint Paul*, 40. Badiou uses Louis Segond, *Le nouveau testament* (London: Trinitarian Bible Society, 1993).

31 Badiou, *Saint Paul*, 40.

32 Badiou, *Saint Paul*, 40.

33 See Benveniste, *Indo-European*, 79; cited from Derrida, *Hospitality*, 21.

34 Cited after Kristeva, *Strangers*, 51. Kristeva discusses the concepts of hospitality and of caritas in Paul's time in 84–95.

35 Derrida, *Hospitality*, 21.

36 Badiou, *Saint Paul*, 58.

37 Badiou, *Saint Paul*, 59.

38 Badiou, *Saint Paul*, 59.

39 Badiou, *Saint Paul*, 59.

40 Badiou, *Saint Paul*, 6.

41 Acts 8.1–30; 22.3–21; 26.9–20.

42 See Jacques Derrida, "Otobiographies: the Teaching of Nietzsche and the Politics of the Proper Name," in Jacques Derrida, *The Ear of the Other*, ed. Christie McDonald, trans. Avital Ronell (Lincoln and London: University of Nebraska Press, [1982] 1985), 14–16.

43 Derrida, "Tours de Babel," 191, 222.

44 Benveniste, *Indo-European*, 79.

45 Derrida, *Hospitality*, 25. Derrida's engagement with Paul is for the most part in passing, and is most relevant for the current inquiry in Jacques Derrida, *Cosmopolites de tous les pays, encore un effort!* (Paris: Galilée, 1997). In *Reading Derrida / Thinking Paul: On Justice* (Stanford, CA: Stanford University Press, 2006), Theodore W. Jennings carefully brings together and analyzes those particular references.

46 Derrida, *Hospitality*, 25.

47 Badiou, *Saint Paul*, 21.

48 Compare the reading of Paul in Jacob Taubes, *Die politische Theologie des Paulus* (Munich: Fink, 1993), 36–8, which differentiates between the Torah, the law of the universe, and natural law.

49 Badiou, *Saint Paul*, 66

50 Derrida, *Hospitality*, 27–9.

51 Derrida, *Hospitality*, 25.

52 For the epistemic difference between the presentation of a "closed cosmos" in Ptolemaic astronomy and the post-Copernican "infinite universe" that, from an astronomical perspective, plays a decisive role here, cf. Koyré, *Welt*; as well as chapter 5 of this book, specifically the section "Humboldt's Cosmos."

53 The exegeses that the transcendence of Pauline theology open up are unending; cf., for example, Taubes, *Theologie*.

54 Badiou, *Saint Paul*, 48.

55 Badiou, *Saint Paul*, 17.

56 For the media-theoretic dimension of this large media-historical thesis, cf. Sibylle Krämer, "Karten—Kartenlesen—Kartographie: Kulturtechnisch inspirierte Überlegung," in *Bild/ Geschichte: Festschrift für Horst Bredekamp*, ed. Philine Helas et al. (Berlin: Akademie Verlag, 2003).

57 Blumenberg, *Vollzähligkeit*, 27.

58 Fabian Steinhauer, "Die Szene ist Rom," in *Römisch*, ed. Walter Seitter and Cornelia Vismann (Zurich: Diaphanes, 2006), 123–5.

59 Kant, "Perpetual Peace," 118.

60 Badiou, *Saint Paul*, 59. For a detailed discursive analysis of the "Universal Republic" of 1789, cf. Wahnich, *Citoyen*, 127–9, 163–5, 347–9.

61 See Judith Butler and Gayatri Chakravorty Spivak, *Who Sings the Nation-State? Language, Politics, Belonging* (Chicago: University of Chicago Press, 2007).

62 Spivak, *Imperative*, 68, 56.

63 Spivak, *Imperative*, 76.

64 Spivak, *Imperative*, 68.

65 Spivak, *Imperative*, 86.

66 Badiou, *Saint Paul*, 56.

10 Finally: East Pole and West Pole

1 Stiftung Entwicklung und Frieden, ed., *Globale Trends: Daten zur Weltentwicklung* (Bonn and Düsseldorf: Stiftung Entwicklung und Frieden, 1991), 19–37.

2 Glissant, *Introduction*, 11; cf. also Glissant, *Poetics*.

3 For this absurdly ingenious concept, I thank my daughter, Vera Neef. The invention of the West Pole and the East Pole would require that the principle of parallel, concentric full circles, which is fundamental for the graticule of latitude, would supersede the principle of half circles for longitude.

Afterword

1 "Vorwort," in Sonja Neef, *Der babylonische Planet: Kultur, Übersetzung, Dekonstruktion unter den Bedingungen der Globalisierung* (Heidelberg: Winter, 2020), 7.

2 Sonja Neef, "Was ist europäische Medienkultur? Oder wie Europa und Atlas Hand in Hand über den nullten Längengrad balancieren, sie Blumen pflückend, er den Globus schulternd," in *Europäische Medienwissenschaft: Zur Programmatik eines Fachs*, ed. Hedwig Wagner (Bielefeld: Transcript, 2020).

Bibliography

Agulhon, Maurice. "Paris. Durchquerung von Ost nach West," in *Erinnerungsorte Frankreichs*, edited by Pierre Nora, 517–41. Munich: C.H. Beck, 2005.

Alpers, Svetlana, and Michael Baxandall. *Tiepolo and the Pictorial Intelligence*. New Haven, CT: Yale University Press, 1996.

Appadurai, Arjun. *Modernity at Large: Cultural Dimensions of Globalization*. Minneapolis: University of Minnesota Press, 1996.

Appadurai, Arjun. *Fear of Small Numbers: An Essay on the Geography of Anger*. Durham, NC, and London: Duke University Press, 2006.

Arago, François. *History of My Youth: An Autobiography*, translated by W. H. Smyth, Baden Powell, and Robert Grant. Boston: Ticknor and Fields, 1859.

Assheuer, Thomas. "Die Erdflüchtlinge." *Die Zeit*, July 16, 2009, 40.

Assmann, Aleida, and Jan Assmann. "Einleitung. Schrift—Kognition—Evolution: Eric A. Havelock und die Technologie kultureller Kommunikation," in Eric A. Havelock, *Schriftlichkeit: Das griechische Alphabet und die kulturelle Revolution*, edited by Aleida and Jan Assmann, 1–35. Weinheim: VCH, 1990.

Atget, Eugène. "Zonier de Paris," in *Paris: Eugène Atget (1857–1927)*, edited by Hans Christian Adam. Cologne: Taschen, 2000.

Aubin, David, Charlotte Bigg, and H. Otto Sibum. "Introduction: Observatory Techniques in Nineteenth-Century Science and Society," in *The Heavens of Earth: Observatories and Astronomy in Nineteenth-Century Science and Culture*, edited by David Aubin, Charlotte Bigg, and H. Otto Sibum, 1–32. Durham, NC: Duke University Press, 2010.

Austin, John L. *How To Do Things With Words*. Oxford: Clarendon Press, 1962.

Badiou, Alain. *Saint Paul: The Foundation of Universalism*, translated by Ray Brassier. Palo Alto, CA: Stanford University Press, [1997] 2003.

Bakhtin, Michael. "Discourse in the Novel," in Michael Bakhtin, *The Dialogic Imagination: Four Essays*, edited by Michael Holquist, translated by Caryl Emerson and Michael Holquist, 259–422. Austin and London: University of Texas Press, [1975] 1981.

Bakhtin, Michael. *Rabelais and his World*, translated by Helene Iswolsky. Bloomington: Indiana University Press, [1965] 1984.

Bal, Mieke. *Double Exposures: The Subject of Cultural Analysis*. New York and London: Routledge, 1996.

Bal, Mieke. "Preisgabe der Autorität oder Pläydoyer gegen den Begriff der Intention," in Mieke Bal, *Kulturanalyse*, edited by Thomas Fechner-Smarsly and Sonja Neef, translated by Joachim Schulte, 295–334. Frankfurt am Main: Suhrkamp, 2002.

Bal, Mieke. "Heterochrony in the Act: The Migratory Politics of Time," in *Art and Visibility in Migratory Culture: Conflict, Resistance, and Agency*, edited by Mieke Bal and Miguel-Angel Hernandez-Navarro, 211–37. Amsterdam: Rodopi, 2011.

Beck, Hanno. "Zu dieser Ausgabe des amerikanischen Reiseberichts," in Alexander von Humboldt, *Die Forschungsreise in den Tropen Amerikas*, 3 vols., edited by Hanno Beck, vol. 3, 371–489. Darmstadt: Wissenschaftliche Buchgesellschaft, 1997.

Benjamin, Walter. "The Task of the Translator," in Walter Benjamin, *Selected Writings*, vol. 1: *1913–1926*, edited by Marcus Bullock and Michael W. Jennings, translated by Harry Zohn, 253–63. Cambridge, MA, and London: Belknap Press, [1923] 1996.

Bennington, Geoffrey, and Jacques Derrida. *Jacques Derrida*, translated by Geoffrey Bennington. Chicago and London: University of Chicago Press, 1993.

Benveniste, Emile. *Indo-European Language and Society*, translated by Elizabeth Palmer. Miami: University of Miami Press, [1969] 1973.

Berger, Hugo. "Europe," in *Paulys Real-Encyclopädie der Classischen Altertumswissenschaft*, vol. 6/I, edited by Georg Wissowa, col. 1298–1309. Stuttgart: J. B. Metzler, 1907.

Blume, Dieter. *Regenten des Himmels: Astrologische Bilder in Mittelalter und Renaissance*. Berlin: Akademie Verlag, 2000.

Blumenberg, Hans. "Das Fernrohr und die Ohnmacht der Wahrheit," in Galileo Galilei, *Sidereus Nuncius*, edited by Hans Blumenberg, 5–73. Frankfurt am Main: Insel, 1965.

Blumenberg, Hans. *The Genesis of the Copernican World*, translated by Robert M. Wallace. Cambridge, MA: MIT Press, [1975] 1987.

Blumenberg, Hans. *Die Vollzähligkeit der Sterne*. Frankfurt am Main: Suhrkamp, 1997.

Boris, Staci. "The Process of Change: Landscape, Memory, Animation, and *Felix in Exile*," in *William Kentridge: Exhibition catalogue*, edited by Neal Benezra, Staci Boris, and Dan Cameron, 28–37. Chicago: Museum of Contemporary Art; New York: New Museum of Contemporary Art, 2001.

Borst, Arno. *Der Turmbau von Babel: Geschichte der Meinungen über Ursprung und Vielfalt der Sprachen und Völker*. Munich: dtv, [1957] 1995.

Botting, Douglas. *Alexander von Humboldt: Biographie eines großen Forschungsreisenden*. Munich: Prestel, 2001.

Brecht, Bertolt. *Life of Galileo*, edited by John Willett and Ralph Manheim, translated by John Willett. London: Bloomsbury, [1939] 1995.

Bredekamp, Horst. "Gazing Hands and Blind Spots: Galileo as Draughtsman," in *Galileo in Context*, edited by Jürgen Renn, 153–92. Cambridge: Cambridge University Press, 2002.

Bredekamp, Horst, Birgit Schneider, and Vera Dünkel. "Editorial: Das technische Bild," in *Das Technische Bild: Kompendium zu einer Stilgeschichte wissenschaftlicher Bilder*, edited by Horst Bredekamp, Birgit Schneider, and Vera Dünkel, 8–13. Berlin: Akademie Verlag, 2008.

Bryson, Norman. *Vision and Painting: The Logic of the Gaze*. New Haven, CT: Yale University Press, 1987.

Buci-Glucksmann, Christine. "Der kartographische Blick der Kunst. Beschreibung und Allegorie," in *Atlas Mapping: Künstler als Kartographen. Kartographie als Kunst*, edited by Paolo Bianchi and Sabine Folie. Vienna: Turia & Kant, 1997.

Bühler, Winfried. *Die Europa des Moschos: Text, Übersetzung und Kommentar*. Wiesbaden: Steiner, 1960.

Bunbury, Edward Herbert. *A History of Ancient Geography among the Greeks and Romans from the Earliest Ages till the Fall of the Roman Empire*. London: John Murray, 1883.

Butler, Judith, Ernesto Laclau, and Slavoj Žižek. *Contingency, Hegemony, Universality*. London: Verso, 2000.

Butler, Judith, and Gayatri Chakravorty Spivak. *Who Sings the Nation-State? Language, Politics, Belonging*. Chicago: University of Chicago Press, 2007.

Calcagno, Antonia. *Badiou and Derrida: Politics, Events and their Time*. London: Continuum, 2007.

Castells, Manuel. *Local and Global: Management of Cities in the Information Age*. London: Earthscan, 1997.

Chirac, Jacques. "Retrouvez l'intégralité du discours de Jacques Chirac prononcé le 30 janvier 2006 lors d'une réception en l'honneur du Comité pour la mémoire de l'esclavage au Palais de l'Elysée." https://www.lefigaro.fr/politique/le-scan/2014/03/27/25001-20140327ARTFIG00102-le-discours-de-jacques-chirac-sur-l-esclavage.php.

Cooper, Jerrold S. "Sumerian and Accadian," in *The World's Writing Systems*, edited by Peter T. Daniels and William Bright, 37–57. New York: Oxford University Press, 1996.

Coulmas, Florian. *Writing Systems of the World*. Oxford: Basil Blackwell, 1989.

Dante. *Divina Commedia*, translated by Georg Peter Landmann. Würzburg: Königshausen und Neumann, [1472] 1997.

Dante Alighieri. *The Divine Comedy. In three volumes, Vol. II.—Purgatory*, translated by Charles Eliot Norton. Cambridge: Riverside Press, [1472] 1892.

Dendane, Sid Ahmed. *Algerie intérieure: De 1936 à 1996*. Algiers: ENAG, 2008.

Deroo, Eric. *L'illusion colonial*. Paris: Tallandier, 2005.

Derrida, Jacques. *Of Grammatology*, translated by Gayatri Chakravorty Spivak. Baltimore, MD: Johns Hopkins University Press, [1967] 1976.

Derrida, Jacques. "Otobiographies: The Teaching of Nietzsche and the Politics of the Proper Name," in Jacques Derrida, *The Ear of the Other*, edited by Christie McDonald, translated by Avital Ronell, 1–40. Lincoln and London: University of Nebraska Press, [1982] 1985.

Derrida, Jacques. "Signature, Event, Context" [1972], in Jacques Derrida, *Limited Inc*, translated by Samuel Weber and Jeffrey Mehlman, 1–21. Evanston, IL: Northwestern University Press, 1988.

Derrida, Jacques. *The Other Heading: Reflections on Today's Europe*, translated by Pascale-Anne Brault and Michael B. Naas. Bloomington: Indiana University Press, [1991] 1992.

Derrida, Jacques. *Cosmopolites de tous les pays, encore un effort!* Paris: Galilée, 1997.

Derrida, Jacques. *Politics of Friendship*, translated by George Collins. London: Verso, [1994] 1997.

Derrida, Jacques. *Monolingualism of the Other or the Prosthesis of the Origin*, translated by Patrick Mensah. Stanford, CA: Stanford University Press, [1996] 1998.

Derrida, Jacques. *Of Hospitality: Anne Dufourmantelle Invites Jacques Derrida to Respond*, translated by Rachel Bowlby. Stanford, CA: Stanford University Press, [1997] 2000.

Derrida, Jacques. "Des Tours de Babel," in Jacques Derrida, *Psyche: Inventions of the Other*, translated by Joseph Graham, 191–225. Stanford, CA: Stanford University Press, [1987] 2007.

Derrida, Jacques. "Racism's Last Word," in Jacques Derrida, *Psyche: Inventions of the Other*, vol. 1, edited by Peggy Kamuf and Elizabeth Rottenberg, 377–86. Stanford, CA: Stanford University Press, [1987] 2007.

Edgerton Jr., Samuel Y. "Galileo, Florentine 'Disegno,' and the 'Strange Spottedness' of the Moon." *Art Journal* 44 (1984): 225–32.

Eisele, Petra. *Babylon: Götterpforte oder große Hure.* Bern: Scherz, 1980.

Ette, Ottmar. "Der Blick auf die neue Welt," in Alexander von Humboldt, *Reise in die Äquinoktial-Gegenden des neuen Kontinents*, 2 vols., edited by Ottmar Ette, vol. 2, 1563–1597. Frankfurt am Main: Insel, 1999.

Ette, Ottmar. "Zu dieser Ausgabe," in Alexander von Humboldt, *Reise in die Äquinoktial-Gegenden des neuen Kontinents*, 2 vols., edited by Ottmar Ette, vol. 2, 1605–1608. Frankfurt am Main: Insel, 1999.

Ette, Ottmar. *Alexander von Humboldt und die Globalisierung: Das Mobile des Wissens.* Frankfurt am Main: Insel, 2009.

Finkelde, Dominik. *Politische Eschatologie nach Paulus: Badiou—Agamben—Žižek—Santner.* Vienna: Turia & Kant, 2009.

Foucault, Michel. "The Confession of the Flesh" [1977], in Michel Foucault, *Power/Knowledge: Selected Interviews and Other Writings 1972–1977*, edited and translated by Colin Gordon, 194–228. New York: Pantheon Books, 1980.

Freud, Sigmund. "The Uncanny" [1919], in Sigmund Freud, *The Standard Edition of the Complete Psychological Works of Sigmund Freud*, vol. 17, translated by James Strachey et al., 217–56. London: Hogarth Press, 1971.

Gerhardt, Volker. *Immanuel Kants Entwurf "Zum ewigen Frieden": Eine Theorie der Politik.* Darmstadt: Wissenschaftliche Buchgesellschaft, 1995.

Glissant, Édouard. *Poetics of Relation*, translated by Betsy Wing. Ann Arbor: University of Michigan Press, [1990] 1997.

Glissant, Édouard. *Introduction to a Poetics of Diversity*, translated by Celia Britton. Liverpool: Liverpool University Press, [1996] 2020.

Guattari, Félix. "Pratiques écosophiques et restauration de la cité subjective," in *Qu'est-ce que l'écosophie?*, edited by Stéphane Nadaud, 31–58. Paris: Lignes.

Haarmann, Harald. *Universalgeschichte der Schrift.* Frankfurt am Main: Campus, 1991.

Hamy, Ernest-Théodore. "Préface," in Alexander von Humboldt and François Arago, *Correspondance d'Alexandre de Humboldt avec François Arago (1809–1853)*, edited by Ernest-Théodore Hamy, vii–x. Paris: Guilmoto, 1907.

Hanimann, Joseph. "Unerwünscht. Ungeliebt. Die *Cité de l'immigration* in Paris öffnet ihr Museum." *Frankfurter Allgemeine Zeitung*, October 12, 2007, 43.

Harries, Karsten. "Unterwegs zur Heimat," in *Bauen und Wohnen/Building and Dwelling: Martin Heidegger's Foundation of a Phenomenology of Architecture*, edited by Eduard Führ, 101–20. Münster: Waxmann, 2000.

Hart-Nibbrig, Christian, ed. *Übersetzen: Walter Benjamin*. Frankfurt am Main: Suhrkamp, 2001.

Havelock, Eric. *The Literate Revolution in Greece and its Cultural Consequences*. Princeton, NJ: Princeton University Press, 1982.

Hecker, Judith. *William Kentridge: Trace*. New York: Museum of Modern Art, 2010.

Hegel, Georg Wilhelm Friedrich. *Aesthetics: Lectures on Fine Arts*, vol. 2, translated by Thomas Malcolm Knox. Oxford: Clarendon Press, [1835] 1975.

Heidegger, Martin. "Building Dwelling Thinking," in Martin Heidegger, *Poetry, Language, Thought*, translated by Albert Hofstadter, 143–59. New York: Harper & Row, [1951] 1971.

Heidegger, Martin. *Parmenides*, translated by André Schuwer and Richard Roicewicz. Bloomington: Indiana University Press, [1943] 1992.

Herodotus. *Histories*, edited by James Romm, translated by Pamela Mensch. Indianapolis: Hackett, 2014.

Hirsch, Alfred. *Der Dialog der Sprachen. Studien zum Sprach- und Übersetzungsdenken Walter Benjamins und Jacques Derridas*. Munich: Fink, 1995.

Hirsch, Alfred. *Übersetzung und Dekonstruktion*. Frankfurt am Main: Suhrkamp, 1997.

Humboldt, Alexander de. *Personal Narrative of Travels to the Equinoctial Regions of the New Continent, During the Years 1799–1804*, 7 vols., translated by Helen Maria Williams. London: Longman, Hurst, Rees, Orme, and Brown, [1807–34] 1814–29.

Humboldt, Alexandre de. *Correspondance scientifique et litteraire*, vol. 1, edited by J. B. de la Roquette. Paris: E. Ducrocq, 1865.

Humboldt, Alexander von. "Einleitung," in Franz Arago, *Sämmtliche Werke*, vol. 1, edited by W. G. Hankel. Leipzig: Otto Wigand, 1854.

Humboldt, Alexander von. *Reise in die Aequinoktial-Gegenden des neuen Kontinents*, 4 vols., edited by Hermann Hauff. Stuttgart: J. G. Cotta, [1807–34] 1859–60.

Humboldt, Alexander von. *Die Forschungsreise in den Tropen Amerikas*, 3 vols., edited by Hanno Beck. Darmstadt: Wissenschaftliche Buchgesellschaft, [1807–34] 1987–97.

Humboldt, Alexander von. *Reise in die Äquinoktial-Gegenden des neuen Kontinents*, 2 vols., edited by Ottmar Ette. Frankfurt am Main: Insel, [1807–34] 1991–9.

Humboldt, Alexander von. *Cuba-Werk*, edited by Hanno Beck. Darmstadt: Wissenschaftliche Buchgesellschaft, [1829] 1992.

Humboldt, Alexander von, and François Arago. *Correspondance d'Alexandre de Humboldt avec François Arago (1809–1853)*, edited by Ernest-Théodore Hamy. Paris: Guilmoto, 1907.

Irigaray, Luce. *This Sex Which Is Not One*, translated by Catherine Porter and Carolyn Burke. Ithaca, NY: Cornell University Press, [1977] 1985.

Jarrasse, Dominique. "Le décor du palais des colonies," in *Le palais des colonies: Histoire du musée des arts d'Afrique et d'Océanie*, edited by Dominique François, 83–126. Paris: Réunion des musées nationaux, 2002.

Jennings, Theodore W. *Reading Derrida / Thinking Paul: On Justice*. Stanford, CA: Stanford University Press, 2006.

Jobard, Olivier, and Florence Saugues. *Kingsley, carnet de route d'un immigrant clandestin*. Paris: Édititons Marval, 2006.

Kant, Immanuel. "Idea for a Universal History with a Cosmopolitan Intent," in Immanuel Kant, *Perpetual Peace and Other Essays on Politics, History, and Morals*, translated by Ted Humphrey, 29–40. Indianapolis and Cambridge: Hackett, [1784] 1983.

Kant, Immanuel. "Perpetual Peace: A Philosophical Sketch," in Immanuel Kant, *Perpetual Peace and Other Essays on Politics, History, and Morals*, translated by Ted Humphrey, 107–44. Indianapolis and Cambridge: Hackett, [1795] 1983.

Kant, Immanuel. "Universal Natural History and Theory Of The Heaven" [1755], translated by Olaf Reinhardt, in Immanuel Kant, *Natural Science*, edited by Eric Watkins, 182–308. Cambridge: Cambridge University Press, 2012.

Koyré, Alexandre. *Von der geschlossenen Welt zum unendlichen Universum*, translated by Rolf Dornbacher. Frankfurt am Main: Suhrkamp, 1969.

Krafft, Fritz. "Wissenschaftshistorische Einführung in Kants Kosmogonie," in Immanuel Kant, *Allgemeine Naturgeschichte und Theorie des Himmels*, edited by Fritz Krafft, 179–93. Munich: Kindler, 1971.

Krämer, Sibylle. "Kann das 'geistige Auge' sehen? Visualisierung und die Konstitution epistemischer Gegenstände," in *Mit dem Auge denken. Strategien der Sichtbarmachung in wissenschaftlichen und virtuellen Welten*, edited by Bettina Heintz and Jörg Huber, 347–64. Zurich: Edition Voldemeer; New York: Springer, 2001.

Krämer, Sibylle. "Karten—Kartenlesen—Kartographie: Kulturtechnisch inspirierte Überlegung," in *Bild/ Geschichte: Festschrift für Horst Bredekamp*, edited by Philine Helas, Maren Polte, Claudia Rückert, and Bettina Uppenkamp, 73–83. Berlin: Akademie Verlag, 2003.

Krauss, Rosalind. "'The Rock': William Kentridge's *Drawings for Projection*." *October* 92 (2000): 5–35.

Kristeva, Julia. *Strangers to Ourselves*, translated by Leon S. Roudiez. New York: Columbia University Press, [1988] 1991.

Le Hallé, Guy. *Histoire des fortifications de Paris et leur extension en Ile-de-France*. Lyon: Horvath, 1995.

Levitt, Theresa. "'I thought this might be of interest . . .': The Observatory as Public Enterprise," in *The Heavens of Earth: Observatories and Astronomy in Nineteenth-Century Science and Culture*, edited by David Aubin, Charlotte Bigg, and H. Otto Sibum, 285–304. Durham, NC: Duke University Press, 2010.

Luyken, Reiner. "Der Banausen-Bau zu Babel." *Die Zeit*, July 23, 2009.

Mörike, Eduard. *Werke und Briefe*, vol. 8.1: *Übersetzungen*, edited by Ulrich Hötzer. Stuttgart: Klett-Cotta, 1976.

Morra, Joanne. "Utopia Lost: Allegory, Ruins and Pieter Bruegel's *Towers of Babel.*" *Art History* 30, no. 2 (2007): 198–216.

Moschos. "Europa," in *Greek Bucolic Poets*, translated by J. M. Edmonds, 427–41. Cambridge, MA: Harvard University Press, 1912.

Murphy, Maureen. *Un palais pour une cité: Du musée des colonies à la Cité nationale de l'histoire de l'immigration*. Paris: Réunion des musées nationaux, 2007.

Neef, Sonja. "M/Othering Europe. Or: how Europe and Atlas are Balancing Hand in Hand on the Prime Meridian—she carrying the Alphabet, he Shouldering the Globe they are Walking on." *Journal of Visual Culture* 6, no. 1 (2007): 58–76.

Neef, Sonja. *An Bord der Bauhaus: Zur Heimatlosigkeit der Moderne. Einleitung*, in *An Bord der Bauhaus: Zur Heimatlosigkeit der Moderne*, edited by Sonja Neef, 11–26. Bielefeld: Transcript, 2009.

Neef, Sonja. "Badiou von Rabat über Paulus von Tarsus: Universalismus, Kosmopolitanismus und das Denken des Planetarischen," in *Treue zur Wahrheit: Die Begründung der Philosophie Alain Badious*, edited by Jens Kipp and Frank Meier, 119–40. Münster: Unrast, 2010.

Neef, Sonja. "À la plage du musée: la Cité nationale de l'histoire de l'immigration," translated by Cathérine Rogister. *Les Cahiers du GEPE* 3 (2011).

Neef, Sonja. "Au bord de la langue de la Cité nationale de l'histoire de l'immigration," translated by Cathérine Rogister. *Multitudes* 46 (2011): 127–37.

Neef, Sonja. *Imprint and Trace: Handwriting in the Age of Technology*, translated by Anthony Matthews. London: Reaktion Books, 2011.

Neef, Sonja. "Interstellar Hospitality: Missions of Star House Enterprise," in *Art and Visibility in Migratory Culture: Conflict, Resistance, and Agency*, edited by Mieke Bal and Miguel Á. Hernández-Navarro, 277–96. Amsterdam: Rodopi, 2011.

Neef, Sonja. "'Video-Graphie' und die Ästhetik der Apartheid." *Rheinsprung* 11 (2012): 89–109.

Neef, Sonja. *Der babylonische Planet: Kultur, Übersetzung, Dekonstruktion unter den Bedingungen der Globalisierung*. Heidelberg: Winter, 2013.

Neef, Sonja. "Outre mèr(e): Jacques Derrida and the Language of the M/Other," in *(M) Other Tongues: Literary Reflexions on a Difficult Distinction*, edited by Juliane Prade, 114–26. Newcastle upon Tyne: Cambridge Scholars, 2013.

Neef, Sonja. "Planetarische Ästhetik: Kosmopolitismus bei Jacques Derrida und Ingo Günther," in *Astroculture: Figurations of Cosmology in Media and Arts*, edited by Sonja Neef, Henry Sussman, and Dietrich Boschung, 143–58. Munich: Fink, 2014.

Neef, Sonja. "The horizon to come: Planetary aesthetics in William Kentridge's *Felix in Exile* and Galileo Galilei's moon drawings," in *On not looking: The Paradox of Contemporary Visual Culture*, edited by Frances Guerin, 164–84. New York: Routledge, 2015.

Neef, Sonja. "Was ist europäische Medienkultur? Oder wie Europa und Atlas Hand in Hand über den nullten Längengrad balancieren, sie Blumen pflückend, er den Globus schulternd," in *Europäische Medienwissenschaft: Zur Programmatik eines Fachs*, edited by Hedwig Wagner, 211–36. Bielefeld: Transcript, 2020.

Neef, Sonja, and Henry Sussman. "The Glorious Moment of Astroculture: Introduction," in *Astroculture: Figurations of Cosmology in Media and Arts*, edited by Sonja Neef, Henry Sussman, and Dietrich Boschung, 7–30. Munich: Fink, 2014.

Neef, Sonja, Henry Sussman, and Dietrich Boschung, eds., *Astroculture: Figurations of Cosmology in Media and Arts*. Munich: Fink, 2014.

Nietzsche, Friedrich. "Star Friendship," in Friedrich Nietzsche, *The Gay Science*, edited and translated by Walter Kaufmann, 225–6. New York: Vintage Books, [1882] 1974.

Nietzsche, Friedrich. *The Antichrist*, translated by Henry Louis Mencken. New York: Cosimo, [1895] 2005.

Ossendrijver, Mathieu. "Astronomie und Astrologie in Babylonien," in *Babylon: Wahrheit*, edited by Joachim Marzahn and Günther Schauerte, 373–92. Munich: Hirmer, 2008.

Ouaknin, Marc-Alain. *Mysteries of the Alphabet: The Origins of Writing*, translated by Josephine Bacon. New York: Abbeville Press, [1997] 1999.

Pamuk, Orhan. *The White Castle*, translated by Victoria Holbrook. New York: Vintage Books, [1985] 1998.

Pisters, Patricia. "The Mosaic Film: Nomadic Style and Politics in Transnational Media Culture," in *Art and Visibility in Migratory Culture: Conflict, Resistance, and Agency*, edited by Mieke Bal and Miguel Á. Hernández-Navarro, 175–90. Amsterdam: Rodopi, 2012.

Renger, Almut-Barbara, ed. *Mythos Europa: Texte von Ovid bis Heiner Müller*. Leipzig: Reclam, 2003.

Robin, Régine. "Autobiographie et judéité chez Jacques Derrida." *Études françaises* 38, no. 1–2 (2002): 207–18.

Rosello, Mireille. *Postcolonial Hospitality: The Immigrant as Guest*. Stanford, CA: Stanford University Press, 2001.

Sala-Molins, Louis. *Le Code Noir ou le calvarie de Canaan*. Paris: Presses Universitaires de France, 1987.

Salje, Beate. "Vorwort," in *Babylon: Wahrheit*, edited by Joachim Marzahn and Günther Schauerte, 10–12. Munich: Hirmer, 2008.

Salzmann, Siegfried, ed. *Mythos Europa: Europa und der Stier im Zeitalter der industriellen Zivilisation*. Bonn: Arbeitskreis selbständiger Kulturinstitute e.V., 1988.

Schuster, Peter-Klaus. "Vorwort," in *Babylon: Wahrheit*, edited by Joachim Marzahn and Günther Schauerte, 7–8. Munich: Hirmer, 2008.

Schwab, Gustav. *Die schönsten Sagen des klassischen Alterthums: Nach seinen Dichtern und Erzählern*. Gütersloh: Bertelsmann, [1877] 1974.

Segond, Louis. *Le nouveau testament*. London: Trinitarian Bible Society, 1993.

Sloterdijk, Peter. *In the World Interior of Capital*, translated by Wieland Hoban. Cambridge: Polity Press, [2005] 2013.

Sobel, Dava, and William J. H. Andrewes. *The Illustrated Longitude: The True Story of a Lone Genius Who Solved the Greatest Scientific Problem of His Time.* London: Walker, 1995.

Spivak, Gayatri Chakravorty. *Outside in the Teaching Machine.* London: Routledge, 1993.

Spivak, Gayatri Chakravorty. *Imperative zur Neuerfindung des Planeten / Imperatives to Re-Imagine the Planet.* Vienna: Passagen, 1999.

Spivak, Gayatri Chakravorty. "Translation as Culture." *Parallax* 6, no. 1 (2000): 13–24.

Steiner, Dietmar, "Die Hure Babylon und One Mile High," in *Der Turmbau zu Babel: Ursprung und Vielfalt von Sprache und Schrift,* vol. 1: *Der Babylonische Turm in der historischen Überlieferung der Archäologie und der Kunst,* edited by Wilfried Seipel, 95–7. Graz: Kunsthistorisches Museum, 2003.

Steinhauer, Fabian. "Die Szene ist Rom," in *Römisch,* edited by Walter Seitter and Cornelia Vismann, 121–32. Zurich: Diaphanes, 2006.

Stevens, Mary. "Designing Diversity: The Visual Identity of the "Cité nationale de l'histoire de l'immigration." *Eurodiv* 56 (2007).

Stiftung Entwicklung und Frieden, ed. *Globale Trends: Daten zur Weltentwicklung.* Bonn and Düsseldorf: Stiftung Entwicklung und Frieden, 1991.

Taffin, Dominique. "Les avatars du musée des arts d'Afrique et d'Oceanie," in *Le palais des colonies: Histoire du musée des arts d'Afrique et d'Océanie,* edited by Dominique François, 179–223. Paris: Réunion des musées nationaux, 2002.

Taubes, Jacob. *Die politische Theologie des Paulus.* Munich: Fink, 1993.

Tawada, Yōko. *Überseezungen.* Tübingen: Konkursbuchverlag, 2002.

Toubon, Jacques. "Editorial: Changer le regard contemporain sur l'immigration," in *Ouverture de la Cité nationale de l'histoire de'l immigration* (exhibition brochure), 4–5. Paris: CNHI, 2007.

Treidler, Hans. "Europa," in *Der kleine Pauly: Lexikon der Antike,* edited by Konrad Ziegler and Walter Sontheimer, 446–9. Munich: J. B. Metzler, 1979.

Treps, Marie. *Les mots voyageurs: Petite histoire du français venu d'ailleurs.* Paris: Seuil, 2003.

Valéry, Paul. "Fonction de Paris," in Paul Valéry, *Œuvres complètes,* vol. 1, edited by Jean Hytier, 1009–25. Paris: Gallimard, [1927] 1960.

Valéry, Paul. "Présence de Paris," in Paul Valéry, *Œuvres complètes,* vol. 2, edited by Jean Hytier, 1011–15. Paris: Gallimard, [1937] 1960.

Van Dale. *Etymologisch Woordenboek: De herkomst van onze woorden,* edited by P. A. F. van Veen. Utrecht: Van Dale Lexicografie, 1989.

Vismann, Cornelia. "Sprachbrüche im Nürnberger Kriegsverbrecherprozess," in *Rechenschaften: Juristischer und literarischer Diskurs in der Auseinandersetzung mit den NS-Massenverbrechen,* edited by Stephan Braese, 47–65. Göttingen: Wallstein, 2004.

Voltaire. *Philosophical dictionary (A–I),* translated by Peter Gay. New York: Basic Books, [1764] 1962.

Wahnich, Sophie. *L'impossible citoyen: L'étranger dans le discours de la Révolution française.* Paris: Editions Albin Michel, 1997.

Welwei, Karl-Wilhelm. *Die griechische Polis*. Stuttgart: Steiner, 1998.

Werner, Petra. *Himmel und Erde: Alexander von Humboldt und sein Kosmos*. Berlin: Akademie Verlag, 2004.

Wetzel, Michael. "Unter Sprachen—Unter Kulturen: Walter Benjamins 'Interlinearversion' des Übersetzens als Inframedialität," in *Medien in Medien*, edited by Claudia Liebrand and Irmela Schneider, 154–75. Cologne: DuMont, 2002.

Wetzel, Michael. "Alienationen: Jacques Derridas Dekonstruktion der Muttersprache," in Jacques Derrida, *Die Einsprachigkeit des Anderen oder die ursprüngliche Prothese*, translated by Michael Wetzel, 141–54. Munich: Fink, 2003.

Williamson, Sue, and Ashraf Jamal. *Art in South Africa: The Future Present*. Cape Town: David Phillip, 1996.

Wolff, Hans, ed. *Vierhundert Jahre Mercator, vierhundert Jahre Atlas: "Die ganze Welt zwischen zwei Buchdeckeln." Eine Geschichte der Atlanten*. Weißenhorn: Anton H. Konrad Verlag, 1995.

Wullen, Moritz. "Mythos Babylon," in *Babylon: Mythos*, edited by Moritz Wullen and Günther Schauerte, 11–21. Munich: Hirmer, 2008.

Wullen, Moritz, and Günther Schauerte, eds. *Babylon: Mythos*. Munich: Hirmer, 2008.

Zeuske, Michael. "Humboldt, Historismus, Humboldteanisierung: Der 'Geschichtsschreiber von Amerika,' die Massensklaverei und die Globalisierungen der Welt." *Alexander von Humboldt im Netz* 3, no. 4 (2002).

Zeuske, Michael. *Schwarze Karibik: Sklaven, Sklavereikulturen und Emanzipation*. Zurich: Rotpunktverlag, 2004.

Zimmermann, Klaus. "Eratosthenes' Chlamys-Shaped World: a Misunderstood Metaphor," in *The Hellenistic World: New Perspectives*, edited by Daniel Ogden, 23–40. London: Duckworth; Swansea: Classical Press of Wales, 2002.

Index

www.ingramcontent.com/pod-product-compliance
Lightning Source LLC
Chambersburg PA
CBHW050436280326
41932CB00013BA/2136